Healing the Effects of Psychic Trauma

A Soul's Evolution

By
Laura Schwalm

Healing the Effects of Psychic Trauma: A Soul's Evolution - Laura Schwalm

Copyright © 2019 by Laura Schwalm

Copyedit by Karin Nicely

Cover design and layout by Troika Studios Inc.

Healing the Effects of Psychic Trauma: A Soul's Evolution - Laura Schwalm

330. pgs

ISBN 978-1-935795-59-9

1. Education

2. Self Help Techniques

Library of Congress Control Number:2019909216

All Rights Reserved. No part of this book may be reproduced, stored in a retrieval system, or transmitted in any form or by any means, electronic, mechanical, photocopying, recording, or otherwise, without permission in writing from MRK Publishing.

The information provided in this book is designed to provide helpful information on the subjects discussed. This book is not meant to be used, nor should it be used, to diagnose or treat any medical condition. For diagnosis or treatment of any medical problem, consult your own physician. The publisher and author are not responsible for any specific health or allergy needs that may require medical supervision and are not liable for any damages or negative consequences from any treatment, action, application or preparation, to any person reading or following the information in this book. References are provided for informational purposes only and do not constitute endorsement of any websites or other sources. Readers should be aware that the websites listed in this book may change.

MRK Publishing
PO Box 353431
Palm Coast, FL 32135-3431
www.MichaelRayKingPublishing.com
Printed in the United States of America

Table of Contents

Foreword
Dedication
Introduction
Before We Begin

My Story

The Beginning 2
Electroencephalography Test 13
Christmas Eve 18
Laid Off 25
The Playroom 28
Andrea's Birthday Present 32
Grammar School 34
Asthma Attacks 39
Third Grade 46
Lori 54
Early Church Days 63
Zena Clairvoyant 67
Nassau Community College 71
Kidney Stones 78
Roger's Family 91
LA Hair Salon 95
Baby Shower 99
Baby Roger Comes 103
Roger's Baptism 115
How I Left–My First Apartment 116
Farmingdale to Queens 120
Leaving The Lemon Tree 130
International Haircutters 135
Dramatics and Meeting Ace Miami 148
My Spiritual Gifts 166
Radio Show 167
Ace's Accident 173
Healing with Awareness and Proactive, Positive Steps 178

Table of Contents

Let's Heal!

Healing Spiritual Disease Patterns 181

Healing Psychic Trauma (Emotional, Physical, and Psychological Abuse) 185

Codependency and Trauma 188

Meditation 194

The Importance of Prayer 198

Endocrine System (Healing Psychic Trauma Manifested as Sickness, Disease, and Imbalances in the Physical Body) 201

How Emotions Affect the Meridian System 206

Psychological and Metaphysical Meanings and Healing Solutions of the Systems of the Body (Healing Body, Mind, and Spirit) 212

Psychological Spiritual Meanings of the Systems and Metaphysical Healing 214

The Anatomy of Your Energy System and How It Relates to Your Health 218

The Connection between Spiritual Imbalances and Imbalances in the Endocrine System 221

Toxic Relationships/Psychic Trauma 226

Healing Adrenal Fatigue with Ayurvedic and Chinese Medicine 230

The Spiritual Message behind Candida 242

The Sacral Chakra 247

Table of Contents

Cosmic Laws 250

Healing Spiritual Blocks to Restore Spiritual Equilibrium 253

Channel Building for Psychic/Spiritual Healing 256

Spiritual Integration of the Shadow Self 259

Soul Relationships, Spiritual Tests, Karmic Programs, and Humanity's Evolution 264

Psychic Cords (Healing Yourself of Toxic Relationships and Healing Second-Chakra Imbalances) 266

Healing Depersonalization Disorder (Healing First-, Second-, and Third-Chakra Imbalances) 271

Healing and Full Body Consciousness (Healing Root-Chakra Imbalances) 274

Finding Your Soul's Purpose 278

The Healing and Therapeutic Benefits of Drumming (Healing the Body/Mind Connection) 282

Healing Colon Cancer (Healing Root Chakra Imbalance) 286

Healing Inflammation Holistically 392

Emotional Intelligence 395

Acknowledgements 297

Foreword

They say our psyche is one with nature and the universe. Like nature, the manifestations that come from it are limitless. It's hard for the human mind to comprehend there is a lot more going on than our own mind takes in. Our senses take in stimuli via our senses—sound, sight, taste, smell, and touch—and are then translated from our own narrow perception of reality into the mind, where they become psychic events.

Transpired psychic events causing detachment soul fragmentation are caused by experiences of which we aren't fully conscious. They have been absorbed subliminally. We only become aware of them when we are triggered emotionally and intuitively.

All our emotional baggage makes up an energetic pain body, and our complexes are all repressed emotions which have themes—feelings of unworthiness, of not being good enough, of being somehow defective, of shame and victimization. These emotions may manifest as digestion problems in one person and breathing problems in another, depending upon one's unique body constitution, family heredity, and genetic makeup. Physical conditions trouble us unconsciously but mirror out within our dreams, behaviorisms, and outer-world life experiences.

Understanding Our Thoughts and How They Affect Our Health

The autonomic nervous system is linked to the subconscious intuitive survival part of our mind. Our amygdala is the center of emotion that connects to our endocrine system. Our thoughts have the power to create biochemical change by secreting chemicals that create chemical pathways in the brain triggered by memories, feelings, and circumstances. The overabundant surge of chemicals in the body manifests as tension, stress, and hormonal and emotional imbalances. Tension in the body makes it difficult for blood to circulate and bring oxygen and nutrients to cells, organs, and organ tissue throughout the body, thus resulting in disease.

Dedication

I dedicate *Healing the Effects of Psychic Trauma* to my parents, John William Schwalm and Suzanne Marie Schwalm, otherwise known as Jack and Sue.

To my father for loving me unconditionally, regardless of who I appeared to be. I thank him for showing me the power of the mind that regardless of the circumstances and odds, your mind can heal, grow, and transcend any situation. I thank him for the intention of wanting to be a good parent.

To my mother for doing the best she could do with the circumstances she was born into and the limited spiritual education available when she most needed it. I am thankful for the spiritual lessons which brought me to my path of purpose. Through her example, I learned the gifts of strength and determination.

Introduction

Everything that happens is in divine order. Spiritual law tells us that every situation we go through and every person who comes into our life here on earth doesn't come by chance. They have come to help us grow, heal, and evolve. We are born into families. We form relationships that teach us to learn and to acquire the different forms and layers of love because God is love. We are here in physical form to learn we are not separate from him. We are here to experience these different forms of love to really understand and know him.

We all go through experiences which create trauma. Whether it's physical, emotional, or psychological trauma, the mind doesn't know the difference. These traumas are held in the body as stress, acted out through our unconscious behaviorisms, and mirrored within our everyday experiences.

Many times, these situations leave a karmic imprint or wound which plays out as undesirable experiences. These experiences have the same themes of abandonment, shame, victimization, and betrayal called *karmic loops*, which block us from obtaining good health, wealth, success, and fulfilling relationships as well as overall emotional fulfillment. Without awareness, healing, and integration of these karmic wounds, we become a magnet for more of the same.

Man is made up of half dust and half deity. The deity part of self is the God part of self. It is known as love and felt as empathy. Since love is such a complex subject, love's definition is different for everyone, so God made a man to depict his character of himself. Like father, like son. Through the bible and other spiritual scripture, we learn that we are in physical form to learn, because of love, we are not separate from God. We are to give and receive love through our soul's purpose. Our free will is to choose what our work will be.

Our physical body has an energy system interconnecting our nervous system, *chakras*, and *nadis*. Since the body is the mind's faithful servant, every spiritual/psychological imbalance is manifested in the physical body. Our circulatory system brings oxygen, food, and nutrients to our cells, tissues, and organs. Spiritual blocks feel like stress. Tension makes it difficult for blood to circulate throughout the body, causing inflammation and physical imbalances. We continually create the same spiritual blocks. If we never learn how to integrate the spiritual cause into our awareness, we become energetically, emotionally, physically, and spiritually sick over time.

Our energy body is a complex structure. In many ways, it can be likened to a subtle energy reflection of the physical body, composed of highly structured etheric matter. Etheric matter is not scientifically recognized, but metaphysically speaking, it is the binding substance existing between matter and non-matter, the substance that binds physical with non-physical.

Everything in the universe consists of energy. Everything is interconnected. All our thoughts and mental states are energy. As parts of a cosmic organism, we are energy beings.

Every living thing which has a spirit also has an electromagnetic field around its physical body. This field is nonmaterial and is associated with human emotions and thoughts, both of which are forms of energy. Any live organism also has an aura consisting of subtle bodies with energetic potentials. These give strength and power to the biological field.

Spiritual blocks affect circulation because over time they create inflammation. When a chakra becomes out of balance, physical, emotional, mental, and spiritual imbalances manifest.

The *root* or *base chakra* (earth) is located at the base of the spine and is associated with survival as well as the right to be here, to simply exist, to take care of ourselves, and to have possessions. It's our connection to our ancestors and our unique DNA as well as to mother earth, father up in heaven, and the physical body. It represents all currencies of the physical world and all major structures that support the physical body: the endocrine system, nervous system, immune system, and skeletal system. Individuals who suffer from spiritual imbalances in the root chakra are likely to have issues relating to support, finances, emotions/relationships, and health.

The second chakra (water), called the *sacral* or *sacred center*, is located in the lower abdomen below the navel and is associated with emotions and sexuality. It is also where our pain body is. This chakra is associated with what comprises our unique individuality such as our passions, interests, and hobbies. This center represents the right to feel, to express and understand one's emotional needs and wants. It also represents balance. Through our unique individuality, we find balance in life through investing in our passions, dreams, and desires. When we shift our focus onto our passions, we escape from the daily stresses of life. We find our balance.

The third chakra (fire), the *solar plexus* chakra, is located above the navel at the solar plexus and is considered the God center because it is associated with intuition, power, and will. The solar plexus has more neurotransmitters than the brain. It gives us the drive and need to act. It is associated with our desire to be innovative and free.

The fourth chakra (air), known as the *heart chakra*, is located just over the sternum, in the middle of your chest, and is associated with love. This chakra allows us to experience the giving and receiving of love. It is another true connection we have to God and humanity. To give and receive love through one's own free will, through one's unique individuality, is the link between ourselves, God, and humanity. The heart chakra helps us determine the right to love and be loved as well as the right to freedom from projected or received prejudice, low self-esteem, and violent conflict. God is unconditional love. Unconditional love has no expectations or ownership.

The fifth chakra (ether), known as the *throat chakra*, located at the base of the throat and is associated with sound, communication, and creativity. This chakra determines the right to speak and hear truth. Our voices allow us to set boundaries and ask for what we need in order to create the life experiences we want to have. In the Book of Genesis, we learn that God created the world with his voice and God created man in his image. Like God, we are always manifesting and creating,

The sixth chakra (light), known as the *brow* or *third-eye chakra*, is considered the seat of our soul. Located in the center of the forehead, behind the center of the brow line, it is associated with intuition and imagination. It is a metaphysical and spiritual law: if you can imagine it, you can create it or become it. The disciple Matthew in the bible said, "Truly, I say to you, unless you turn and become like children, you will never enter the kingdom of heaven." In Luke 17:21, Jesus says, "The kingdom of God doesn't come to the observation, nor will they say, 'See here!' or 'See there!' for indeed the kingdom of God is within you."

The seventh chakra (thought), known as the *crown chakra*, is located at the top of the head and is associated with knowledge and understanding. It also represents internal psychic knowing, one consciousness, and unity consciousness.

In addition to the chakras, your subtle energy body or energetic anatomy also includes your aura, meridians, and nadis.

The Aura

This magnetic energy field is made up of individual yet interrelated subtle energy bodies, also referred to as *auric bodies*, as well as the seven layers of etheric energy: the *etheric layer*, the *emotional layer*, the *mental layer*, the *astral layer*, the *etheric template*, the *celestial layer*, and the *ketheric template*.

Diseases are caused by the depletion, congestion, or blockage of life force (*prana* or *Chi*) in your energy body. These imbalances are distinguished by the aura's width, color, and vibration. It is a good idea to practice spiritual hygiene by healing any negative thought patterns and moving stagnant energy with yoga, acupressure, Energy Medicine, or acupuncture to rejuvenate life-force energy.

Having a clear understanding of the anatomy of your aura will enable you to take control of your life. Your aura, more than any other human trait, manifests your life as an endless life in the universe.

The bible states that the kingdom of heaven is within you and that one day heaven will be on earth. These two statements predict individual healing as well as mass healing. This is inevitable for the world's evolution. God will return again through the character of man, through his higher and spiritual character.

Before we begin:

What follows will be my story. A story of extremes. A story of pain, struggle, bad decisions, and unfortunate situations. Please know that the revealing of these experiences is intended to show a portion of the psychic trauma I've suffered and have worked diligently to overcome. Although you will not have gone through the same experiences, everyone has experienced traumatic events that have created fear and changed their perception of life or themselves and sometimes not in the most productive of ways.

I originally wrote this as a blog over many years. I now pass this on to you, in the hope you may engage and seek the healing you desire.

www.HealingWithLauraSchwalm.wordpress.com

Blog post: December 6, 2018

Many people who know me and who have worked with me know it has been my own healing which led me to become a Master Psychic Healer.

I believe I am at the point within my transformational journey with a lifetime of experiences qualifying me to talk about the effects of psychological trauma.

I grew up in a spiritually imbalanced home where I watched my father spend most of his young-adult, adult, and senior years struggling financially and being debilitated by severe health issues. These included two hip replacements, upper- and lower-back surgeries—which totaled over twenty surgical hours—and many different forms of cancer.

My mother was as emotionally and psychologically imbalanced as my father was physically imbalanced. I learned by seeing firsthand at a very young age how similar energies act like a magnet to resonating energies.

You may think my parents weren't good people, but this is quite the contrary. They were good people who for the most part had good intentions. They were spiritually imbalanced and as a result, formed behaviors which blocked them from creating good health, wealth, and overall emotional fulfillment. I not only inherited certain behaviors from my family; my environment conditioned me to rely on these sabotaging behaviors for my survival.

Living out of balance due to my stress-coping skills, I reaped the consequences of many karmic situations that manifested as physical ailments, financial and relationship issues, and emotional ups and downs. After many years of reading self-help books and attending classes and seminars, I got the courage to enroll in Holistic Health School, which taught me about the body/mind connection.

Being born a highly sensitive person, my psychic abilities have always been my greatest asset. But being conditioned in an imbalanced environment also made my abilities my largest downfall. For me, saying affirmations and having good intentions were not enough.

I had to recondition my body/mind connection and change my diet and lifestyle habits. Then I saw changes. The hardest obstacle I had, and I see my clients have, is reacting to internal and external stimuli that create and compound emotional triggers. Many times, these triggers lead to sabotaging behaviors like addiction and codependency.

As a psychic healer, I hear from clients almost daily about how they have forgiven their parents and whoever else has hurt them. They don't even remember what transpired that could affect them and how they are creating their reality.

But they don't realize it's their own unconscious behaviorisms that are blocking them, and awareness is crucial to their own healing. They need to have an understanding that their ancestors, many times, were conditioned in environments that taught them to undervalue themselves. As a result, they grew up to choose partners, relationships, and living/working environments that reinforced the negative message, making the individuals feel as if they can't move forward in their life, which ultimately causes resentment.

Awareness is nonlinear. It concerns time. Cultivating it is something that happens over time. In the "Now Movement" happening across the planet, as related to Eckhart Tolle's various writings about spiritual enlightenment, *now* refers to our own personal, global, and spiritual awakening, which is ever changing and encompasses the past, present, and future.

When we experience undesirable life experiences that create trauma, whether physical, psychological or emotional, it changes the way we view not only the situation but ourselves. We begin to experience many different emotions. We feel shame, guilt, or feelings of not being worthy or good enough. These thoughts create feelings which, if not integrated, become unconscious and sabotaging habits, conditions, and reflexes that mirror out into our behavior and character.

We live in a society that constantly associates our worth and success with outside worldly possessions. What we need to realize is that we can redirect our behavior by creating a new intention along with a daily practice in order to create situations and outcomes we want to have—instead of reliving undesirable ones that are considered karmic.

Disease, poverty, and toxic relationships hold the same low vibration in energy. With so many people going through health crises, some severe and even life-threatening, it is important to note at this point in our evolution we must understand the cause of disease and where its roots lie.

All pain is the result of living out of alignment with God's laws, the laws of love. It is a choice we make at the "soul level" in order to expand our hearts, raise consciousness by learning, and to cultivate Christ-like character traits.

Bad relationships, poverty, and disease are all excellent teachers, not only for healing but also for one's spiritual growth and evolution. Undesirable life situations give us vital information about our behaviors that have evolved through many lifetimes. Many times, this brings a new level of consciousness or an awakening to new spiritual paths and truths.

The secret to moving through any undesirable life experience is to seek the knowledge, growth, and evolution within it. For without understanding the underlying purpose for the undesirable life experience (sickness, toxic relationships, or money problems), these things will eventually manifest later in our life as physical health issues, how well we prosper financially, and how emotionally fulfilling our relationships are.

Cultivating awareness is key for healing. It is to understand that emotional triggers are subconsciously chosen default reactions to traumas out of fear from experiences and situations we've lived through. We repeat behaviors once created out of survival but now repeated due to lack of presence.

If an emotional trigger causes an unconscious reaction, this condition can also be reconditioned to not be reactionary but to be in the moment by practicing body/mind medicine such as yoga, weight training, and energy psychology. Emotional reactions are unhealthy defaults. They reflect a lack of control and a lack of being present that can be transmuted by doing body/mind medicine. Practicing yoga and doing weight training are two simple forms of body/mind exercise that help individuals who have suffered psychic trauma to heal detachment issues and to retrain their nervous system to no longer be over-responsive.

Steps to Healing

First, identify and acknowledge how you are feeling. Scan your body for tension. Do you feel tightness, heaviness, buzzing, or tingling? Do you feel hot or cold? Stagnant energy held in the body is perceived as stress but is experienced differently by all individuals.

Some helpful things to remember when reading energy: The body/mind connection doesn't just happen on a physical level but on a chemical one, as well. Our mind encompasses all mental states, beliefs, attitudes, and emotions which change our biological function. This is because our endocrine system, nervous system, and immune system are in constant communication and are relying on the same chemical language. Emotions such as fear, guilt, anxiety, sadness, and jealousy manifest within the body as disease.

There are only two emotions: love and fear. All other emotions stem from these two. Anger, anxiety, and jealousy all come from fear and create stagnant and toxic energy blocks.

We express sadness and grief by crying, and crying involves our entire respiratory system—our throat, lungs, ribs, nose, etc. When we suppress the energy of grief and sadness, it is held within these areas of the body and over time inevitably affects the heart.

Anger triggers the body's fight-or-flight response. The adrenal glands flood the body with stress hormones, such as adrenaline and cortisol. The constant flood of stress chemicals and associated metabolic changes causes a slew of problems that include digestive and abdominal pain, increased anxiety, depression, high blood pressure, skin, and heart problems.

To release stagnant energy, make a statement of intention. Say it out loud a few times then do something that is in alignment with the statement. Pairing an action that directly correlates to your intention lets your body and mind get into sync.

Accept, embrace, and treat yourself with love, for you have chosen these experiences on a deep level as part of your personal growth and your soul's evolution. It is important to release any associated feelings. Take a deep breath and forgive yourself and replace the negative (habitual) behavior by incorporating a new habit that is supportive to your intentions and goals.

Due to the body/mind connection, the way we think and feel, and the deep-seated habits and conditions we hold, contribute to developing imbalances in the body and mind that lead to mental and physical disease. Learning to work with our emotions allows us to become more conscious of our thoughts that need to not only heal but also be integrated.

Healing requires a combination of body, mind, and spirit protocols. No one protocol is more important than another, but depending on how far along a person is within their physical healing of their disease, a strict nutritional and supplement regimen based on one's unique physical constitution needs and goals should be integrated daily, throughout the day, with their spiritual practices.

It is helpful to look at all undesirable life experiences, including disease, with a spiritual perspective. It helps us embrace all our situations with love and helps us work with the Divine to discover the true meaning of the Divine. This is the key to permanently overcoming all obstacles as well as achieving overall wellness.

The first half of this book is a good precursor to what follows. I will first give you my story, my trauma, my life struggles, and then I will follow up in the second half with ways and means to counteract, reduce, and even eliminate psychic trauma in your life. I truly hope the information I've put together here helps you in your journey, because that is my intention.

                                                        Laura

The Beginning

Anne Patricia Conol was my father's mother's maiden name. For all anyone knew, she hadn't any living relatives aside from a great-aunt who lived in the boarding house where she was raised. My father's father, on the other hand, came from a large supportive and loving family, surrounded by aunts and uncles and extended family.

In 1935, on a beautiful May afternoon, my grandfather was driving down the block in his 1934 Cabriolet convertible when he spotted, walking down the street with another gentleman, a fair-skinned, tall, lean, beautiful woman, with soft-blond, wavy hair. My grandfather thought to himself, "I think that woman needs to be my wife." Three years later, they got married and had a house built in the Whitestone area of Flushing, New York, where they went on to raise three boys and one girl. The eldest son is my father, John William Schwalm.

My father's family was very family oriented. They would take vacations with their extended family, and life was very enjoyable in their younger years. My father was a whiz in school. He had a photographic memory, so he never really had to study. In 1951, he was accepted into Brooklyn Tech, a very prestigious school you had to pass an exam to get into. But halfway through his senior year, he failed English. Rather than make it up in summer school, he decided to transfer to Bayside High School, where the credits he'd already earned would meet the requirements for graduation.

This, of course, made my grandfather angry because he felt my father ruined some of his opportunities since Brooklyn Tech was a more high-ranking school.

After graduating high school, my father only applied to one college. Despite his brilliant mind and grades, his focus was on basketball. He was a decent player but feared if he applied to a large college, he wouldn't get on the team, so he decided to apply to only one small school, which was Providence College.

By the second season, even though he was chosen to be on the team, he didn't get much time playing, so he decided to quit in his senior year. He later asked my grandfather if he could transfer out of Providence and go to school locally.

My grandfather declined because he worried that if my father transferred out, he may not graduate college at all, so Dad decided to join the Reserve Officer Training Corps in college on top of taking his required academic courses. Upon graduating, he was supposed to be an officer in the army.

Unfortunately, in his senior year, he was kicked out of the ROTC program for drinking. No longer being enrolled in ROTC, he would no longer be classified with the U.S. military Selective Service System as having a 1-D status once he graduated school. Therefore, he would no longer be deferred or exempt from the draft. His new classification was 1-A, which meant he could be drafted at any time, and the following March, he was.

Once again, due to his intellect, he didn't have to fight in the field and instead landed an office job in Germany for two years in 1959 during the Vietnam War.

Back home, my grandmother was in and out of many doctors' offices. The physicians ran many tests, trying to figure out why she was rapidly growing more ill. My father's younger siblings often waited in the car for hours at a time for my grandparents to come out of the doctors' offices. Although my grandparents, like many people at that time, didn't speak of cancer and sickness as freely as they do today, everyone knew there was something seriously wrong.

By 1962, my father returned home from Germany. A few months later, he met my mother, Suzanne Marie Higgins. She was an only child born into an Irish Catholic family.

Her father and mother were married by a justice of the peace when Suzanne's mother was sixteen and her father was fifteen. Their relationship was always tumultuous and full of drama.

Before Suzanne was born, my grandfather got called to serve during World War Two. He was to be stationed in Bombay, India. Right before he left, however, he walked in on my grandmother as she was putting pin holes into a condom.

He exclaimed, "Margaret, what the hell are you doing? Why are you popping holes in the condoms?"

She said she thought he was going to die oversees and she would have nothing except possessions from him. While he was stationed in India, my grandfather received a letter from my grandmother, saying she was pregnant. In October 1942, my mother, Suzanne Marie, was born.

My mother was the apple of my grandmother's eye until my grandfather came home four years later in 1946. When he returned home, he was hallucinating from alcohol withdrawal, was suffering from post-traumatic stress, and seemed to be very psychotic at times. Even with his own spiritual, emotional, and psychological trauma from his turbulent childhood and the war, my grandfather was captain of the New York City fire department in Hell's Kitchen. He truly cared about people in spite of his own imbalance. But because he believed my grandmother was too lenient on my mother, he disciplined her more harshly himself. It didn't take long for my mother to become terrified of her father.

He made it clear that he viewed my mother as defective, so when he came home from the war when she was four years old, he worked to change my mother into what he thought was acceptable. The methods did not matter as long as he did what he saw fit and my grandmother did not take a stance against it.

In the seventh grade, my mother was friendly with a boy named Don who lived a few houses away. They used to walk to and from school together. One day, Don's mother came running over to my grandparents' house and banged on the door, all the while holding a condom in her hand.

When grandfather opened the door, she accused Suzanne of being promiscuous with her son. My grandfather didn't even wait for an explanation. He simply commenced verbally and physically abusing his daughter.

This was one of the many times my mother would run into other people's opened garages, back yards, or anywhere else she could find to escape his wrath. But her father would always find her and beat her on the spot. This particular time, he did not just beat her. He asked her to prove to him that she was still a virgin. This was just one incident of many.

Despite Suzanne's home life, she had plenty of friends who helped her deal with her chaotic parents. And through these friends she met the man she would marry.

My father had just come home from serving his two years in Germany. His buddies, Jimmy Shroder and Phil Alsing, liked to play basketball and go out drinking. They frequented the Harmony Bar. Phil was dating a woman named Pat, who was friends with my mother. She later became my godmother. It was late November when my parents met at the Harmony Bar.

Their relationship was a bit touch and go in the beginning. My father was ten years Mom's senior and was seen as a perpetual bachelor by my mother's controlling father. My mother had a very similar personality to her father. She tried not to let the age difference and his bachelor-attitude discourage her, but on their third date, my mom and dad got into an argument. She stormed out of the restaurant into the pouring rain without her umbrella.

"Suzanne, why didn't you respond to Jack's letters? That is really shitty of you," Pat accused one day.

"I don't know what you're talking about," my mother said.

"Jack put a lot of time and effort into writing those letters. He's not the kind of guy who opens up and shares his feelings the way he tried to."

"I never got them. I swear I never got them!"

Later that evening, after dinner, my mother was helping my grandmother wash the dishes in the kitchen and my grandfather went to sit in the living room to have his after-dinner cigarette. My mother took the opportunity and asked, "Did anything come in the mail for me lately?"

My grandmother began to fidget and tried to change the subject. After a long pause, my mother said, "Mother, what came in the mail for me?"

They both looked up to see my grandfather standing behind them. He said, "Yes, I threw out his letters. I don't want you with him."

He then spewed out everything he'd noticed, in the short time they'd dated, that appeared to be wrong with Jack and his family.

"Dames are stronger than men. They carry babies. When a woman gets sick often and still gets her period, there is something wrong. And look at him with his bad back. The only thing he's good at is drinking in a gin mill."

Jack didn't let my grandfather's view of him stop him, even when my grandfather threatened to throw him out the door without opening it. For months on end, Jack continued to date Sue.

Sometimes it wasn't all debates and arguing, though. Sometimes Grandpa would be working, and my father would sit for long periods of time, listening to my grandmother's stories about her large, close-knit Irish family. It was a family that shared a lot of love but also a lot of sibling rivalry.

On a particular winter night in 1963, the evening started out like many others with my father calling my mother to set up a time to get together. My father drove over to my mother's house, and grandpa wasn't there. After a few hours of grandma's stories and eating dessert, my mother asked my father, "Is everything okay? You seem quiet."

My father said, "I'm sad. I am sad because today, my mother died."

My grandmother said, "Why didn't you say anything?"

He took a sip from his beer and shrugged. My mother then asked, "Where were you before you came here?"

"I sat by the river, staring at the Whitestone Bridge for what seemed to be an hour but was actually about four. I felt numb and guilty for not visiting her the night before she passed away. Then I went out drinking with my buddies."

My parents got married November 11, 1965. They moved out of Queens into the Bronx, where they then had my older sister, Andrea. My mother would sit outside the adjoining mother/daughter homes and talk with the neighbors.

The neighborhood at the time was predominantly made up of Italians and Orthodox Jews who were very family oriented. My mother took a lot of comfort in that atmosphere while my father was at work.

One day, while she was sitting out on the front steps of the house, she was sobbing. One of the neighbors came out and said, "Suzanne, what's the matter? Why are you crying?"

My mother replied, "I am pregnant with another child. I cannot imagine being able to love it as much as I love my daughter."

The neighbor, who was much older than my mother, laughed and took my mother's hand. She pointed to a finger and said, "You like having this ring finger as much as you like having your pointer finger, don't you?"

My mother sat first in amazement at the neighbor's analogy and then began to laugh.

At that time, my father was going to law school all day and working at night. Many evenings, he liked to stop off at the bar. On his way home one evening, he got pulled over by a police officer who asked where my father was coming from, and my father answered, "Law school."

The officer asked my father if he'd had anything to drink. My father admitted that he'd had a few beers but had also mentioned how he'd just worked nine hours and had gone to school prior to that. He said, with a screaming baby at home he didn't usually get much sleep, and he was tired. (My sister Andrea was a colicky baby who screamed many a night.)

The police officer asked my father to get out of the car and then took out his Breathalyzer. My father tested at a 0.4 blood alcohol level, was arrested, and had to spend the night in jail. He laid there in the cell and thought of committing suicide. Later, he would say he hadn't had the nerve to do it.

The neighborhood where my parents were living in the Bronx was growing more and more dangerous. In the prior weeks, for example, there had been two burglaries and then a shooting which had taken the molding right off the neighbor's door.

While my father was in law school, he made very little money doing apprentice and accounting work. My mother was savvy with money, though, and she would scrimp and often 'take from Peter to pay Paul.' That way, they would have enough to celebrate the holidays and go away on vacations.

While on vacation at Glenn Brook Farm in 1969, they met Robert and Vivian McTernan. The McTernans already had a son, Robert, at the time, and Vivian was having trouble getting pregnant with a second child. The couples sat together at meals for the week and shared many good conversations.

Over breakfast one morning, Vivian turned to Sue and said, "You mentioned you were looking for a house away from the city. I think you should look in our neighborhood in Long Island."

About a month after my parents returned from vacation, my mother made plans with Vivian to go out and look for a house. My mother was about seven months pregnant with me, and money was tight, but Vivian assured her she would find a home in their price bracket.

My mother fell in love with a home that was right across the street from an elementary school and just around the block from the McTernans' home. However, my parents were concerned they wouldn't be able to afford that house if there were any problems with my mother's pregnancy, so they decided on a smaller house a few weeks later.

The house had three finished bedrooms, an unfinished attic, one bathroom, a small kitchen, and a living room/dining room combo. But the roomy back yard was what sold them on the place. The house had brown paneling that always felt cold and moist, and there was a lot of paranormal activity, which contributed to my fears.

On September 21, 1970, much to my older sister's dismay, my parents moved into 824 South Gate, and only two weeks later, I was born.

Right away, it seemed, my mother noticed I was much different than my sister. Whereas Andrea had been colicky and hypersensitive, I was hyposensitive and slept seven to eight hours a night almost immediately. I also was not finicky as a child and was able to eat most things, while my sister couldn't.

My earliest memory of my mother was when I was a few months old in my basinet and mother jumped out of bed, hysterical. She picked me up and began shaking me, and I started to cry.

My father asked her, "Sue, what is wrong with you?"

She stood there with her mouth open and a puzzled look on her face and said, "I thought she was dead. She never woke up crying for her bottle at 7:00 a.m., and it's almost 9:00 a.m."

By this point, my father was in his last year of law school. Money was still tight. My parents were living on thirty-five thousand dollars a year, and there were five of us.

My father had always had a drinking problem, but the added stress of law school, two children, and an unstable wife made him into a full-blown alcoholic, which made it impossible for him to provide for his family. Codependency, addiction, abandonment, and betrayal set the tone of not only their marriage but also of the living conditions for us girls.

My mother, coming from a very unstable background herself and then marrying an alcoholic, was not equipped emotionally or psychologically to deal with the stresses of a colicky baby (Andrea) or a baby whose development seemed to be slower than what she considered normal (me). And when I was five, my younger sister, Christine, was born.

Because my father was at the bar so much, my mother would escape by locking herself in her room then just sit on the edge of her bed and listen to the radio. She also liked to drink a glass of wine and chain smoke while talking to herself. When my father finally made it home, she would scream and threaten him that she was going to go back home to her parents. There were many evenings dinner was put on the table after 10:00 p.m. if at all.

When I was five months old, my mother took me to the doctor because I wasn't sitting up on my own. Before the doctor came in, she had put me on the table. When I fell over, she smacked me on my legs with disgust and kept me lying down.

When the doctor came in, she frantically conveyed her own ideas about how fast she believed I should sit up in comparison to how quickly her first child or other children had achieved this. The doctor said I was a slow learner but not to worry. Finally, when other babies typically were learning to crawl and take their first steps, I finally sat up.

By the time I was seventeen months old, my parents became concerned because I still wasn't walking and doing what the other children my age were doing. The earliest memories I have of being physically in my body are those of feeling numb, disconnected, and even foggy in my mind.

In kindergarten, the teacher suggested to my parents they put me in special education or repeat the year. Half the school year was over. I couldn't remember where my seat was, nor was I able to keep up with the other children in the classroom.

I can remember the children not liking me and calling me names. I can remember desperately wanting to be loved, to be accepted and included. I didn't seem to fit in anywhere. In the first grade, I was placed with a school psychologist because I started to steal.

I can remember how a lot of the children in my class had their hair done by their mothers. They looked well put together with cute outfits, matching lunch boxes, and warm, frilly coats. I wanted to look like them. I wanted to have what they had. I wanted to be who they were. The only way I saw to fit in was to steal the things they had. I thought those things would bring me happiness and love.

My mother thought it would be useless to keep me back in kindergarten and suggested I be put into first grade. If I had repeated the year, I would have been reinforcing key skills like reading and writing, but my mother didn't think those things were important enough to suffer the stigma of having a child who was held back.

However, they ended up holding me back in first grade anyway, so I was now seven and in the first grade with the kids from the year behind me.

School was difficult. Entire lessons would be taught, and I would daydream and not learn. Every lunchtime was spent doing makeup homework. Soon, I was not feeling good at home or in school. By the end of first grade, they knew I would be repeating the year.

My mother and Vivian worked hard to get me into a class with Vivian's son Joey, which emotionally had helped me a lot. They also got me into remedial writing, reading, and speech. Unfortunately, I was out of the classroom more than I was in it and kept falling behind. My teachers were at a loss as to what my mother could do for me. They even admitted to looking the other way with my poor grades.

At the end of the school year, my parents were advised to take me to a brain specialist to run some tests.

Electroencephalography Test

I graduated kindergarten the summer of 1974. My father had taken off work to take my mother and me to my appointment with a brain specialist in Queens, New York. I was asked to sit in the hallway while the doctor sat with my parents inside an office for a long time.

They had given me a plastic toy to play with while I waited. I remember sitting on the chair, watching my feet dangle above the floor. I picked up the toy, which had a plastic pencil with a magnet at the end of it, and turned it over to see a picture of a man's face.

I saw that there were hundreds of little black-metal shavings inside the toy. The object was to use the magnetic pencil to move the metal shavings around to form the man's hair.

Finally, my parents came out of the office to bring me in. Soon, a nurse came into the doctor's office and took me into another room, where she had me change into a white robe. Then, they sat me down and started to put my hair into tiny pig tails.

They attached small white electrodes over the pigtails that were all over my head. Then they poured a solution over the pig tails. I remember it feeling cold and sticky as I tried to stop it from dripping down my neck.

The doctors had suggested to my parents that I have two tests done: an MRI and an EEG. An MRI (Magnetic Resonance Imaging) monitors the brain's activity due to changes in blood oxygenation. It is useful for mapping which regions of the brain get activated during certain activities.

First, they did the EEG (Electroencephalography) to monitor my brain's electrical activity. The gel they poured over my head was to enable high temporal resolution, which is good for detecting epilepsy, sleep disorders, or whether someone is in a coma.

Once the electrodes were on my head and hooked into a machine, I wasn't aware of most of the testing being done on me. When they were almost finished with the EEG, another practitioner came into the room and asked me to shut my eyes and to say the color which flashed inside my head.

First, I saw red then green, blue, orange, yellow, and violet. I remember asking the practitioner if we could do the test again, but he replied with a stern, "No." His negative answer made the hospital feel colder and made me think the tests showed something more concerning—and that he didn't like me either because of it.

A few weeks later, the test results came back saying there was nothing wrong, though I still couldn't remember anything or learn new concepts. My mind was always fogged, and my body was always fatigued.

The following school year, I, along with Robbie Clappi, a boy who lived across the street, had Mrs. Momanis for a first-grade teacher. Robbie and I used to play hide-and-seek and tag with all the neighborhood kids. He was athletic and had a lot of friends. I remember being happy, at first, that we were in the same class, but that quickly changed. Right from the beginning, I was falling behind. And when the other kids started to make fun, Robbie began to act like everyone else did to me.

I never felt as if I belonged anywhere. I felt so disconnected from the other students, the teachers, and myself. It seemed like an endless losing battle, so I didn't mind that I spent most of my lunch periods and playtimes trying to complete makeup work.

Before school one day, I found my mother's large gold, clip-on, triangle-shaped earrings in the bathroom while I was brushing my teeth. I was desperate to be liked, and I believed the earrings would make people like me.

I slipped the earrings into my school bag and figured I would put them on before I got to school. Then I would take them off before I got home and put them back into the bathroom.

That day, my sister Andrea and I walked to school. When we went our separate ways, I clipped the big earrings to my ears and walked into the classroom. Right away, everyone noticed.

All the girls in the classroom were suddenly talking to me. They seemed to like me because of the earrings. Even the teacher had greeted me with a big smile, saying how lovely I looked with them on. All the girls in the class always looked well-kept with their pretty outfits on and their hair done. I felt that the earrings and whatever stuff I could acquire was the answer to all my problems.

Later that day, when I returned home from school, my mother was crazy, in a manic mood because my sister, Christine, had made a mess. It was easy for me to slip back into the bathroom and put my mother's earrings back into the bathroom.

Every day, it seemed that Christine had been unattended for a long time, so she would create havoc in my mother's life. And every day, my sister Andrea and I would wonder before entering the house from school, "What did she do today?"

Andrea and I dreaded having to deal with our mother. Our fear of her and the way she made us feel was the only thing we both could relate to or seem to have in common.

My mother was a very charismatic person outside our home. She was active with the PTA when Andrea and I were in grammar school, so she made a lot of friends, which I believe was our saving grace in many instances.

The day I returned the earrings to the bathroom was a day my mother was supposed to carpool for my soccer practice. When I came out of the bathroom, my mother looked at me angrily and said, "I don't have time for this shit. It's already 3:45, and your practice is at 4:30. And it's my fucking day to carpool. I must run around all day for you kids. It's a thankless job."

I felt sick. I remember thinking it wasn't even my idea to join soccer. *You signed me up for soccer because your friend Ginny signed her daughter Dolores up for it.*

My mother never took an interest in or made much time for anything we did unless there was some emotional fulfillment in it for her. She could never handle or follow through on her part of the responsibility without making us feel as if we were unworthy and ungrateful for it.

At 4:00 p.m., the phone rang. I could hear her pick up the receiver in the other room and answer in an angry voice that felt more like 'what the hell do you want?' than hello.

A second later, I heard my mother completely change her tone into a demure one and say, "Cathy, thank God you called! I am really running very behind. Christine took off her diaper and smeared her shit all over the wall." After a short pause she continued, "Oh, Cathy. These kids are going to be the death of me. Thank you, thank you so much."

The call had been from Mrs. Terrano. Since it was our day to carpool, we should have been picking up her daughter Mary.

I do not know who was more relieved, my mother or me. On the rare occasions she couldn't get anyone to pick up her end of the stick, she would let us sit wherever we were for hours at a time, waiting for her to arrive.

When Christine was in junior high school, she needed transportation for her after-school activities. Mom agreed to share the responsibility with Christine's best friend's mother, Annmarie. Many times, when it was my mother's turn, she wouldn't show up and they would be stuck at school until 8:00 at night. Christine would call and call, and I would hear the phone ringing for hours.

My mother would scream, "Don't pick up that fucking phone or I'll break your ugly face! I don't have time to jackass across town to pick her and her slut friend up."

As if standing everyone up wasn't bad enough, eventually my mother sabotaged our friendships when other parents would confront her. On occasion, a few friends' parents would get home from work and pick up their children and not drop me off. They would make excuses, but I knew it was the lack of reciprocation.

It seemed my mother was stuck in the same pattern of trauma her parents had inflicted upon her. She played it out in my and my sisters' lives. The constant messages of unworthiness, not being good enough, not having enough, abandonment, and betrayal were the ongoing themes for us in everyday life. She loved to pit friends against friends and cause paranoia, which made long-term relationships for us impossible.

Christmas Eve

The smell of cigarettes and ammonia permeated the house while my father was at work. It was around 8:00 p.m. one Christmas Eve. My little sister and I were sitting in our snow-covered front yard in lawn chairs. Her freckled white skin was red from the winter air.

Christine asked me through chattering teeth, "Can we go in the house yet? I am so cold."

I told her, "In a little while. We have to wait until Dad gets home."

I always thought it was better to have adult witnesses around my mother as much as possible. I figured she would act out less when triggered, but in the end, that never seemed to matter.

The cab finally dropped my father off around 8:30. I was relieved to see him since my hands and feet were burning from the cold. Christine and I walked behind our father into the house.

My mother pointed her finger at him as she glanced at the clock and said, "Pissing money away that we don't have. I married the LAWYER, the big lawyer! What a joke! You're a joke, Jack!"

My little sister and I ran upstairs. My older sister was in what once was our playroom but now was her room. I hated that she had taken over the playroom. There wasn't any other place in the house we could go to get away from my mother. And Andrea didn't really care.

Many days, I was stuck playing on the landing outside her bedroom, but at least it was warm. The house was as imbalanced as the people who lived inside. The main floor was always ten to twenty degrees colder than the upstairs. I would dread having to leave the warmth of the upstairs to come downstairs for dinner.

Before a holiday or right before we went away on vacation, my mother would go off on a tangent and my father would decide to disappear to the bar. When he got home, our version of World War Three would erupt. The energy of the house was so heavy. Often, I could see what appeared to be a black blob-like energy that had a dark presence.

Years later, I found out a son of the house's previous owner had hung himself in his bedroom, which was first our playroom and then Andrea's bedroom. As an energy healer, I realize now that my parents had the same energy the previous owners had. It was the same energy that brought "like" situations, people, and experiences to not just my parents but to my sisters and myself as well.

It was 1979, and my father was home in his bed. I could see that the light was on from outside since it had just turned dark. I had gone to a friend's house after school, so I was getting in late. I cannot remember my father ever staying home from work because he was sick, but I could hear my mother through the thin walls, asking my father to get out of bed. She asked him to stand and hold his knee to his chest. She asked him if he was having any pain.

My father was in so much agony he fell back onto the bed. My mother called Vivian and shared my father's symptoms. They both concluded through their own observations that my father should go to the hospital because they thought he had appendicitis.

At 5:30 p.m., my mother called Dr. Gerber, the family doctor. She asked if she could make an emergency appointment. By

6:00 p.m., Dad was admitted into the Nassau Community Medical Center for tests. By 8:00 a.m. the following morning, my father was diagnosed with colon cancer.

The MRI showed the mass was as large as a man's closed fist. The mass's location appeared to be near the lymph nodes, which most likely meant the cancer had spread. My father was forty-five and my mother was thirty-five at the time. They were barely making ends meet as it was. And neither of my parents had any help or support from their families.

If that wasn't bad enough, the night my father found out he had cancer was the anniversary of his mother's death from esophageal cancer.

The doctors didn't want to wait, so that evening, they wheeled Dad into the operating room and took the cancer out. We had waited in the waiting room the entire time although Mom went outside often to smoke. The surgery took nine hours from start to finish. When the surgeon came out, he was smiling from ear to ear. He said, "Mrs. Schwalm, your husband was very, very lucky. Even though the mass was very large, it was not near the lymph nodes. The x-ray we took before the surgery had cast a shadow that was so large it looked like the mass was on his other side near some lymph nodes, but in actuality it was not."

Even though the doctor recommended chemotherapy, he was almost positive the cancer had not spread.

My mother was a stay-at-home housewife. She had done well enough in high school but was beaten down by her father and had never tried to get a college diploma. My father had always been the bread winner, but he was then apprenticing at a law firm, waiting to take the Bar Exam.

He had medical insurance, but the chemotherapy wasn't fully covered. It covered everything except twenty percent, but my parents were very concerned because they didn't know how much the actual chemotherapy cost would be.

While my father was in the hospital, my mother arranged for Aunt Nonie, her mother's sister, and her husband, Jimmy, to stay with my sisters and me. Dad had to stay in the hospital for two weeks for post-op.

I remember a gray Lincoln pulling up to the front door and a tall, thin woman wearing a pantsuit and sunglasses pushing open the door. In a loud voice, the woman said, "Goddammit, Jimmy, we were supposed to be here four hours ago. If you had half a brain, you would be dangerous." She flicked her cigarette after a lengthy drag, looked at me, and said, "Well, you must be Laura Bell. You look exactly like your grandma." She handed me a medium-sized plastic bag that had a few wigs in it. I was shocked because I had never known anyone who wore a wig.

Nonie had cancer herself, but at the time we didn't know it. I liked when people came and stayed over because my mother would be busy trying to accommodate them and spending less time on what we kids were doing. My father had gone in for surgery in August. I shared with my Aunt that my birthday was coming up and asked if she thought I would be able to have a birthday party.

She assured me she thought I would. That evening, Nonie mentioned my concern to my mother. The next morning before anyone else was up, my mother woke me up violently out of a sound sleep. "You selfish little bitch—going around crying over having a birthday party while your father has cancer cut out of him and is laying in a hospital bed. You pathetic piece of shit!"

She stormed out the door and sped to the hospital.

My father came home the next day. When he walked through the door, he looked taller and thinner than I remembered. His cheeks were flushed. My mother was behind him and told him to go lay down and relax.

My father said, "I just laid down for the past three weeks." He walked over to the refrigerator and took out a beer and then sat across from me on the living-room couch. I remember he seemed detached and angry.

I said, "Dad, this is great! You don't have cancer anymore!"

He sat back on the couch, shook his head, and took a sip from his beer. I was surprised at his response, so I continued and said, "Dad, why are you sad? They got the cancer." But he didn't answer. He took another sip and looked away.

After a few moments, my mother came into the living room and said, "Get the hell outside and leave him alone!"

As I got up to go outside, I glanced over at my father with sadness because he was different. Even though the cancer hadn't taken him, I felt it had taken him in another way.

My father's cancer was a big distraction from my school issues. With all the running around for my father, no one had the time or patience to review my IEP or lesson plans. (An IEP is an Individualized Education Program for children who need special education. It is where parents are supposed to go over the plan with teachers, psychologists, and school administrators so they can help reinforce the child's studies and educational plan at home.)

Due to the chemotherapy costs not being fully covered, my mother took odd jobs and worked nights for extra money.

Many nights, she would leave me and my sisters home, assuming father would be in shortly after she left. Unfortunately, my father would take the opportunity to go to the bar while my older sister and I attended to my little sister, cooked dinner, and helped with chores. The next day, Andrea and I would lie and tell my mother our dad had gotten home much sooner than he really had in hopes it would keep the peace.

This tactic rarely ever worked, though, because she would almost always find out the real story. My sisters and I would beg my father to lie to our mother. But he never did, regardless of the consequences. We even went as far as to make up stories that he could tell her, but he always told her the truth when she asked.

When I was in grammar school, I had four friends who were born in the same month as I was. I knew these girls because they were daughters of my mother's friends.

It was a Saturday in late September. I was at my classmate's nine-year birthday party. My mother was taking care of my little sister at home and asked my father to pick me up at the birthday party, which was a few blocks away. My father came and got me. We went up to the stores on Carmen Avenue, where he gave me five dollars for milk, told me I could get some candy for myself, and told me to meet him in the bar.

First, I went into the deli and bought the milk and candy. Then, as I walked into the bar, I immediately got hit with the smell of beer and cigarettes. Every stool in the bar was full, and there was a pool table in the middle of the room. My father introduced me to the bartender and to some of the people sitting around him. The bartender asked me whether I'd ever played pool and pushed two quarters across the bar. My father took a swig of beer, walked over to the pool sticks, and nodded at me.

I jumped off the bar stool in excitement and chose my stick. We played pool for what seemed a few minutes but was really a few hours. That day, my father taught me how to play pool. Finally, we left the bar after the sun had gone down. By then it was a lot cooler outside.

The plastic seats in the car felt moist and cold against my legs. I began to feel nauseated and became anxious. I told my father I did not think it was a good idea to tell my mother I had been at the bar. I pleaded with him, but he chuckled beneath his breath. Then he turned to me and assured me everything was fine.

Soon, we pulled in the driveway and walked through the front door. My mother came running out of the kitchen, clutching a potholder in one hand and a serrated knife in the other. She walked up to us, pointing the knife, and got in my father's face.

"Where the fuck were you for the better part of three hours? I asked you to pick her up, not go to the bar, and not to piss money away." She then turned to me and held the knife up against my face and said, "I'll kill you if you step one fucking foot into that bar again. I am telling you, Jack, you will come home to a bunch of dead children if you keep this shit up. Now go pick up Andrea from soccer practice and take her"—indicating me—"with you."

Crying and sobbing, I followed him out. I could feel pins and needles shooting through me. I felt numb. My father didn't say anything during the drive to pick up my sister. When we arrived, my sister came running out of practice and jumped into the back seat.

She then saw by my swollen eyes that I had been crying and asked, "What is the matter? What happened?"

I tried to get the words out but couldn't. I just cried louder. My father then grabbed me and yelled, "Shut up! Just shut up!"

I stifled myself as best I could as we drove the rest of the way home in silence.

Laid Off

One morning, it was almost 7:30 a.m. one morning, and the cab would soon be pulling up to the front door. Dad would tiptoe into my room to make sure he didn't wake up my little sister, and he would whisper, "It's time to get up," while he tickled my face before he would flee out the front door.

I looked forward to the few seconds he and I had in the mornings, because I didn't see my father much during the week when I was growing up. He worked late and many times would go to the bar after work. Also, he had over an hour commute each way. After he left for work, I knew well enough to get up and get ready on my own.

Mother was a late riser, and she expected us to feed and dress ourselves. This was not the easiest task as I didn't have many clothes that fit correctly and I didn't know how to tie my shoes.

As far as breakfast, I used to skip it a lot of the time because I didn't like cold cereal. Whenever I ate it, it made me nauseous and I would vomit most of it back out. So I used to make it look like I was eating by pouring a little milk in a bowl. Then I threw a few flakes in. I knew by the time my mother woke up, she would see the soggy flakes and assume I had eaten.

One morning, at almost 8:30, an hour after the normal time Dad would have gone to work, I woke to the sound of glasses clanging together. I walked out into the living room and saw my father dart past me as he was running around the house in his three-piece suit. He was holding a bottle of brown liquor in one hand and a glass in the other. His energy seemed scattered and frazzled, and he radiated anxiety. He glanced over at me but didn't say anything before dashing out the door.

After he left, I walked over to a dish filled with quarters on top of the liquor cabinet. I took two fists full and filled my pockets. I had wanted to walk up to Carmen Avenue to the discount store to buy candy. I then sat down and contemplated where my sneakers were while waiting for my sister so we could walk together to school.

Every now and again, like that morning, my mother would wake up before I left for school. She would start screaming about what I was wearing and how I looked. I remember feeling frozen while she screamed at me and belittled me.

"Where are your sneakers? Where the fuck are your sneakers?" She came at me with the clenched sneaker in her hand and started hitting me in the head with it. Finally, she dropped the sneaker. "Hurry up, you useless piece of shit, and get to school."

Terrified she would still be standing over me, I hurriedly tucked my laces into my shoes and ran out the door.

My older sister and I walked to school together most every morning. But there was always a heavy feeling of awkwardness and embarrassment between us, either because of what our mother did to us in front of each other or because of all the thoughts and feelings we had on our own as a result of it. We rarely spoke of the experiences that went on in the house, and once we got to school, we had plenty of our own challenges to deal with.

Even though the environment was different at school than at home, my sister and I kept recreating the same internal living hell we had at home, feeling shameful, defective, not worthy, and not good enough.

That particular morning, I didn't wait for my sister. I had about five dollars in change from the dish, enough money to buy twenty packs of Bubble Yum gum.

After I bought the gum, I walked back to the school and waited outside for the teachers to open the doors. As children started to congregate around the doors, one girl noticed I was chewing gum and asked for a piece.

Before I knew it, I felt like the entire school had surrounded me, and within a few minutes, all my gum was gone. I remember having the gum to give to others made me feel important. I liked the feeling, but it was very short-lived. Some of the children ridiculed me anyway, pointing out I was still a nothing, regardless of my generosity. The gum didn't win me any friends.

When I was lucky enough to make a friend and not sabotage the relationship by being detached, stealing, lying, or gossiping, my mother would do her best to sabotage the relationship.

Stuck in the torture of what her father had done to her, she continued the narcissistic patterns deliberately, consciously, and repeatedly. The greater the scene she created, the more damage she did to our relationships and our self-worth. Over time, as she thrived on this, we just stopped bringing anyone around.

The Playroom

When Andrea and I were little, we spent a lot of time in the upstairs room of my parents' house that was made into a playroom. My mother very rarely came upstairs unless she wanted to yell at us or hit us for one reason or another.

For the most part, when my sister and I got home from school, we were either sent outdoors to play or sent upstairs out of our mother's sight. The bathroom was across the hall from her bedroom, and we would watch her since she would many times leave the door open a crack. This was her regular place of retreat. She would sit on her bed in her bedroom for hours, rocking back and forth, listening to music, drinking wine, and smoking cigarettes. And not until my father came home would she run around frantically trying to do a day's worth of house chores and start preparing dinner. So dinner was put on the table late and with rage.

One day, Andrea said to me, "Let's make Mommy think it's really windy outside by moving this cable back and forth really fast."

She took the window off the track and laid it on the floor of the playroom. After about thirty minutes, my mother ran up the stairs. As she did, my sister and I ran away from the window.

My mother lunged at Andrea, demanding, "What the hell are you two doing?"

As Andrea stepped away from my mother, she knocked over a ceramic bank in the shape of baseball mitt. The bank fell onto the glass window she had placed on the floor. My mother grabbed her by the arm and said, "Look what the hell you did. What's wrong with you? If you had half a brain, you would be dangerous."

During our younger years, Andrea and I would make fun and reenact arguments my mother had with my father.

One evening, we were in the playroom, waiting for my father to come home. It was already 7:45 p.m., and we hadn't eaten yet. Andrea let out a big sigh. She looked at me and shook her head.

She said, "Mom has been downstairs cleaning since the moment I got home. I haven't eaten since 11:00 this morning, and Dad—God only knows when he will walk through the door."

It was the dead of winter, and the neighborhood was silent. My sister went back to reading her book. I could hear my mother talking to herself downstairs as she slammed doors and banged things around. She often would work herself up with drinking and rehearsing what she was going to say to my father. By the time he got home, she would get violent.

I sat on the floor, going in and out of consciousness by daydreaming. When I drifted out of consciousness at one point, I had a vision that my father got stabbed in the back. When I came back into consciousness, my sister asked me what was the matter. I must have had a weird look on my face, and I started to cry.

She said, "Wait, why are you crying?"

I replied, "I had a vision that Father was going to somehow hurt his back very bad."

Andrea assured me that no one, including our mother, was going to hurt our father.

Finally, by 9:15 p.m., my father walked through the door. My mother had been waiting for him to arrive, so as soon as he did, she lashed out. She was so angry she picked up a kerosene heater while it was on and tried to throw it at my father.

My father was so accustomed to my mother screaming and abusing him that he seemed immune to her abuse. He never yelled back—he wouldn't even raise his voice—or challenged her in any way.

The lack of reaction he gave made her crazier and even more violent. My parents had a large circular coffee table in the middle of the living room. It had a large piece of glass that sat on top of it. She smashed it with her fist during one heated argument, and a piece of glass flew into my father's back.

This wasn't the first time she had had hurt him out of frustration. My father's detachment and lack of emotion would only add fuel to this. Because my mother felt miserable, she felt we all should be and would turn her anger on us.

Once, my little sister had an allergic reaction to seafood and she started to swell up. My mother told her not to worry about it and to take an aspirin.

She was so fixated on getting revenge on my father that Christine had to get a ride to the hospital from someone else. When my father came home, my mother had been drinking and she threw a VCR tape at his head. The corner of it hit his eye and he had to get stitches.

I walked home from Nassau Community College to find no one home and blood all over the bathroom. I thought for a moment Mom had stabbed Dad.

The next day, as my father dropped me off at school, I saw the yellow stain on his face from the iodine the hospital had put on his cut.

I pretended I didn't know what had happened. He said he had hit his head. It seemed to me that my mother could do whatever she wanted to whomever she wanted whenever she wanted without any consequences, which made me feel unsafe.

I was terrified of her. I was constantly in the fight-flight-or-freeze survival mechanism. From her bullying and isolating me to abusing my sister and father, I didn't only have anxiety and learning issues; I could feel actual resulting physical sensations for long periods of time, as well. Some of the physical sensations felt like pins and needles at the base of my spine and in my legs from my nervous system being in overdrive.

Andrea's Birthday Present

Aside from one birthday party when I was in first grade and a party I had in seventh grade, my mother did not like anyone to celebrate my birthday. It was one of my mother's favorite forms of psychological abuse. Isolating and ignoring me meant not acknowledging anything I ever did nor celebrating anything related to me. This behavior covered birthdays, holidays, and graduations and continued into my adult life as well, showing up when I graduated from beauty school, got married twice, and gave birth to my son.

It wasn't until I was married to Roger that he said to me after I had come home with bags of Christmas presents for my family, "Why do you go out and buy these people anything? They ignore you! Your sisters and family either hand you nothing or gifts that are cheap and reflect no thought. They treat you like you are less than them, like a dog."

For whatever reason, I knew in my heart Roger was right, but I thought I could make them like me by buying them stuff. Unfortunately, that never happened, and my gifts became expected.

For many years, Andrea would take my gifts and say, "Thank you. Oh, I left your gift at home by accident. I'll send it to you."

I couldn't fathom taking a gift from anyone on Christmas and not giving something in return without feeling bad or guilty. I assumed she was the same, because I had remembered a time when she had gone all out.

The night of my tenth birthday, right before bedtime, I heard Andrea say, "Wait, she cannot go to sleep! I want to give Laura her birthday gift."

She came into the bedroom and handed me a box and a tube, both wrapped in colorful birthday wrapping paper. She said with excitement, "Happy Birthday, Laura! You're a whole decade old. Do you know what that means?"

I shook my head *no*. As she explained what it meant, I first ripped open the tube, which was a Salvador Dali painting called *Persistence of Memory*. Then in the box, I found a Magic Eight Ball. Billed as a fortuneteller ball, it looked like a black pool-hall ball that had the number eight on the outside of it, but when you flipped the ball over, it revealed a window that would give you a fortune after you shook it.

At that time, my sister had known I was obsessed with witches. I wasn't a good reader, but if I had to take a book out from the library, it was always one about witches. I was ecstatic with my gifts. After my sister left my bedroom, I heard my mother questioning her in the hallway right outside my door, asking her why she gave me anything and not to do it anymore. We were all equally terrified of my mother, and Andrea and Christine learned early it was best to go along with everything she said. Over time, it became comfortable treating me like I was an outsider.

Grammar School

Jana lived around the corner from me and was my first friend. We had met one day while I was sitting on the stoop down the block from my house. I was sitting on the curb by myself when she rode up on her bike and boldly introduced herself. From that day forward, we were inseparable.

She was a lot smarter academically than I was. Her love and kindness gave me strength, and she cared for me like a mother. When I was having problems in school, Jana spent many days teaching me how to read and write. She also made sure I had a place to stay and food to eat, and she gave me her old clothes to wear so I could look more kempt, because I was always self-conscious about looking the way I did.

It didn't take long for my mother to notice how nice Jana treated me, and she didn't hide the fact she didn't like it. She would complain that Jana was spoiled. Every chance she could, she accused Jana of being bossy and controlling and that I was her doormat. When Jana would call on the phone or come by the house, my mother would deliberately go out of her way to be rude and make Jana feel unwelcome and not liked. My mother continued to repeat this behavior with everyone who showed me love or any type of caring.

Luckily, Jana was not afraid of my mother and continued to call for me regardless of how mean my mother was to her.

Unlike my birthdays, Jana's were celebrated, and she was allowed to invite the entire class to her parties. She had games like "spin the bottle" and "seven minutes in paradise"—kissing games where someone needed to pick you to be their partner. I would always complain and find a way not to play in fear that no one would pick me.

By the time I was fourteen, I had moved out of my parents' house three to four times. My father already had cancer and had undergone two major surgeries: one back surgery, lasting thirteen hours, and a hip replacement.

My mother was always in a bad mood. She let it be known that she didn't want to work. She would belittle and insult my father, saying things like, "I married the big lawyer. Ha! Isn't that a joke? You're a joke, you noodle dick!"

As I was growing up on Long Island, we lived in the suburbs. The homes were built close to the other homes. Everyone knew everything about everyone since the town was small, but that didn't stop my mother from expressing herself. When my father came home late because he'd gone to the bar, she would say, "You got your wife working while you sit at a bar and piss money away that we don't have. You do not care that you let your kids run around the streets like NIGGAS!!!"

She fought with him until all hours of the morning, and he often was too tired and too drunk to fight back.

A few times, my father came home and fell asleep on the toilet. Then my mother would wake up the house by pounding on the bathroom door and screaming at him. One time, she saw he hadn't made it to the bathroom and had defecated in his pants. She flipped out, threatening she was going to kill all of us, that he would come home to a bunch of dead children. I remember visualizing in my head our dead bodies with blood and stab marks all over us.

My mother was always on a tirade, spewing her anger and frustration onto us kids, especially me, since I was not particularly good at anything. And I was a horrible student, which made her think people viewed her as defective for giving birth to a child who had a disability.

In addition to learning disabilities, I also had physical problems. Along with severe allergies, asthma, and kidney stones, I had debilitating menstrual cramps. I would dry heave from the pain and lie curled into a fetal position in agony on the restroom floor in the school nurse's office. The pain was excruciating. It felt like knives going in and out of my abdomen.

After a few class periods of lying down at the nurse's and not feeling any better at those times, the nurse would send me home, which would make my mother angry. I tried to deal with it. My mother believed that girls who didn't have sex didn't need to go to the gynecologist, so I self-medicated. I would go to my friends' houses and raid their medicine cabinets for whatever I could find.

Many times, I would mix different over-the-counter pain relievers that wouldn't really relieve the symptoms but instead made me shaky and gave me other symptoms.

Everyone walked on eggshells around my mother because they knew she was severely imbalanced and that she drank heavily to deal to with her life. One time, my parents had gotten money as a gift for their anniversary, so my mother told my father to buy himself a suit since he was starting a new job.

My father, not being the most fashion savvy, went to a department store and came home with a polyester suit. My mother proceeded to set it on fire in one of our garbage cans she had dragged into the living room for that purpose.

She sat there, blank-faced, and cheerfully said, "Jack, look at the nice bonfire in the living room, you fucking piece of shit. I will burn the entire house down with everyone in it."

She always had to take it to the extreme because my father very rarely showed emotion or got upset. That evening, for example, he very calmly walked over to the phone and called the police.

About forty-five minutes later, I heard the police talking to my parents then carrying the garbage can out of the house.

Even though we three sisters were growing up in the same household, each of us had our own ways of dealing with the dysfunction. My older sister, for example, didn't have many friends but loved to read. She could read a novel in just a few days to help her block out the chaos in the house. I, on the other hand, took off to my friends' homes, while Christine was involved in after-school activities that would also take her away from home.

But when we had to be home, it was every girl for herself. My mother always had to be able to dump her animosity about her life onto someone. Whoever that someone was, she expected the rest of the family to follow her lead. If they didn't, she would turn her fury onto them.

My mother's favorite type of punishment for me was gaslighting, where she constantly psychologically and emotionally manipulated me and the people in our environment. After a short while, I wasn't able to think clearly or even trust my own mind, so I became dependent on my psychic claircognizance ("clear knowing") to help me stay safe from her and her wrath.

When I had any good achievement, special occasion, or anything that would give me acknowledgement, she ignored it and expected everyone else to ignore it as well. There were many birthdays that went by without a simple "Happy Birthday" from any of my siblings or either one of my parents.

Each time I moved out, my parents made little effort to bring me home. They were always dealing with an abundance of problems at the time, with me being one of them. A psychic I would visit during that time told me I was my parents' reminder of everything they didn't like about themselves. It made so much sense to me since neither of my parents treated my sisters as badly.

It was just easier to stay at different friends' homes and figure out how to survive by myself. My family never gave me any support, and if they did know of my concerns or problems, they would do more to hurt me than help me.

Asthma Attacks

One of the most prominent memories I have is of being sick when I was seven years old. I had post-nasal drip that wouldn't stop. My head was pounding, I had fever and chills, and worst of all, I was wheezing. My chest was tight, and I couldn't breathe. It was summertime, and my mother wasn't working yet, so she was then home all day "cleaning" the house.

My sisters and I were expected to go outside and fend for ourselves until our father came home. I remember feeling so sick and weak that I sat down on a curb underneath a tree around the block from where we lived and fell asleep. I woke up what seemed to be only a few moments later to a girl was my age riding a pink Huffy bicycle. She had long, thick, brown, wavy hair in two ponytails. Her name was Jana Vosseler, and she became my first friend.

Jana was very confident and assertive. She rode right up to me on the curb and said, "Why are you sleeping on the curb? Are you sick?"

The pressure in my head felt like I had been hit repeatedly with a hammer. I picked it up off the ground. I'm sure my eyes were so glassy and red that it looked as if I'd been crying.

Jana glanced at my face and said, "You look sick. Maybe you should go home. Where do you live?"

I turned and pointed at a large red house with white trim. She said, "That is not your house; I know the people that live there."

I remember feeling ashamed of where I lived. I was always fearful of my mother's reaction to anyone who came around for me, so I was reluctant to tell Jana. But she was not accustomed to not getting what she wanted. She was very persistent in digging through my lies and excuses but still wasn't able to get me to go home.

About an hour later, we could her a woman's voice calling for Jana. I saw an attractive woman with short, wavy, reddish-brown hair with golden streaks in it walking towards us. She had a big smile on her face and said, "I see you have made a friend, Jana."

As she introduced herself to me, she said, "You do not look so well." She reached across, put her hand on my forehead, and said, "You have a fever. I think you should go home. Where do you live?"

I knew I couldn't lie to Jana's mother, so I reluctantly answered her question. She offered to walk me there. I quickly said I would be fine and walked in the direction of my house. Puzzled, yet letting me go alone, Jana and her mother watched me go.

A few hours later, I heard a knock at the door followed by my mother opening it.

"Hello, my name is Barbara Vosseler. I just wanted to come by to introduce myself and to see how your daughter is feeling."

My mother said, "My daughter?"

Barbara then told my mother how she had met me on the curb. I heard my mother say, "Oh, she just didn't get enough sleep last night."

But Barbara said, "I actually felt her forehead, and she felt as if she had a fever."

My mother thanked Barbara for her concern and promised to make a doctor's appointment. After Barbara left, she stormed into my room where I was lying down and said, "What are you, a fucking martyr? You must embarrass me by sleeping on the street? There's always something with you."

I hated being sick. It made me feel as if I was a problem and an inconvenience. It was much easier for me to figure things out for myself than to deal with my mother. But my friends' parents and my teachers often witnessed this and thought they were helping me. In reality, it only made things worse.

By the next morning, I couldn't breathe at all. I wasn't worried about the backlash I would get from being sick anymore because I truly thought I was going to die. My mother thankfully called the family doctor, who saw me right away as an emergency patient.

The doctor didn't need to put his stethoscope to my chest to see the difficulty I was having breathing or to hear the wheezing. The doctor at first assumed I was having an asthma attack. After I had a chest x-ray, it was determined I had pneumonia. This would be the first time out of many that I had pneumonia.

Dr. Gerber, our family doctor, gave me a shot of epinephrine and two breathing treatments to open my airways. He wrote me four prescriptions. One emergency inhaler, prednisone, Theo-Dur, and a steroid inhaler. The medicine made me shaky and jumpy, but I was grateful to be able to breathe again. Before we went home, we stopped off at the pharmacy to fill up my prescriptions.

While we waited, my mother shared with me about the many asthma attacks she'd had when she was young and how she'd grown out of them. I remember feeling the worst part of having asthma was the worry of having an attack.

My parents very rarely went on vacations by themselves. In fact, I can recall only two or three times, if even that much. And I probably remember those few times mainly because of the turbulent situations happening before, during, or after them.

Nothing with our family ever seemed to go smoothly or according to plan. My father had put aside money to take my mother away for their ten-year anniversary, so they asked my grandparents on my mother's side to watch us while they went on a long weekend to the Poconos.

It was winter, and my mother was running around packing and getting her luggage together. My father had just returned from picking up some last-minute things from the store. I was sitting on the couch, staring out the window, when I saw a mid-sized burgundy-red Lincoln pull up outside the house. When the car stopped, a woman jumped out of the passenger's side.

She had big, dark-brown, curly hairy. She had heavy makeup on and wore a full-length mink coat. On the driver's side, a short man with thinning blond hair and wearing a sports coat got out next. He walked to the back of the car, popped open the trunk, and grabbed two suitcases out of it.

I couldn't hear what they were saying, but I could tell they were bickering. I opened the door, and they walked in.

My grandmother said, "Hello, Laura Bell. How are you?" Without waiting for a response, she looked around nervously and asked, "Where is your mother?"

My mother came running out of the bathroom almost on cue. "I am so sorry to be running late!" She then turned and ran back into the bathroom.

My grandfather had walked into the house and sat down on the couch. Aside from looking up at her and nodding, he didn't acknowledge her. He did, however, point out the dusty floorboards that she'd missed cleaning.

Grandma was trying to lighten up the atmosphere with some small chit chat. Finally, as my parents were leaving, they gave my grandparents Vivian's phone number and kissed us goodbye.

When my parents had gone, my older sister and I went upstairs to the playroom. We hadn't been there long when we could hear yelling downstairs. My older sister crept halfway down the stairs to see my grandparents arguing. Then she saw my grandfather leave and came running back upstairs to report her findings to me.

She suggested I go downstairs to keep Grandma distracted while she tried to quickly gather any bottles of alcohol and hide them in our storage closet where we kept all our cleaning supplies. But by the time we got to play out our plan, my grandmother had already started drinking.

My sister told me to continue keeping our grandmother busy anyway while she hid the rest of the bottles. A few hours later, our grandmother was having intense mood swings—one moment spewing anger, the next hysterically crying, then acting above it all and as if everything was fine.

Around dinner time, even though my mother had prepared food, my grandmother decided she was going to take us to Mimmo's, an upscale Italian restaurant. Since Grandpa had taken the car, she called a cab. As we waited on the couch, my grandmother poured herself another drink and blurted out, "I didn't have to marry your grandfather, you know. I have had many men want to be with me."

As she told us this, she became more and more hysterical. As the tears streamed down her face, she squealed, "Harry was a handsome man. He was considerate and wanted to be with me. Harry was going to take me to Bermuda."

Finally, the cab arrived, and my older sister and I took our little sister into the back seat of the cab. Grandma sat in the front, and off we went to Mimmo's.

As soon as we got to the restaurant, Grandma asked the waiter to bring her a dirty martini and then continued to rant about someone named Charlie and all the other men who'd treated her better. She had passed them up to be with my grandfather. My sister and I had noticed a pay phone in the lobby of the restaurant when we walked in, and we took turns trying to contact Vivian on it. We also kept diluting my grandmother's martinis.

My grandmother kept on, telling us again and still emotionally about Harry taking her away. The people at the surrounding tables looked up at us and chuckled. I decided to run back to the pay phone and try Vivian one more time. I tried the number a few more times, but nobody picked up.

As I hung up the phone, a man in the lobby looked at me and chuckled. He said, "Try another. Maybe the next one will be home."

He had seen me all night trying to get through to Vivian. He assumed I was prank-calling people and shooed me back to my table.

After dinner, my grandmother asked the maître d' to call a cab for us while she paid the bill. Grandma stumbled to get up, knocking a glass off the table. As she walked into the lobby, Andrea and I followed her, holding on to Christine. The cab pulled up, we jumped in, and the driver headed back to our house.

Once at home, we jumped out of the cab and my grandmother paid the driver. As my sisters and I went into the bedroom to change for bed, we heard my grandmother screaming. She was on the floor, banging her fists on the ground, crying.

My older sister and I ran to her to see what all the commotion was about. In between sobs, Grandma explained she'd lost her bag either in the restaurant or in the cab—and in her wallet in the bag was $10,000.

My older sister called the cab company, and the dispatcher promised to relay the message to the driver. About two hours later, there was a knock at the door. By now, I was in bed, and

I could hear the familiar voice of the cab driver and then my grandmother thanking him profusely for returning her bag.

A few moments later I heard the door close, then silence, and I fell asleep. The next thing I remember is Andrea waking me up, saying Vivian was coming to get us because Grandma had left with the cab driver, most likely headed back home.

The next day, my parents were coming home, so Vivian called the lodge where my parents were staying to notify them we were with her instead of my grandparents. The following evening, when my parents came to get us, I could feel my mother's embarrassment.

She apologized for some time and then said to Vivian, "It never fails. They can never let me have my time. Every special occasion has always been sabotaged or overshadowed by my parents. My wedding, my honeymoon, the birth of all my children, every holiday, every occasion. They just aren't capable of letting me have anything."

From a young age, I had seen that my grandparents were mean to my mother. She was their only daughter, so we were obligated to spend all of the holidays with my mother's parents unless they would pick a fight and not want to see us.

Holidays consisted of my grandfather berating my father about his political views, my mother making small chit chat and dodging belittling comments, and the three of us girls watching a green TV in the back room. Though this was not really what my mother wanted to do, she didn't have the courage to go against them.

Third Grade

As I began third grade, my mother put me in Miss Skidmore's class. She had been my older sister's third-grade teacher a few years prior. She was an older woman I believe was once a nun in the convent.

Aside from having stern mannerisms, she taught with a military style just like they did in Catholic schools. Miss Skidmore had loved my sister, so my mother thought I might have the same success with her. Shortly into the school year, we found out that wasn't the case.

My older sister had always excelled in writing from a very young age and was a straight-A student. Miss Skidmore almost seemed offended by the contrast between my sister's and my learning capabilities. It seemed she thought if she had me read some of my sister's poems, her smartness would rub off on me.

By the end of the first quarter, we both knew that wasn't going to happen. On my report card, she gave me one C and the rest Ds, which were equivalent to Fs.

When the grades came out each grading period, the kids at my school always gathered around the back doors of the building before, after, and during lunch to share what grades they'd gotten.

The night before we got our grades that particular time, I had just gotten screamed at by mother. When one of my schoolmates asked me the next day how I did, I began to cry as I held the report card in my hand. The girl grabbed it from me and then told everyone my grades.

When Miss Skidmore opened the door, she saw me crying and asked, "Why are you crying?"

I told her about the kids making fun of me for getting straight Ds. She glared and said, "You didn't get straight Ds. Why are you telling people what is on your report card?" But she never once reprimanded the kids who were making fun of me.

After having put me into remedial everything and a year of working with a school psychologist, my parents were advised to transfer me out of Miss Skidmore's class after the first quarter.

Home life at this point was very turbulent. I remember walking into an argument between my parents and overhearing my father say, "Sue, we cannot afford another baby!"

My mother started bullying and berating him, screaming about the lawyer that isn't a lawyer. "If you had balls and were a man, you would be able to provide."

She would scream about the women who she perceived to be living better than she was. When I walked into the room to get something, I could feel my father's shame as he looked at me from the corner of his eye. I could also feel my mother had a plan for the financial problems and her desire to have another child.

From that day on, she began ignoring me and isolating me from the family. My intuition had clearly shown me that my mother's plan was to phase me out.

It was the first Monday of the second quarter at school, and the bell had just rung. Miss Skidmore read the class criteria for the day. At the end of the announcement, she asked if anyone in the class would want to escort me down to the principal's office.

I was in shock. I had no idea why I was being escorted down to see the principal. The classroom started to buzz with whispering. Miss. Skidmore, noticing the puzzled expression on my face, blurted out to the class that I was being transferred out of her class into Special Education.

A few seconds later, there was a knock at the door from a small, pale-skinned woman with glasses and frizzy brown hair. She excused herself to the class, turned to Miss Skidmore, and said, "I am here for Laura Schwalm. My name is Mrs. Miller."

Miss Skidmore looked at me and nodded, so I collected my things and followed Mrs. Miller out the door.

We headed down the corridor to her classroom, where there were students sitting scattered all over the room. Mrs. Miller announced to the class that I was a transfer student from Miss Skidmore. The class broke into whispers. As I took my seat, I scanned the room to look at the other children's faces.

Krista Blakeman, the only other girl in the class aside from me, was sitting at her desk with a glazed look on her face. Her mouth hung wide open. It was obvious she was close with one of the boys in the class, because he seemed very protective of her. I guessed he must have known her from home.

The rest of Mrs. Miller's students were boys who just glared at me. After about an hour, a boy named Joey, who looked a lot older and bigger than the rest of the class, turned to me and said, "Why did you get transferred to our class? You know, we don't know you, so you're not one of us."

Mrs. Miller walked around the class, stopping at every desk. She asked me, "If you were in trouble, who would you ask for help, and who do you consider a close friend in the class?"

I can remember thinking the question was ridiculous because I didn't know anyone in it. I frantically tried to tap in and pick someone from the sea of faces in the classroom. I heard an Italian boy, Richard, say, "Krista Blakeman," so I said her name.

Mrs. Miller then informed me that no one had chosen my name.

Soon after that, Mrs. Miller told everyone to get settled in. "Prepare to fill out the sheet I am handing out," she stated as she walked around the classroom, distributing the papers. Then she stood in front of the class and told everyone to not be concerned with anyone else's paper. She admonished us to pay attention to our own because everyone's assignment was different.

I settled back in my chair, grabbed my pencil, and began to read the sheet which had the alphabet in dotted lines, ready to trace for script. I felt instantly that the teacher must have made a mistake because I had remembered doing that same assignment a year back in school.

I raised my hand and said, "I think my assignment is a mistake. I learned this already."

Without hesitation, Mrs. Miller exclaimed, "You are in this class because you failed and they don't want you there." With that, I learned not to say anything.

After the first part of the day was over, the class headed off to lunch. I saw Vivian's son Joey and some of the other kids from the regular mainstream class. I got excited when I saw Joey, but he was standoffish. I started to get upset and went to sit in the corner until recess was over.

I remember looking around at all the kids playing on the playground with their friends, laughing and giggling. I remember feeling very numb and disconnected. I wondered why no one liked me, and I wondered what I could do to be liked.

Anna Haberxettle was the smartest and prettiest girl in the third grade. She had been in my class the previous year and was in the other Mrs. Miller's class, which was down the hall. Her script penmanship was as perfect as her bob haircut. She always looked well-kept, did well in her studies, and was praised by her teachers. Everyone wanted to be her friend, and her parents obviously loved her.

I remember thinking I wanted to be her and wondered how I could become her. I noticed she had a large white pencil case with animals on it. Inside the pencil case, she had three number-two pencils, five Hello Kitty pencils, a sharpener, and a white envelope with five dollars in it.

One afternoon, I took a hall pass to go to the bathroom, and on my way back, I noticed the other Mrs. Miller's classroom was empty but the door was open. I looked around the room and out the door to see if anyone was coming. Quickly, I ran over to Anna's desk, took out the pencil case, and stuffed it down my pants.

My hands were shaky, and I could feel the adrenaline pumping through my body. I ran back to my classroom. About forty-five minutes later, Mrs. Miller from the other class walked down to our classroom and poked her head in the door. She asked my teacher to step outside. I knew intuitively that Mrs. Miller was telling her that I had stolen from the classroom. My mind raced as I tried to logically to talk myself out of what I already knew.

During lunchtime, Mrs. Miller came over to me and asked me to give her the pencil case. I tried to deny I had it, but she wouldn't stop threatening, saying, "Children that steal get sent away."

I confessed after a short while. I remember feeling frozen in shame and wishing the school day would never end. I knew I was going to be punished and beaten once Mrs. Miller told my mother what I had done.

When I arrived home, however, my mother seemed to be in good spirits. I thought maybe, by the grace of God, Mrs. Miller hadn't said anything. But a few hours later, the phone rang, and I could hear my mother say, "Good evening." Then I heard a long pause.

I could feel the energy in the room change. I started to feel overstimulated. She hung up the phone and raced over to the chair I was sitting in and grabbed a fist full of my hair. She threw me across the room and screamed, "You ungrateful little bitch! Who the fuck are you to disgrace me? You're an embarrassment! You can go to your room with no dinner."

Even though I never ate breakfast and lunch consisted of a small lemonade and a bag of barbecue chips most every day, I didn't care. The following day was Saturday, and I could hear my parents and my sisters eating around the table.

My father asked if I was allowed to eat, and I could hear my mother say, "She will eat when I feel she should eat."

A half hour later, my mother yelled, "Laura, get in here!"

I walked into my parents' room, where my mother proceeded to slap me repeatedly and then threw me to the bed. She picked up my father's belt and started hitting me over the head with the buckle a few dozen times.

After she finished beating me, she said, "I wish you were never born! Now get the fuck out of here, you piece of shit."

I stumbled off the bed in a fog and walked out to the warm, sunny back yard. There, I fell asleep under the tree. I remember drifting into a deep sleep and seeing nothing but black. I heard a man's voice outside of me that had no emotion. It said as if it was speaking to me, "Do you want to come home?"

I didn't say anything back, and the voice repeated the question two other times, each time a little more sternly. I wasn't sure if I was imagining someone talking to me or whether it was God, because the voice had a soothing and calm tone. The voice finally said, "I am going to ask you one more time. Do you want to come home?"

I remember feeling puzzled but grateful I didn't have any pain on my head from the beating. I finally answered the voice that seemed to be in my mind, "No, I will stay."

The voice asked me, "Are you sure?"

I replied, "Yes." A few minutes later, I woke up from my sleep under the tree.

I knew intuitively that if I would have said yes, God would have taken me home.

My entire grammar school days were spent in a fog. I was in a constant state of fear of dealing with the consequences of my mother's wrath, teachers' disappointment, and isolation from students because of my failing grades. Teachers and psychologists moved me around like a piece on a chess board. I would see them glaring and hear them whispering in frustration about how little I could understand and retain. Concepts I learned one day I forgot the next. The more pressure there was, the more overstimulated I got. My nervous system was in a constant state of survival mode, not just from the environment but my own thoughts as well. I felt frozen, I was stuck in the survival mode of fear, making me feel that nowhere was safe. I felt like there was something wrong with me and I was defective.

I tried joining after-school activities, but I was clumsy and uncoordinated, and no one ever wanted me on their team. The other children made fun of me and called me 'corroded.' Everywhere I seemed to go, I was bullied and made fun of. After a while, it was safer to just be in the fantasy and dream state of my mind.

I was also knock kneed and walked funny, which made me feel so uncomfortable in my body. I would detach myself by living in my mind. Unfortunately, this kept all my new experiences in school and in life looking like my old experiences.

On the random occasion a fellow classmate would want to be my friend, I would sabotage it by first wanting them to fix me, care for me, and love me, and then when they wouldn't or couldn't, I retaliated the way I was taught, which was to become manipulative, controlling, hurtful, and deceitful.

Lori

Seventh grade was when I met Lori Wasserman. We were getting dressed for gym when a few girls walked over to where she was standing by the lockers. Some started intimidatingly banging on her locker while the others called her names. After a few minutes, the bell rang and they walked out of the locker room. I decided to walk over to her and introduce myself.

"Hi, my name is Laura and my birthday is next week. I would like you to come to my birthday."

She looked at me, not only puzzled but obviously suspicious as well. She said, "If you really want me to come to your birthday, you will call me and ask me." With that, Lori handed me her phone number and we left the locker room.

Lori came from East Meadow Elementary School. I went to Bowling Green Elementary School. Our junior high and high schools were combined with children from both schools.

As soon as I got home from school, I called the number Lori had given me and she answered the phone. I said, "Hello, Lori. Yes, I am serious about you coming to my birthday party at the roller rink. Are you going to come now?" From that day forward, Lori and I were inseparable.

This would be one of only two times I was ever allowed to celebrate my birthday. Since it was on a Saturday, I asked my mother if Lori could sleep over the night before. Lori had gotten me a black shirt with cats made from sparkles on it. She said she couldn't wait to give it to me. I had admired it a few days before at the flea market.

Every day, Lori invited me over after school and I was more than happy to go. It was always comfortable at her house. There was never anyone home when Lori got home from school, so we were able to do whatever we wanted. Lori trusted me with her house as if I was her sister.

Lori's home life and parents were much different than mine. Everything was pleasant. Her parents gave off the vibe of being successful, and they were so accommodating to Lori's every whim. They lived comfortably, and they were always taking Lori places, exposing her to new things.

One day when we got home from school, I had to use the bathroom, so I went directly to the upstairs bathroom. Lori went into the kitchen to get a drink and then screamed up the stairs to me, "Me meet me on the deck."

As I left the bathroom, I passed her parents' room and saw a stack of money their dresser.

I could feel the adrenaline pump through my veins immediately. I gently stepped toward the dresser and took a few bills from the top. I slipped them into my pocket. When I got downstairs, Lori asked me if I wanted to ride up to the store to get cigarettes.

We both had tried smoking a few weeks before at a party. Every few days, we would buy another pack. Lori would have to pay for them, and I would ride my bicycle to the discount store to buy them. Once I got back to her house, we would smoke a few cigarettes on her deck and talk.

Lori's mother worked for a doctor that was good friends with Ron Delsener, who produced concerts. She was always getting free concert tickets and asking me to go. But I knew my mother would never let me go, so I would lie and say we were doing something for school. Lori and I, for the most part, would finagle and make up stories to get around my mother.

I had anxiety all the time because I was always in fear I would get caught and my mother would do something to sabotage my friendship with Lori. I also had a deep-seated fear that Lori's parents were getting tired of having to drive all the time and pay for me to do things in order for me to keep going places with Lori. Both the temptation of money laying around and the need for security became overbearing. I started to steal money from them regularly.

Every day on his way home from work, Lori's father would bring us a Happy Meal from McDonald's. Around 7:00 p.m., after we'd eaten, he would drop me home.

One day after school, Lori's mother pulled me aside and told me that Lori didn't have friends. I got the feeling she was trying to tell me we were spending too much time together by the comments she made. She would frequently say Lori didn't have any real friends before me and she wasn't used to always having friends around. I knew Lori wanted me to come over every day, though, because she asked me.

I didn't know how to respond to her mother, so I just nodded.

It was obvious Mrs. Wasserman was afraid to discipline Lori because she would become rebellious and defiant to the point of refusing to do anything her parents asked. For example, I remember Lori telling me her grandparents really wanted her to honor their religion by having a bat mitzvah. They would explain to her the importance of celebrating, but she still refused adamantly out of defiance.

During the summer, Lori's parents would sign her up for camp, but she missed most of it because she wanted to spend the summer with me and our friends from school. We would all meet under the overhang in the back of the elementary school and smoke cigarettes. We talked about when we would be old enough to drive.

In the beginning, my mother didn't mind that I was at Lori's. Over time, however, she became passive/aggressive and confrontational with Lori. Mother would deliberately make her feel uncomfortable. Despite all this, for a while, Lori and I remained friends. In the summer of the eighth grade, Lori went to Japan and China for almost the entire month. My family was going to a country club upstate for a few weeks, but our family got back from vacation before hers did.

I kept myself busy with friends from the neighborhood until Lori returned home from vacation on a Saturday. As soon as she did, she called me, wanting to come over. I asked my mother if she could, and after a long pause and sigh, she reluctantly said okay.

After about thirty minutes, I saw Lori's father pull up outside the house. His car stopped, and Lori jumped out of the car as her father popped the trunk. Lori grabbed two large garbage bags from the trunk. She walked in the door with a big smile on her face. She put the two packages down and nodded toward them, saying they were gifts for me and my family.

She handed me one of the bags, and I pulled out one red and one black silk kimono. They both had Chinese lettering representing peace on the back. Underneath the robes was a wooden jewelry box with a jade ring in it. There was also a leather journal with Chinese golden lettering that spelled *Reflections*.

Lori put her hand in the other bag and pulled out a small box for my mother. I excitedly called my mother into the room. She emerged from the kitchen with a glass of wine in one hand and a cigarette in the other, a look of disgust on her face. Lori handed her the box as my mother put down her glass of wine.

My mother opened the box and took out a small figurine, which had a hook on it for the Christmas tree, of a woman with blond hair, wearing a flowing gown and high heels. She looked like a doll from the 1930s. My mother vaguely nodded and barely thanked her for the gifts.

I could tell Lori was disappointed by my mother's reaction. I believe she thought the gifts would win my mother over, but instead my mother became nastier. It was almost as if my mother had realized that Lori really cared about what she thought about her. My mother preyed on her from that moment forward and treated her worse.

The next day at school, Lori approached me and said, "My father thinks your mother has a drinking problem. Every time he picks me up at your house, your mother is drinking a glass of wine. He would prefer that you come to our house."

After a few weeks of going to their house, Lori's father started to complain that my mother never participated or offered to drive. For over two and a half years, Lori's father had driven us to and from their house and everywhere else we wanted to go.

One day when Lori's father called and asked us what we wanted from McDonald's, he told Lori that I would need to call my mother to get picked up from their house.

I started to feel anxiety right away. I knew my mother was going to be livid. I just wanted to walk, but Lori and her father wouldn't let me. I called my mother, and sure enough, I knew she was mad. I knew there would be consequences.

About forty-five minutes later, my mother honked the horn outside Lori's house and I went out. I could see by her face that she was annoyed. I opened the car door and slipped into the back seat since my mother didn't let anyone sit in the front with her.

There were two large jugs of kerosene on each side of the car, so I was forced to sit in the middle. As soon as I shut the door to the car she started screaming.

"You selfish little bitch! Like I don't have enough else to do than pick your ass up! I have been driving around in this fucking development for over an hour! How the fuck do I get out of here?"

I became so overstimulated I couldn't think. I could feel the epinephrine speeding through my body. I became shaky and felt like I was going to pass out. I was frozen.

As she screamed at me, she kept slamming on the breaks so the kerosene and I would jerk forward then slam back against the seat. I screamed for her to stop. She looked at me in the rearview mirror. Through her clenched teeth, she hissed, "Don't tell me what to do."

She then took a long pull from her cigarette and threw it in the back seat, where it landed in between one can of kerosene and my leg.

Frantically, I grabbed the cigarette butt and flicked it out the window with my shaking hand. I felt like I was going to vomit. I knew it wouldn't end there, either. Once I got home, I would be berated in front of the family, and they were going to pretend it wasn't happening or that it was normal. She would then act all giddy and joking around with my sisters. I lived in a constant state of fear because I was constantly being isolated, betrayed, and victimized. Later in life, after many years of being forced to live out these experiences, I unconsciously created new versions of the same.

I told Lori the next day at school what had happened, and somehow after that, Lori convinced her father to let her come over to my house so my mother wouldn't have to pick me up. It became more and more obvious that both parents didn't want us to spend that much time with each other.

One October night, my parents were supposed to go to my aunt and uncle's house for a visit. My parents got into a fight, and my father went by himself while my mother stayed home.

Since I thought my parents would be gone for the evening, Lori and I had invited over a bunch of kids from our school that we regularly hung out with. Lori and I were upstairs at my parents' house with a mutual friend, wondering what to do. We kept hearing the phone ring, but when my mother would answer it, the callers obviously hung up. After this happened a third time, my mother staggered over to the foot of the stairs and yelled, "Are you expecting anyone? Someone keeps calling and hanging up."

I denied any knowledge of anyone coming over. Once my mother walked away from the stairs, I turned to Catherine, our mutual friend, and told her to go downstairs and tell my mother she had to go home for her brother's birthday. I didn't want to ruin anyone's Saturday night. After fifteen minutes, I told Lori to tell my mother she was going to go to Catherine's brother's birthday, too. I knew my mother would eventually feel bad for me and let me out.

About ten minutes after Lori left, my mother called me downstairs. She was in the kitchen, cleaning, with her cigarette and glass of wine, wearing an inside out T-shirt and oversized sweat pants. She glared at me from across the room and said with a slur, "If that is true about your friend Catherine's brother, give me Catherine's parents' phone number."

I gave her the phone number and she got Catherine's father, who confirmed that it was his son's birthday. She said I could go, so I quickly ran up the stairs, put on my shoes, ran back down and then out the door.

My mother yelled after me, "Call me when you get there."

I said okay. I got up the block to where my group of friends stood on the corner. Lori and Catherine were telling everyone what was going on. I got to the corner and said, "If she comes out, get out of here, because I am dead."

A few seconds later, I heard the front door slam and my mother's voice again reminding me to call her when I got there. All of a sudden, I saw my group of friends run across Stewart Avenue and up the block.

Then I heard, "Laura, get your ass back in the house."

My stomach sank to the floor. I felt my head pound, I felt dizzy, and I thought I was going to vomit. I walked in the door and my mother asked me, "Does Lori's mother think she is staying here tonight?"

I said, "Yes."

She giggled and said with a smile, "Give me her phone number." I knew this was the moment she had been waiting for, the excuse she needed to justify tearing our friendship apart. I wanted to die because I knew it was the end of my friendship with Lori and I knew I had caused it myself.

I could taste the cortisol in my mouth as I yelled the number from the top of the stairs. I could hear the rotary dial on the phone spinning with each number. After a short pause, I heard, "Hello, Susan. This is Suzanne Schwalm. I am calling you to let you know that your daughter is not sleeping here tonight. I think she went to Catherine's. I do not know whether Lori was going to tell you. It seems you run a very loose house." I could tell from her tone my mother was passive/aggressively egging Lori's mother on.

I learned later that Lori's mother then took the opportunity to say, "Suzanne, there have been so many times I have wanted to call you, but I didn't exactly know how to confront the situation."

It was as if they had both been waiting for the right moment to dig up every little thing that Lori and I had ever done. The animosity between the two had silently built up over the past two years. Also, every lie Lori and I had ever told came out that day, and things which Lori had told her mother in confidence to get her to be more understanding to me and my situation came out.

The exchange between our mothers escalated into a screaming match and ended in threats.

I sat upstairs with my stomach in my mouth. I was once again frozen numb. Right before my mother hung up the phone, I heard her. I knew my friendship with Lori was over and the group of friends we had obtained together would no longer be.

My mother walked to the foot of the stairs and yelled up the banister, "You are grounded until further notice, and you are forbidden to see Lori Wasserman." This was exactly what she had wished to say for so long.

The next morning, I saw Lori moving her stuff from the locker next to mine. I tried to talk to her, but she wouldn't make eye contact and brushed me away. We never spoke again.

My Early Church Days

My family wasn't really religious as I was growing up. When I was younger, we usually went to church on Christmas and Easter. We also went to catechism so I could make my Holy Communion and Confirmation. For this, usually the parents of one of the kids in the class would volunteer to teach for the semester.

I went through the motions of going, but I had trouble comprehending what I read. Very rarely did I have my homework done. I mainly learned about Jesus from the discussions we had in the class.

It felt to me like the only time you went to church was when you needed something. I never really experienced the church giving anything except during mass—a stale wafer and a sip of cheap wine. I do not have a lot of memories from the church aside from the priests. They were always boring, so it was hard for me to pay attention.

I also recall my mother going to church when my father had gotten sick in my younger years, but it was never consecutively. Which church we went to was dependent upon where my mother thought her friends would be.

As a young child, I would curse God for my learning disability, awkwardness, parents, and all my other perceived failures. It was like God didn't like me or he'd forgotten about me. I wanted answers. Everyone talked of a man who loves us but who didn't do anything. Just like my parents. They were supposed to show love and support, but mine didn't. I saw my friends had parents who did; I saw strangers who did. I did not understand why God gave me my parents.

I thought since I had the opportunity to talk to a priest for my confession, I might as well bring up my observation when I had my turn. The church was packed with kids doing their confessionals. My mother sat with Vivian at one of the back pews while Joey and I waited in line for our turn at the confessional. After thirty minutes, I entered the confession box. The priest swung open the window to where I could see him. There was no partition between us anymore.

He was very overweight with a red, rounded face. He began to recite the Our Father. Once he finished, he asked me to tell my confessions. I quickly thought of something to make up. I didn't think I was going to be looking at someone's face.

I said I fought with my sisters a lot. He said, "Is that it?" in an angry tone like he didn't believe me. He then sat back in his chair and said, "Is there anything else?"

I said, "Yes, I don't believe in God."

He looked at me in shock. In a high-pitched voice, he said, "What do you mean, you do not believe?"

I could tell by his expression and reaction he was angry. I tried to say, "Never mind," but he wasn't having it. I realized at that time it wouldn't be wise for me to tell the priest I didn't believe in God because of the parents he gave me.

If I'd told him that, I was sure he would have had a word with my mother, so instead I said, "I have a hard time believing in God because we do not see him. I do not know him, and he doesn't seem to care too much about me."

The priest, still looking annoyed with me, did not offer any explanation or words to give me peace of mind. Instead, he told me to say twelve Acts of Contrition, gave me a made-up confession to recite—a poem I didn't know or even understand the meaning of. His reaction lacked not only advice but empathy. Once again, I felt shameful and awkward.

Years later, when I was in my first year of college, my sister Andrea had her wedding rehearsal dinner. She had forgotten to bring the donation check for the church. The woman from the church, who was giving direction and supervising the rehearsal, started clapping her hands and stomping her feet, threatening to stop the rehearsal when my sister told her the check was at home.

Of course, my mother took the opportunity to scream and embarrass my sister in front of her soon-to-be-husband's entire family. I felt my sister becoming overstimulated and emotional, and even from across the room, I saw her eyes fill with water.

My father said in an embarrassed tone that he would go home and get a check. But that didn't stop my mother from continuing her rant about my sister being stupid and not knowing anything and being selfish because my parents had to flip the bill. Finally, after a few minutes, one of Andrea's soon-to-be brothers-in-law told my mother to shut up, that it wasn't appropriate for her to be berating her daughter the evening before her wedding.

My sister thought because she'd supplied the priest and organist, there wasn't any charge. The woman from the church who was taking us through the rehearsal didn't seem to care, which completely was a turn-off.

The church was supposed to represent support, forgiveness, and compassion, but instead the church was selfish, not patient, and seemed very unforgiving. For years on and off, I began to look for God through different religions and customs, with the catalyst usually being a psychic.

I became fascinated with Santeria after frequenting a botanica where I met my Godmother Maria, who took me under her wing. She taught me about the different Orishas, rituals, customs, and prayers. After five years of working with her diligently, she baptized me into the religion. Though I loved Maria and a lot of the customs, I didn't feel any more connected to God and still longed for a personal and fulfilling relationship with him.

Zena Clairvoyant

It was my mother who got me into psychics. I never knew what the big deal was about getting a reading until I experienced one. But after my reading with a clairvoyant, I was intrigued to find out everything there was about spirituality, healing, and the psychic world. All the information I came across put me on my path.

When I was twelve years old, I went into the city with my sister and a few of her friends. We came across a psychic named Zena. She was located on the corner of Bleecker and Fourteen Street and 7th Avenue. Her place was a very narrow corner unit where one exterior wall faced Bleecker Street and another faced 7th Avenue. Her building stood three stories tall. The rooms were all in the shape of a corner.

Zena was a tall blond woman with fair skin and light hair. She spoke with a Romanian accent but claimed she was from Cannes, France. After my sister and her friend got their cards read, it was my turn.

I sat across from Zena at a round wooden table on which sat a crystal ball and very large tarot cards. The table was positioned right in front of her storefront window. The cards were not your standard Weight and Rider deck.

She asked me to shuffle the cards then proceeded to tell me a lot of very accurate information about my family and myself. The reading only lasted thirty minutes, but her accuracy stayed with me. I longed to hear what else she had to say, but we lived on Long Island.

It wouldn't be until I was a freshman in high school that I was able to coerce two of my friends to go with me to see Zena again. One friend, Susan, and I went to high school together, and the other person, Katherine, and I worked together over the summer at the pool.

Susan was interested to see whether her relationship of seven years was ever going to get easier. Katherine wanted to know whether she would be reunited with her father. She had been estranged from him since her parents had gotten a divorce.

We took the Long Island railroad into the city and walked down to Bleecker. Susan was not overly impressed with her reading even though Zena's prediction about her relationship turned out to be accurate. Katherine, on the other hand, left her session extremely happy. She was told that even though she hadn't seen her father in years, she would reconnect with him and live with him again within one year. Eventually, Katherine did move in with her father. As for my own reading, it was a much quicker one than the time before.

Every year after that, I went back to Zena for readings. During one visit, she said I was blocked, a spiritual term meaning I was unable to obtain financial stability or an emotionally fulfilling relationship. She said she could help me for five hundred dollars. Though finances were tight, I found a way to get Zena the money, and I returned to her the following week.

After I gave her the money, she asked me to go across the street to Woolworth's to pick up a tube of thread. She said to tie a piece of the thread in three knots and then to call her once I got home. When I got home, I took out the thread from my wallet and noticed the piece now had one large knot in it.

When I called her with my findings, she said I would have to bring her an additional five hundred dollars because her work wasn't complete. I was devastated and crushed. I couldn't believe she was asking for more money, knowing my situation.

I didn't bring her any more money, and it was a while before I saw her again.

Five years passed, and I was working as a hairdresser on the Upper West Side of Manhattan. Often after work I would go gallivanting through the city. One evening, I found myself in the West Village and my curiosity got the best of me.

I walked over to her building to see she was offering a reading to someone. She looked up and ran over to the door as I was about to walk away. She seemed really happy to see me, complimenting me on the way I looked and about my energy, so I asked her if I could get a reading.

She looked at me hesitantly and answered, "No, you know how to do this now," and she pawned me off on her niece, who didn't have any psychic ability and gave me a very general reading.

I didn't understand what Zena had meant when she said I knew how to do readings until later when I realized psychics don't just pick up on things which happen in the moment. Years later, when I started up my own spiritual practice, I went back to visit Zena only to find she had sold her business. The law had finally caught up with her and her daughters. She needed to sell the business to help her daughter with the lawyers' fees. Her daughter Sylvia had been caught for swindling $138,000 from clients and was convicted on ten counts of grand larceny.

I learned firsthand from Zena what it was like to be perceived as gifted and what happens when you work for the Divine and abuse your gifts. No one is immune to karma, especially psychics. I was determined to run the most ethical business I could, so I enrolled in Bible School Fellowship. Though the fellowship didn't teach how to use your intuition, it did teach what the symbolization in the bible means and how to apply the information to your life.

After learning in class, doing the homework, and reviewing again, we would meditate and share. Hearing what the other students learned was great reinforcement for me. I would often find myself channeling and teaching scripture to my clients in their private sessions.

My clients were then not only learning how to create the life experiences they wanted to have; they were able to heal themselves and prevent the same karmic patterns from repeating. And if that wasn't good enough, they learned how to have a personal relationship with God so they would learn not to become dependent on anyone or anything of the physical world.

Whether Zena knew it or not, she intrigued me, empowered me, humbled me, victimized me, and betrayed me, but most of all, she influenced me to always be ethical in my practice, and I will always be thankful for that.

Nassau Community College

I was in my senior year in high school, and I would be graduating without regents. (Regent examination scores are one of the things colleges look at when determining admittance.) Instead, I took just a standard test, which can help get you into community college. I still didn't know how to write or do basic math correctly. The school selection was limited. My dream at the time was to become a cosmetologist or a photographer.

I had absolutely no interest in going to college and voiced it regularly. However, it just so happened I got a small scholarship of a thousand dollars when I graduated from the special education department that could only be used for college.

When I had graduated high school, I assumed I would work for a few years to accumulate the money for either photography or cosmetology school, since my mother had made it clear there wasn't money for what I wanted to do. On the day I graduated, in fact, my mother took me aside, away from everyone, into the kitchen.

With her pointer finger pushed into my chest, she demanded, "What are you planning to do now?"

I said, "Cosmetology or photography school."

She suggested Nassau Community College, which I had absolutely no desire to go to, nor did I have the basic academic requirements to pass most of the math, English, and science classes there. I also mentioned I didn't want to live at home while in school. In addition, if I went to a local school, I would need a car.

In the end, knowing I had no choice but to do as she pleased, I lived in the house. My mother loved the idea of not having to pay a dime for my school since the scholarship covered it. She would justify her cheapness with me by saying, "We had to put the money where it's worth it." Obviously, my grades showed her I wasn't worth it, and she said this to anyone who would listen.

My mother also promised to buy me a car if I went to Nassau. I didn't agree but walked out of the kitchen without saying so aloud. Our conversation ended with her last words being that I was going to Nassau Community.

When school started, my mother reneged on the car, denying she'd ever agreed to buying one, which forced me to rely on friends and strangers for rides. Every morning, I would go through my list of friends to see who would pick me up.

My sister Andrea, of course, chimed in how she agreed that I shouldn't get a car. It seemed Andrea liked to side with my mother because it gave my mother fuel and kept the focus off herself. She often dealt with my mother this way, knowing very well my mother would turn up her wrath, but as long as Andrea didn't have to deal with her, she didn't care.

I remember being terrified that I wouldn't be able to make it to classes and tests half the time. I knew if I failed because I'd missed a class, I would be punished. One day, during my first semester, I had a friend, Karen, who was only going to Nassau for a semester and then transferring out. She offered to pick me up whenever our classes coincided.

It was around 8:30 in the morning in the middle of the semester. A downpour kicked up, and Karen pulled up to the driveway. As I ran out to the car with my backpack, my mother started running and passed me to reach the car ahead of me.

She poked her head in and thanked Karen for coming to pick me up. As I approached the car, she grabbed me to the side. She got in my face and said, "I feel I owe the world because of you." She then pushed past me and stormed away.

I remember the September mornings being cold, but by midafternoon I was peeling off clothes in order to not overheat. My mother had expected me to graduate with my Associate's Degree within the two-year requirement, which meant I had to take at least five classes per semester.

Carrying a coat and the three to five books for classes was a lot to lug around. I would get dehydrated and have an empty stomach to boot. Walking was even worse in the winters because of the sleet, snow, and ice.

Thankfully, there were some places on the Nassau campus where I could go to shield myself from the rain and the cold. I had plenty of friends, but I didn't have any money for photography paper, food, or transportation. If I was lucky, I was able to scrounge around for a few dollars for the local Arby's.

To get some money, I decided to get a job at the school art gallery. I worked there for a few months after classes until around 9:00 p.m. It was difficult to get home that time of night with all my books and no car. And after a few months, I quit anyway because I never got paid.

Luckily, God gave me a great friend at that time named Susan. Susan's house was one of the only places I could go to escape my mother. She not only gave me rides to and from Nassau even when she didn't have classes; she also got me a job at Life Uniform, where she worked.

I looked forward to work because it meant freedom. Money gave me independence from my mother. Most of the time, Susan and I worked together and many nights, we went out right after work and stayed out until we had to go back to work the next morning since it was a weekend.

We would take turns taking naps in the dressing rooms, trying to sleep off our hangovers. Susan had dysfunctional issues within her own family, so she thankfully never judged or gossiped about my parents' drinking problems. It felt good to be around someone I didn't need to explain anything to and who accepted me.

One day, we were working and I had a sharp pain that went across my back and down my side. I felt pressure as if I had to use the bathroom. I felt nauseous and had dry heaves. I ran to the bathroom and sat on the toilet, slumped over. The pain was excruciating.

I would go from sitting on the toilet to hovering over the toilet every few minutes. I was trying to get comfortable, but there was no relief.

Susan yelled from outside the door, "Are you okay? Should I call someone?"

I didn't want anyone to call my mother because there were always consequences for inconveniencing her. The pain was agonizing. I couldn't hold back the moaning and cries no matter how much I tried. I could not stifle the sound. It seemed to echo through the door.

Just then, the regional manager happened to visit us unannounced. She walked in to see Susan whispering through the bathroom door and the store manager threatened to call an ambulance if I didn't give them a number. I gave the store manager the number of my mother's friend Vivian.

I figured Vivian could calm my mother down when she would inevitably go at me because I was sick. Vivian did a lot for her children. Almost too much. I always would ask Vivian to help in situations like that in hopes that her patience, kindness, and compassion would rub off on my mother.

Unfortunately, Vivian wasn't home, so I called Jackie Davis, my friend Doreen's mother. Doreen at the time was my best friend. Her mother, despite being married to an alcoholic, having a daughter in rehab, having a son with diabetes, and many times working two jobs to make ends meet, always showed me kindness and generosity.

I gave the manager her number. The manager came back over to the bathroom door after hanging the phone up with Jackie and said, "She will be here in about thirty minutes. Hang tight."

When Jackie got there a short while later, I was lying on the floor in a fetal position. The manager, Jackie, and Susan carried me to the car.

With sweat pouring off me, I was shaking and feverish. The pain was nothing I had ever experienced before. After I was in the car, Jackie sped to my parents' house while trying to calm me down.

I stumbled into the house, and my mother was home. I ran past her into the bathroom and fell to my knees in front of the toilet. I could hear Jackie telling my mother that I should go to the hospital. Then I heard her leave. A few minutes later, my mother came running to the bathroom. She swung open the door and stared at me from the doorway.

She said, "What's the matter with you now? There is always something wrong with you. I don't have time for this shit!"

She left me whimpering on the floor for what seemed an eternity then came back to the bathroom and said, "Get the hell up and get your ass in the car!"

When we arrived at the hospital, they first gave me a cup to collect a urine sample. In the bathroom, I filled the cup, and to my horror, saw that my urine was full of blood.

I went back into the waiting room. My mother had already left, and a few minutes later, a nurse came and got me. I was still sobbing from the pain, so she started an IV to give me pain medicine.

The nurse said, "You'll feel a lot better once you pass that kidney stone. Hopefully it will come down in your sleep."

I woke up a few hours later and saw my mother for a moment through the glass. Still groggy from the painkillers, I was drifting in and out. A while later, a nurse came over to me and asked if I had another contact because it had been over two hours since the desk had left a message on my parents' answering machine.

I gave the nurse Jackie's number. About forty-five minutes later, she was at the emergency room to pick me up. This time, she looked upset. I could feel she was annoyed. Once I got in the car she said, "Why can't your mother ever get you? How come you always ask me?"

I began to cry and started to threaten that I would rather be homeless than live with my mother. I shared many stories, knowing in my heart that Jackie wouldn't let me live on the streets. I knew she would have mercy and let me stay with her.

The next day, I waited until my parents were at work to go back into the house to pack up some clothes and then headed back to Jackie's before they got home. I was nervous that my mother or father would call and be confrontational. Mother knew most people didn't want to get involved.

But that evening, no one called to see where I was. For weeks, I lived there before I went back home.

Every time I would come back after escaping her torture, I was isolated and ignored by my family even more. If one of my sisters acknowledged my birthday or treated me nicely, there were consequences. They would get belittled, bullied, and threatened if they were even decent to me.

A few years later, when I was out of college, my mother and Christine got into it one night after Christine and I had seen each other. She was still living in my parents' house. My sister came home around 11:00 p.m. after having dinner with me and went into the kitchen for a glass of water.

My mother stormed in after her and said, "How's your sister?"

Christine told her I was doing well and quickly changed the subject to the groceries she'd bought on sale. My mother opened the refrigerator and started to throw the food out onto the floor, complaining that my food was taking up too much room in the refrigerator.

Christine knew my mother was only picking a fight with her because she had seen me. She also suffered many incidents of physical and psychic trauma from our mother and knew at this point she would have to move out in order to have any type of relationship with me.

The following day, Christine signed a lease on an apartment. My mother said she didn't have to follow through and she wished Christine would have changed her mind. She didn't, and two weeks later she was living on her own.

Kidney Stones

I'd had blood in my urine for as long as I could remember. My parents would get a phone call from the school nurse every year, from kindergarten through senior year in high school. By the time I was in seventh grade, I was passing kidney stones regularly. As a result, I developed a lot of scar tissue in the bottom of my urethra, where over time the stones were getting stuck.

After four semesters of Nassau Community College and still too many credits short to graduate, I decided to take a semester off. That way I could take driving lessons and make money to buy a car. My mother was annoyed I had taken the semester off but didn't give me too much flak about it at first.

One day, I answered the phone when Vivian called. She asked me in a confrontational way, "Laura, do you think it is wise you take a semester off? Most people who take time off from school never finish."

Without pause, I replied, "The agreement was if I went to Nassau, my parents would get me a car. But they didn't, so I have no car and no money to get back and forth to school."

Vivian went silent and apologized. Later that night, Vivian must have repeated to my mother what I'd said about her reneging on her promise about my car. Of course, this made her furious.

She said, "You piece of shit. I would never say I would buy you a car. For all I care, you can walk to and from until the end of time."

From that moment on I decided that when I got my car I would move away once and for all.

I obviously knew her statement about never saying she would buy me a car was untrue because after we had initially talked about it, my Aunt Pat and Uncle Phil gave my parents my cousin's old car to use. It needed new brakes and a few minor repairs, which of course they never fixed, and eventually they had the car towed away.

My mother was the master of gaslighting, so I knew my godparents had given her the car for me because she'd acted concerned, but she never had any intention of fixing the car. She loved to stage that she was a caring parent to the faces of everyone we knew, but behind closed doors, she was self-absorbed and got off on causing pain.

Having been fired from my job at the uniform store, I got a job at a bagel store from 5:00 a.m. until noon. After my shift there, I would go home and sleep for a few hours before having to go to Sears' portrait studio and work until 11:00 p.m. Susan and I remained friends, but we barely hung out any more because of our busy schedules. At the portrait studio, though, I met a nice Spanish-looking boy named Rob who trained me, and over time we became friends.

We used to go out to eat after work and share our stories about life. He was a refreshing change from most of the people I spent time with because he was easygoing. He never expected anything and would let me drive his car for hours, which eventually helped me get my license.

The next day I went to work at the bagel store, I had an aching pain in my lower back that just wouldn't let up. After a few hours of work, the pain was unbearable. I kept running to the bathroom, hoping I could find some relief, but the pain continued to get worse.

Rose, the owner of the bagel store, and I also became close over a short period of time. She knew a little bit about my parents but not everything. I had learned at a young age to not air my dirty laundry because people tended to look at me as if I had done something to deserve the treatment.

After seeing I wasn't returning to the counter, Rose came into the bathroom and stood outside the stall, asking me what I wanted to do. I told her to give me a few more minutes, but the pain was getting unbearable. She decided to call an ambulance. About thirty minutes later, the ambulance came and took me to the ER, where they put in an IV to administer pain medicine to me.

Before I went to my assigned bed, the nurse gave me a cup and asked for a urine sample. When I filled the cup with urine, it again was filled with blood but this time was bright red. When I handed the nurse the cup, she gasped.

When the hospital released me later that evening, I had already made up my mind that I was never going to go home again. It was time to quit the bagel store and the Sears portrait studio, go back to school, and get a job with enough hours to earn what I needed to support myself.

I went to my Doreen's house to recuperate and to settle into the new job I got at a deli. My plan was to move out of Doreen's and get my own apartment. I had gotten the job from a high school friend whose sister worked there. It wasn't my ideal job—being a sensitive, I don't work well under pressure—but it was a paycheck.

There was a trucking company next door to the deli called United Van Lines. They moved people and businesses. Every morning, I would see the same group of fellas come into the deli and order their breakfast before they went out for the day in the trucks.

There was one guy named Roger who stood out among the group. He seemed serious and shy and was very handsome, with black hair, dark eyes, and olive skin. One day after I'd worked there a few months, he stormed back into the deli with his bag containing his just-purchased breakfast.

He looked me in the eye and said, "Why is it that every morning I order the same breakfast—a bacon, egg, and cheese on a roll and chocolate milk—and every day my order is wrong? This morning, I got a bag that has a BLT and a large tea."

I apologized and tried to explain that I was new and working with a man who didn't speak English very well. During my explaining, the owner, Jimmy, came out from the back and waited for Roger to leave...and then fired me.

A few minutes later, I was pulling out of the deli and I saw Roger in his truck, ready to head out for the day. He said, "Short day today?"

I replied, "From here on out." He looked at me, puzzled. "I just got fired for screwing up your order," I said, embarrassed.

His mouth opened in shock, and he said, "I didn't think that was going to get you fired."

I quickly brushed off the incident and chalked it up to not being in the right profession. He said to me, "This may not be the most appropriate time, but do you think I can have your number?"

As I wrote my number on a piece of paper, I reassured him I would be fine. I passed the paper to him through my rolled-down window. He thanked me and said he would speak to me soon.

About a week later, Doreen and I were hanging out in her room when her landline rang and it was Roger. I remember being hesitant about taking his call, but Doreen talked me into it. She felt I needed someone to take me out to get my mind off everything.

Roger invited me out to go bowling that evening with him and a few of his friends and their dates. He picked me up, and we wound up having a great time. I didn't tell Roger about my living situation right away, but as time passed, I had no choice.

Doreen's house was getting unbearable. They had their own demons to deal with, and everyone was in need of their own space, not to mention Roger and Doreen started to have control issues about my relationship with each of them.

Doreen's mother started to reprimand me over the smallest of things, while her children were twice as wild and she never disciplined them. I felt she was trying to make me the example, and I wasn't having it. I was tired of being the outsider, the black sheep, and the one who was called out on everything because I didn't belong anywhere.

I knew how much Roger cared about me. He drove over an hour to see me every day after work. Many times, we would spend the entire night together, and he would have to pull over on the side of the road on the way to work to carve out an hour of sleep.

One night after work, he came over to see me at Doreen's house. The energy was heavy. I definitely felt I had overstayed my welcome there. I told Roger I would have to get a night job and most likely would have to cut the time we spent together.

Roger feared he was going to have to see me less, so he told me not to worry and brought me to his house, where I crawled and shimmied myself through the tiny basement window that was in his bedroom. We were quiet enough to not let anyone know. As he later left for work, he promised to help me look for an apartment when he got home.

After a few weeks of looking for an apartment, Roger approached his father and said he was going to move out and get an apartment with me. Instead, his father agreed that I could move into Roger's basement apartment. During the summer, when Roger's sister Stephanie was home from college, she stayed with us in her own bedroom in the basement.

I had been living at Roger's for a few weeks when my mother tracked me down. She had only met Roger once, and of course she was furious that someone was looking after me and treating me nicely.

She said, "So I see you moved in with your boyfriend. Have you been to the urologist? Laura, you're going to lose a kidney. Oh, by the way, since you took the semester off, I am going to take you off my medical. My work insurance policy doesn't allow me to cover any child that isn't in school."

I replied, "But I had to take the semester off for the kidney stones."

"Then I suggest you get your boyfriend to put you on his policy."

Even though I wasn't living with her, I was still terrified of her and allowed her to manipulate me. After I hung up the phone, Roger could tell I was upset. He dragged the conversation I'd just had with my mother out of me. He picked up the phone and called his grandfather, who owned the moving company, and asked him to put me on his insurance. A few weeks later, I was insured.

When my mother called around that same time, she started the conversation off by yelling at me over the insurance. "Did you get the insurance? I don't know how you're going to come up with four hundred dollars a month for insurance, but you are not a healthy person and you need medical."

I couldn't wait to shut her down. "Roger added me to his insurance," I said very cheerfully. I could tell instantly my mother was livid. I could feel her jealousy through the phone, but thinking she would fool me, she said, "Good, good," and made an excuse to hang up the phone.

Roger had had his share of trauma, too. He'd lost his mother in a car accident. His father was as emotionally and mentally imbalanced as my mother, and Roger had also struggled with dealing with him appropriately.

Roger's father did love him very much, though.

A few weeks after I'd moved in with Roger, my mother invited herself over to our apartment. It was a fall day, and we figured we would take a ride out to Port Jefferson to do some shopping and walk along the boating docks. When my parents arrived at the apartment, my mother walked in as if she was about to do an inspection.

Even though I was living on my own, she continued to talk down to me, insulting and gaslighting not just me anymore but Roger, too, even after we were married, as well as Roger's family.

My mother knew Roger's grandparents had raised Roger after their daughter, his mother, had died. So when she realized Roger and I couldn't be broken up easily, I found out she called Roger's grandmother, Marie.

We were at Roger's grandparents' house for dinner. Marie had just cleaned off the dishes from dinner and was setting dessert plates. Without making eye contact, she quietly said to me, "Your mother called me the other day and said that I should tell Roger to not be with you because there is something wrong with you, that she'd had to 'put the money where it was worth it.'"

She said my mother had told her I was not mentally stable and had always created problems. And that for his own sake, her grandson should find someone who didn't have so many problems.

Roger looked at me, and I looked at Marie. I replied, "She always does stuff like that."

I had no words, really. I was used to my mother betraying me, sabotaging me, and trying to ruin my life. I was equally aware that most people didn't have mothers who were deliberately trying to destroy them, so I had to be careful about what and how much I said.

There were just too many times where she had singlehandedly ruined relationships I had with friends, friends' families, and teachers. I never knew exactly what she said or did, but whatever it was, it always cost me.

I knew Roger's family didn't think I was the ideal catch, but we all tried to get along. Roger saw, for example, that I made an effort to take time out of my day to talk to Marie.

Roger would argue with me about my mother, saying she was a "buttinsky," that his parents had problems with her butting in where she didn't belong. I was desperate to fit in somewhere, though, so I continued to talk to her when she called. I thought during this time that I could win her over.

After a few months of living with Roger, we got engaged and I decided I wanted to go to beauty school. Marie had overheard our conversation and said to me, "Maybe your parents can pay for it."

I knew Marie felt her grandson already did a lot for me and felt he shouldn't have to do for me what my parents should have done. I explained to her that I'd always wanted to be a hairdresser, but my mother had always talked negatively about the profession and would say, "If you really want to be a hairdresser, you can go after you graduate college." In the end, Roger, against his grandmother's advice, funded my school.

I remember seeing my mother shortly after that and telling her the news about enrolling in beauty school. I could tell she was annoyed but was pretending to be happy for me. She even offered to give Roger money every month to help fund it, but after one month of giving some money, she never gave any again and we never asked.

It was late December, and I was attending beauty school in Babylon about forty-five minutes away from where we were living. I loved learning and designing new styles, and I had made a ton of friends.

Roger and I had our own routines. We began looking for wedding venues. I felt as if I was finally coming into my own. When I arrived home that evening, Stephanie, Roger's sister who was a few years younger than him, was home from college to celebrate the holiday.

When I got in, she told me how her friend Jennifer had invited her to spend New Year's Day at Walt Disney World with her and her family. Stephanie was afraid to ask her father because he tended to give his kids a hard time about everything.

The next day, I asked Roger's stepmother, Arleen, whether she thought Stephanie would be able to go. She said she didn't see why not. When her father came home, Arleen asked for her, and Stephanie was able to go.

Stephanie was home for about a week before she left. Since Roger had to be up early for work, he would turn in early. But I would stay up with Stephanie, talking about everything under the sun until early morning.

The day after Christmas, Stephanie's friends picked her up, and they headed down to Florida in a rental car. Everyone in the car aside from Stephanie took turns driving. Stephanie had always been nervous about driving ever since she'd lost her mother in the car accident.

A few days later, Stephanie called home to say they had arrived and were enjoying the sights. After Christmas, Roger and I went back to our busy lives of work, school, maintaining a living, saving, and seeing friends when we had the time.

The following Saturday, Roger and I went late-night bowling with a few friends. The night seemed to fly, and we all had a great time—especially me, because I scored high and did very well for being a horrible bowler. I even said to Roger that I felt someone from the other side had helped me.

After we dropped everyone off, we headed home and pulled up to the back of the house to the basement steps. I noticed that the kitchen light was on upstairs. All of the basement lights were on, also, and I remembered we had shut everything down before we had gone out for the evening.

I mumbled under my breath that something had to be up because Roger's father was way too frugal to have all these lights on when no one was home. As we made it through the front door, I heard footsteps coming downstairs.

Roger's father, Roger Sr., came staggering down the stairs. At first, he looked drunk, but as he walked towards us, he told us to have a seat on the couch. I noticed he was crying.

Roger and I sat.

Roger's father said, "There's been an accident. Stephanie has been in an accident."

Roger sat up and touched his father and said, "Dad, it's okay. Everything is okay. Where is she?"

His father shook his head, began to sob loudly, and said, "She's dead."

After everyone calmed down, Roger Sr. asked me if I could pick up Christine, Roger's little sister, from her girlfriend's sleepover in the morning. He said not to tell her about Stephanie.

I agreed, and we all tried to go to sleep, knowing the following day would be a long one. Roger drifted off after lying on the bed, numb, for a bit. I couldn't sleep. I had a need to go into

Stephanie's room and look around for anything that could give me comfort.

Her room was messy from her packing. Her Christmas gifts had not been put away. An elliptical exercise machine stood in the middle of her room. I looked for the eight-by-ten picture of her mother that she always had on the headboard of her waterbed, but I noticed it was gone—there was still a space where there wasn't dust from where it used to be.

I rummaged through her room a little more and found a notebook with a will she had written, saying that she wanted to leave her sister, Christine, everything of hers.

The next day, I picked Christine up from her friend's house. She asked me why I was there so early and why I was the one to pick her up. I made up an excuse, and thankfully, she didn't question me too much.

When we got home, we made it downstairs to the basement where the entire family was waiting to tell Christine that her sister had died. Roger's father broke the news to Christine, and she broke down, sobbing.

Stephanie's suitcase was shipped back to us from the police station a few days later. In the bottom of the suitcase was the picture of her mother. About a week later, her body was flown up from the office of the coroner who had inspected her in Florida.

Roger's father talked with the undertakers at the funeral home and requested an open casket since Roger, Stephanie, and Christine had never had closure when their mother died.

Unfortunately, the funeral undertakers said it was impossible to make her look bearable because the accident had decapitated her. To allow the family to have some sort of comfort, the funeral parlor opened the bottom half of the casket so everyone could hold her hand before the actual service started.

Life seemed to become more chaotic after the funeral. Arleen and Roger Sr. filed for a divorce. Roger's father wanted us to move upstairs and live in his space. He wanted to take ours, instead, and he wanted us to look after and raise Christine.

Christine was wild, dating numerous men, doing drugs, and had already had two abortions by the age of seventeen. Christine didn't take orders or listen to anyone. Life was only going to be that much more impossible now that Stephanie was gone.

Roger Sr. and Arleen's marriage was doomed from the beginning due to Roger's grandmother coaching Roger and Christine on how to create havoc in Arleen's life. For a while, Roger's grandparents on his mother's side (Marie and Michael) had tried to move past the incidents that had transpired with their daughter. They would still get together for Sunday family dinner—that was, until Roger's father mentioned to Marie that he was engaged. The thought of Roger's father being nice to another woman in her daughter's house and in front of her daughter's children infuriated her.

Although Roger's father's intention was to get remarried and live happily ever after, he and Arleen had problems right from the start because he wasn't used to disciplining his children or having another woman aside from their mother do it. So, Roger's father often sided with his kids and never reprimanded them and did not allow Arleen to, either.

The energy of the house felt heavy and stale. It reminded me of the house I grew up in. Stephanie was gone, Roger and I were moving out, and Arleen and Roger Sr. were about to finalize their divorce.

It was late afternoon when I walked past the spare upstairs bedroom were Arleen was staying. I poked my head in the door, and she invited me in. I apologized for all she was going through. I knew I would miss her. There were many morning conversations we'd shared over coffee and cigarettes.

Arleen told me she'd overheard Roger Sr. on the telephone mentioning how we were switching living arrangements. She said that Roger Sr. wasn't capable of giving.

I told her I didn't feel good about switching our living spaces with Roger Sr. and I was afraid Christine would cause too many problems for us, as well.

Roger wasn't capable of talking to his sister without it ending in an argument, which meant I was the middleman. I didn't want the responsibility of taking care of anyone. Once again, I felt family was manipulating our lives.

I was also concerned because Roger Sr. wanted us to take over the payments and repairs of the house without actually signing the house over to us. He had a history of spending everyone else's money on fixing his stuff and not being able to keep his word.

During that time, we were in constant communication with Roger's grandparents on his mother's side. Marie had told me to make sure Roger Sr. put the house in our name before we made the switch. I told Roger what his grandmother had said, and he assured me he was going to say something to him, but after a few days had transpired, I saw he wasn't going to. Roger was afraid to ask, so I called a family meeting that evening, during which Roger's father decided to decline my request. Right then and there, we said we were going to move out.

The next day, Marie called us and said her daughter Naunie had a small house in Massapequa that she was about to put on the market. She offered for us to stay there for one year rent free so we could save money and buy our own home.

Roger's Family

I had moved in with Roger, into the basement of his father's house, in September. Roger had all the qualities of the perfect guy when I met him. He was hardworking, caring, sensitive, and had a deep empathy for not only people but animals. He had more animals for friends than humans, but like me, he'd had a turbulent upbringing.

Roger grew up in a relatively wealthy home because his parents had inherited a moving company from Roger's grandmother Marie on their wedding day. Roger's parents had gotten married when Ruth, his mother, was twenty-two and his father was twenty-five. And though the family seemed to have everything a good life had to offer, there were the same heavy energy and spiritual issues present as were in my house.

Roger grew up watching his father emotionally and physically abuse his mother. She would constantly be trying to escape with the kids away from his wrath. Many times, Roger and his sisters would see their mother with a black eye and bruises, crying.

One time, Roger recalled having to wait until his father left for work to let his mother back into the house after his father had locked her outside in ten-degree weather with no coat or shoes for about an hour.

Once Roger had let her back into the house and she thawed out, she called her mother. She then frantically started throwing as much of their clothes as she could into black plastic garbage bags and took a few possessions of her own.

As they were pulling out of the driveway, Roger's father pulled in. Ruth was determined to get away, so she stepped on the gas and drove up the block to a shopping center. She got out of the car with her three kids and ran into a craft store, trying to find a place to hide and to use a phone, but unfortunately, Roger's father had followed close behind them. He went into the craft store and dragged them out.

After this incident, Roger's mother talked to her parents and some legal advisors about a divorce. Unfortunately, after much pleading and apologizing, Roger Sr. then convinced Ruth to go up to Walden, New York, for a "Let's make it work" weekend.

They had once talked about building a log cabin and raising their children up there. Roger Sr. loved to hunt. They all enjoyed the outdoors and country living. "This could be the beginning of a new and better life for us as a family," Roger Sr. had told them.

After about an eight-hour drive, they arrived at Roger Sr.'s mother's house, where they would be staying. They unloaded the car and got the kids settled in the house. They weren't there for very long when Roger's parents decided that they would make a store run to pick up some groceries and DVDs for the evening.

A few hours later, two police cars made their way up to Roger's grandmother's house. Two of the officers from one of the cars came up and knocked on the door.

When Roger's grandmother answered the door, Roger heard one of the officers say, "Excuse me. I am Officer Perry. May I come in?"

He asked if he could speak with her in private, so she took both officers into another room. Roger heard his grandmother gasp and start crying. When the police officers had gone, Roger's grandmother told him his parents had been in a car accident and were at the hospital.

Mary, Roger's father's mother, called Ruth's parents to let them know of the accident. That evening, they drove up to Walden to pick up Roger and his sisters, finally arriving after a ten-hour drive.

As soon as they arrived, they wanted to speak to the police officers who had gone to the accident, so they made a call to the precinct. The same two officers made their way back to Mary's house a few hours later.

When the officers arrived at the house, they were invited in, and they all sat down on the living-room couch. Officer Mason started the conversation with, "I am sorry for your loss," and proceeded to tell Ruth's parents how she had died.

He described how Roger's parents had driven down Elm Road to get to the shopping center. The steeply sloped mountain road was very winding and lined by trees. He said Roger's mother had been driving their Ford truck, which was a stick shift. Roger's father was the passenger.

A deer had run into the middle of the road while they were going about thirty-five miles per hour. As a reflex, Ruth must have swerved out of the deer's way into the trees. The car went off the slope of the hill and into the ditch, where Ruth had somehow fallen onto the stick shift and ruptured her aorta.

The officers then said that the left side of Roger's father's head had severe bruises and looked caved in. He had been unconscious when they arrived at the scene.

Roger had been sitting on the floor of the bedroom with the door cracked, listening to the conversation, while his sisters were napping in another room.

After they had visited the scene of the accident, Ruth's parents drove back to their home in Long Island. They took Roger and his sisters with them to stay for what they thought would be forever. However, the time frame was only a few months because Roger's father came out of the coma and was able to return home eight months later.

While Roger Sr. was still unconscious, Ruth's mother and father decided to have her cremated. Since he was in the hospital for so long and his daughters were young, Roger Sr., along with Ruth's parents, thought it was best, even after he awoke from the coma, that they didn't have a funeral for Ruth. But he asked for Ruth's ashes and kept them in his closet. He obviously wasn't good at saying goodbye and letting go because he kept his father's ashes in his closet, as well.

Aside from what they were told by their grandparents and what they overheard from the police, Roger and his sisters didn't have any other closure until years later, when Stephanie came to me, upset about missing her mother and not having had any closure. It was the second sibling that came to me, crying.

I desperately felt an obligation and a need to help her, so after Stephanie told me where her mother's ashes were, I took them out of her father's closet and brought them downstairs. After everyone else had gone to sleep, Stephanie and I stayed up. I brought out the ashes, contained in what looked like a plain paint can, and we sat on floor, prying open the can.

Stephanie put her hands in her mother's ashes and watched them slide through her fingers as tears streamed down her face. Suddenly, she became nervous about her father finding out we'd stolen the ashes. I assured her not to worry, that I had made arrangements to meet her grandmother, who was bringing me her dog's ashes to put in place of her mother's ashes. Marie had plans to put the ashes in a cemetery near her house.

LA Hair Salon

After Arleen and Roger Sr. got a divorce, we wound up moving into Roger's Aunt Marie's house because Roger's father wanted us to take on the responsibilities of his house and Roger's little sister, Christine, because he couldn't emotionally deal with the responsibilities. But Roger's father didn't want to sign the house over to us, and he had a bad habit of using his children's resources for his needs and wants. Many times, he gave Roger things, Roger would put money and time into them, and then Roger Sr. would later take them back for himself again.

Roger and I didn't want to get stuck paying for a house his father never intended to give us, so we took the opportunity to use Roger's Aunt Marie's house when offered. We were there one year when I got pregnant but moved back into Roger's father's house until I gave birth. Then we got our own place.

The pregnancy made me sick and exhausted right away. It was a few months after graduating beauty school that I got a job working at an upscale salon in Plainview called Frank James.

I was there for a year and a half when one day, James, one of the partners, had taken almost the entire staff and opened his own salon. I wasn't there long enough, nor did I have enough real talent, for anyone to mention to me about the move. With most of the staff gone, and since I was only an assistant, for financial reasons I decided to go up the block to Frank's stepbrother Larry's salon, LA Looks.

During my pregnancy, I was always exhausted, my hair was always flat, and my makeup wouldn't stay on my face. My hormones were all over the place. Being an assistant was demanding. There were only two assistants most days, and there were nine stylists. If we got lunch, we had to eat it in between washing heads. And if you were a good assistant, very rarely did they want to move you onto the floor.

The salon had classes once a week, but the classes were advanced. On the rare occasions they taught the assistants, no one had the patience to teach me, because I wouldn't be able to remember what was taught and the teachers would get frustrated and give up.

My whole life, I had convinced myself I couldn't learn. The beatings over failed spelling tests; being made to eat the paper on which I had misspelled words; being isolated, ignored, and victimized—all threw me right into anxiety. I hated myself because I thought I was stupid. Everywhere I went, I thought people didn't like me because I was stupid.

The thought of not being liked overstimulated me. I desperately wanted to be liked and accepted to the point I would bring the entire salon cookies and cakes whenever I worked.

At the time, I was also trying to keep the peace with my mother by being polite when she called and limiting the time we talked and what I spoke to her about. Unfortunately for me, I made the mistake of telling her where I worked, which was only a twenty-five-minute ride from her house. One busy Saturday afternoon, she came to visit me at the salon without combing her hair or even changing out of her pajamas, which consisted of inside-out, oversized, too-short sweatpants, my father's stained T-shirt without a bra under it, and sneakers.

I was washing hair and assisting both of the owners, Larry and Albert, behind the color station when she walked past me, saying "Hello." I pretended I didn't know her.

Both the owners asked me as soon as she left if I knew her. I said, "No." They had thought she was lost, homeless, or sick. I don't know whether my mother thought I would introduce her and was too prideful to introduce herself or whether she planned to look homeless just to embarrass me, but whatever it was, she never said a word one way or another about me ignoring her.

Marie, on the other hand, tried to support my hairdressing career by getting her hair colored in the salon. She was used to going to upscale salons and got her hair done regularly. I liked it when she came in because we would talk and share lunch. Over lunch, I would tell her about my pregnancy symptoms and she would share some of her Sicilian remedies to relieve whatever I was dealing with at the time.

One day, a man walked into the salon, and he had chunks of what looked like dandruff in his hair that he must not have washed in a very long time. I began to get nauseous, and I asked the other shampoo girl to take over.

I ran into the bathroom but didn't make it to the toilet. I threw up all over the floor and then started to cry hysterically as I quickly grabbed paper towels to mop it up.

Without thinking, I threw the paper towels in the toilet, flushed, and the toilet bowl overflowed. I took the remainder of the paper towels and threw them into the garbage, but now the bathroom smelled like vomit.

I went to get one of the owners, and the other assistant went into the bathroom. She quickly came out, making it known to the entire salon what I had just done. She walked by me, holding a can of Lysol. She started spraying the salon as she held her nose.

The owner came running over to me, grabbed my arm, got in my face, and said lividly, "The next time you want to puke, you can take your ass outside and run into the back woods."

I left early that day. When I got home, I got a phone call from Lori, Larry's wife. It had been a while since Lori and I had worked at the salon together, but from time to time we kept in touch. She had no idea of what had transpired earlier at the salon.

She was calling me to vent about her husband having an affair with one of the technicians. I had confirmed a few facts about Larry when she'd called me, not realizing Larry was having an affair at the salon with one of the nail technicians.

Larry had apparently invited the woman to a family dinner, and Lori thought it was odd. She automatically didn't like the woman, and she didn't like the way Larry and she carried on like long-lost school chums at the dinner table in front of their children.

Once Lori pieced the times together, she said she was going to divorce Larry, but before she did, she was going to march into LA Hair, cause a scene, and make Larry get rid of the nail tech. Before she hung up the phone, she said, "Laura, you got the last laugh. I am going to make sure of it."

I felt horrible. It seemed negativity followed me. I was hurt and mortified. I never returned to work.

Everyone acted as if my pregnancy was the worst thing. Roger wasn't ready to be a father and tortured me every day about aborting. Our plans to have a beautiful wedding were shattered due to the fact I didn't abort.

My mother was angry that I was pregnant and not married, and my father went along with everything she told him to. My friends were still going out and partying, and now my job showed no empathy or compassion for a young pregnant woman.

Baby Shower

After years of having bad relationships, Doreen finally married a guy named Michael. They bought a house near Naunie (Roger's aunt) in Massapequa, and Vicki (a friend of Doreen's) bought a house in Seaport, one town over, and was living with her boyfriend. We all would try to get together during the weekends, but everyone was renovating their new homes. When my friends had time, they wanted to go out to a club and drink. Once Roger and I started to have problems and I got pregnant, my friends stopped asking me to hang out.

Roger and I were fighting horribly all the time while I was pregnant. It was as if he had turned into someone I didn't know. We were moving out of Naunie's and back into Roger's father's house. I was no longer as close with my friends, and my mother was constantly calling me and making me feel bad. My father and little sister were nonexistent during this time, and my older sister was mad that I was the first amongst us three girls to be having a child. My mother had convinced her since she was the oldest it wasn't right that I was having the first born.

Thus, my mother once more took the opportunity to make Andrea feel bad about herself and where she was in her marriage by using me. My mother had conditioned my family to treat me more like a pet or a mentally handicapped person the entire time I lived in the house with them. Even though I was no longer living there, I still felt as if I had to explain about and apologize for my pregnancy.

Early into my pregnancy, I developed full-blown gestational diabetes and toxemia. I was forced to see an endocrinologist right away, who put me on insulin three times a day. He also put me on a strict diet of no carbohydrates or sugars. Everything from my face to my feet were so swollen. I had no energy, and my hormones were all over the place between the stress, the asthma medicine I was on all the time, the toxemia, and the gestational diabetes. I was a walking time bomb.

My friends were slowly getting out of the partying scene, working on their careers, and trying to get their lives together. I was just trying to survive. Doreen and Roger continued to have territorial and control issues when it came to me.

Doreen went out of her way to butt heads with Roger, knowing it made me uncomfortable. It was a tactic I had seen my mother use often when I brought my friends around. Roger many times would hold his tongue for me, but once I became pregnant, that changed.

When he would come out with me and my friends, he was rude. He started to make me question my friendships by saying, "They don't put any effort into the relationship. We do all the work to be in their lives, and they really don't care. If we want to see them, we have to go to them. They never drive to us."

I didn't trust anyone at this point. No one seemed to understand or care what I was going through. And since Doreen had given her baby up for adoption a few years prior, she wasn't overly ecstatic that I was having a baby.

My friends did not understand what my family had done to me my entire life. My mother had spent a lifetime making sure they all ignored me and anything having to do with me or what I cared about. I knew deep down inside my child wouldn't change things. If anything, I was more vulnerable, and my mother would take full advantage of that.

I felt like everyone was going to treat my son the way they treated me. But I was determined to not make that a reality.

As the due date approached, I became anxious that no one was going to throw me a baby shower. I tried to find out whether my friends were going to do anything by hinting to Candy, Doreen's sister. All I wanted was peace of mind, for someone to tell me my son wouldn't be forgotten about and everything was going to be okay.

Candy caught on and wound up saying something to Vicki. Then both Doreen and Vicki confronted me, saying they couldn't believe I would ask. I could tell they were annoyed, so I tried to explain how for years my family ignored me and didn't acknowledge any of my special occasions.

I just didn't want my son to be ignored and not celebrated. Doreen and Vicky didn't understand the lifelong traumas I had experienced around my mother. They told me to grow up since I was having a baby. No one understood the control this woman had over me and how she was able to convince not just my immediate family but distant family and everyone in my community that I was a horrible and useless person deserving of nothing but abuse.

They finally put my mind at ease that they would have something. In January, they wound up having a baby shower for me at Doreen's house. They invited a bunch of my friends, and some family was there also. My mother and grandmother were invited and so was Roger's grandmother, and everyone was on their best behavior.

My mother, of course, didn't bring a gift. She said she would give it to me at a later date but never did. I could tell she was angry that everyone had gotten together to celebrate for me.

Neither one of my sisters acknowledged the baby shower. Roger's grandmother Marie went out of her way to be extra nice to me when my mother was around. I could tell this made my mother uneasy and angry. Every time Marie wasn't around, my mother would bad mouth her to me in hopes of making me paranoid.

I was grateful my friends had the baby shower for me because I knew in my heart my family was not ever going to do anything or give me anything. I felt how irritated my mother was that someone else did throw me a shower.

Baby Roger Comes

Roger's father had been a skilled and avid hunter for many years. He had a room of taxidermy, which he added to regularly, but any other restorations or upgrades to his home died with Ruth. This time, when we moved back to Roger's father's house, we moved upstairs into Christine's old bedroom.

Marie, Roger Sr.'s girlfriend, had her Persian cat locked in the spare bedroom. There were big balls of shed hair all over the room, and the cat had a big box—a zapper, which didn't allow the cat to leave the room—strapped around its neck

As soon as I saw the condition of the room, I immediately reminded Roger about my allergies and how cats triggered my asthma. He assured me that Marie was going to move her cat into the solar room and he would clean the room.

It couldn't have been any longer than a week after we moved back that I wound up in the hospital with asthma. Living in Roger's father's house was a nightmare. I was making regular trips to the emergency room every other night by myself to keep my lungs opened.

Roger was never home. He worked constantly. Aside from the periodic annoying questioning from his grandmother, Marie, and the condescending and belittling calls from my mother, family didn't call. I had lost all my friends. I wanted to die.

After the third visit to the emergency room, the doctors would yell at me and say, "Get rid of the cat! You are severely allergic, and if you aren't careful, you could lose the baby, not to mention how dangerous it is for you."

I tried to explain my situation to the doctors, but they looked at me with disgust, as if I had deserved the situation somehow.

We had been living at Roger's father's house for six months when I got a phone call telling me the doctor wanted me to retake the glucose tolerance test. I had just taken it the week prior when the nurse called and said my levels were too high.

I made an appointment for a few days later, and within forty-eight hours, someone from the doctor's staff called me and said the doctor had requested I see an endocrinologist again and gave me the number of a referral.

The following week, I saw the endocrinologist, who ran several tests. He said my sugar levels were increasing rapidly. I needed to go on a restricted diet. After every meal, I had to take full vials of N and R insulin. By my eighth month of pregnancy, I had full-blown toxemia and was strictly monitored though my stress level was through the roof.

Roger's father made it uncomfortable to be in the kitchen or living area when he was home, so I was restricted to the bedroom for the most part. I was fighting with everyone about the cat and was constantly making doctor and hospital visits to deal with my asthma.

Roger's father had the audacity to tell me there were signs named after me like "one way," meaning I was selfish because I had to eat a specific diet and at certain times. Soon it became unbearable to use the kitchen when he was home.

Roger and I began to eat at the home of our friends Glenn and Patty every night. They were my saving grace and probably the reason I was able to carry my son as long as I did. Glenn was a tenant living in an apartment in Roger Sr.'s house. He worked at Roger's family's moving company and had been living in the house at the time of Ruth's death.

His wife, Patty, moved in a short while after, but they didn't stay long because Roger Sr. raised their rent and made it unbearable for them. Roger Sr. was the male version of my mother. He couldn't stand to see anyone happy or doing well and always found a way to cash in. He never did anything just for the sake of doing it.

Roger and I had been engaged for many years, but once I got pregnant, he started to get cold feet. Roger did everything to convince me to abort the pregnancy. He even tried to bribe me by saying we would have a fancy wedding if I did, but I knew in my heart the baby was supposed to be born. Finally, two weeks before my son's birth, we got married in Glenn and Patty's house.

The baby was due in April. But I wound up being hospitalized for almost a month for having the asthma attack in February. My hormones from the asthma medicine, gestational diabetes medication, and having toxemia made me shaky, moody, hungry, weak, hormonal, and suffer from insomnia.

I literally thought I was losing my mind. I felt like everyone wanted me to lose my baby and that my relationships with everyone, no matter how nice they started, ended in betrayal and with me fighting somehow for my survival.

So there I was, stuck in a hospital bed for nearly a month. There was nothing on except the Colin Ferguson trial. My father had been on the same train but a few cars down the night Colin Ferguson, also a passenger on the train, opened fire with his pistol, murdering six people and wounding nineteen others. I remember thinking he should be happy that he was lucky to be alive and appreciate his family, but the shooting only gave him another excuse to go to the bar.

No friends or family visited me other than Roger, who made out like it was solely my fault I was in the hospital.

I had been in the hospital for about three weeks when my mother called my room. Unsuspectingly, I answered the phone. When I heard her voice, my stomach dropped. She said, "I knew it. I knew you were in the hospital and no one had the decency to call me. How dare Roger? You could die and I wouldn't know!"

So phony is all I could think. *Just one more thing she can twist and gaslight me with.* I quickly changed the subject with a made-up story. I told her that Roger and I had married in the Poconos a few weeks prior, when in reality, we hadn't gotten married yet. There was a long pause on her end. I kept talking to her for a while about the pretend wedding until she conveniently became too busy and had to go.

After I hung up the phone with my mother, a nurse came into my room to check my vital signs. She saw I was upset. She said, "Is anyone going to visit you today?"

I said, "No."

She asked me if I was okay. I nodded, but my face clearly expressed I wasn't. She excused herself from my room for a minute and came back holding a piece of paper with a phone number on it.

She said, "This is the number for the hospital counselors. Maybe you should talk to someone."

After she left the room, I called the number, and shortly thereafter, a young woman in her late twenties came into my room and introduced herself to me as a counselor. She had been assigned to the room.

I told her everything I had been through, and all she could respond to me was, "Well, what do you think?"

After a few minutes, I got very frustrated and asked her to leave.

I sat up in the bed afterwards and turned on the Altar Channel in the hospital and prayed. I asked God to give me a healthy baby. I told him I would forgive everyone for how they'd treated me during my pregnancy. I went home a few days later, and the cat had finally been moved downstairs, and life resumed.

One month later, I went grocery shopping and I could feel the pressure of the baby pushing down. I didn't think anything of it, because the baby was due in April and it was still only March. Once I got home, I put the groceries away and then went to the bathroom.

When I stood up from the toilet, I felt a ton of water come out of me onto the floor. When I looked, there was blood. I started to shake. I ran to the phone and called the doctor.

The nurses at the doctor's office said my water had broken and that I had to come into the hospital. I then called Roger, who at the time was out of the office on a job. Then I called my parents' house. Christine answered the phone. She wished me good luck and quickly hung up the phone.

It was obvious she didn't want me to talk to my mother in fear she would upset me. After I hung up the phone with her, I headed out the door. I could hear the phone ringing. I knew it was my mother, and I intuitively knew why she was calling.

Right after I was admitted into the hospital again, Roger met me in the room they put me in, and it seemed the baby took his time coming out. Every few hours, the doctor would come in to check how dilated I was. For the most part, I fell in and out of sleep all night. At around two in the afternoon, the doctor came in with a few other doctors and nurses. They said a few tests they had run on the amniotic fluid showed the baby's lungs didn't look like they had fully developed since the baby wasn't due for another few weeks.

They concluded that being on all the prednisone and asthma medicine contributed to me going into premature labor. The words weren't even out of the doctor's mouth when I lunged off the table and grabbed Roger's shirt and started punching him.

The doctor pulled me off him and yelled angrily that if I didn't watch myself, I would be restricted. I tried to explain my anger, but the doctor didn't care. Once again, I seemed like the crazy and unstable one. This was the theme that continually played within my life.

Thankfully, on March 22 at 4:30 p.m., a healthy, eight-pound Roger Hilton Spahn entered the world. He was born three weeks early, and he came out with a white veil over him known as a *caul* (the amniotic membrane). Ironically, my mother told me I was born with a caul. Old wives' tales that were passed down and shared in my family said babies born with a caul are born from a witch and have mystical powers.

The labor was exhausting! Once my son was delivered, I started to shake profusely because my sugar levels rapidly shifted back to normal. They wheeled me back into my hospital room, where I found a box of chocolate "It's a boy!" cigars Roger had bought. I ate half the box and drifted to sleep, not waking until the following day when Roger wheeled the baby into the hospital room.

Later that evening, my parents came to the hospital with my little sister. It was obvious my father had had a few drinks before they had gotten there. My mother seemed frantic, barking at me, "Where is the baby?"

I told her the baby was across the hall in the nurse's station. My father and she left the room to see my son, and Christine ran over to the bed.

She whispered, "How are you feeling?" then glanced over to the door and said, "She gave me a lot of shit the day you went to the hospital. She was really angry that I didn't tell her you were on the phone. You know she wanted to talk to you."

I nodded and thanked her.

Christine knew that my mother looked for any opportunity to gaslight and emotionally degrade me, so the day I called, she only spoke to me for those few moments and quickly hung up the phone.

My mother came back into the room with my father, but now Roger's father and his girlfriend, Marie, were visiting as well. Big Roger gave me a peck on the cheek and said, "You did good."

I was still really upset with Marie because of her lack of empathy with me as far as my allergy to her cat, but I tried to be polite. Even though everyone was on their best behavior, I could feel the tension.

After Roger was there for a while, he began bickering with me about how I should take care of the baby a certain way, and his Grandma Marie came in. She seemed very happy to see the baby, but soon she was also putting in her two cents about how the baby needed to be raised.

Meanwhile, all I could think about was how everyone had tried to sabotage my pregnancy, so I wasn't too open for suggestions at that point. After a short time, Marie kissed me goodbye on the cheek, and then Roger walked her to the elevator.

When Roger returned to the room, he said, "I cannot believe your mother."

I said, "What?"

He replied, "My grandmother just told me how your mother called my grandmother to tell her that the baby was born.

"So?"

"My grandmother said your mother made it sound like we weren't going to call."

"I am sure that is not what she meant."

He looked at me and shook his head. "Your mother is constantly calling my grandmother and either insulting you or her, and I am tired of it. I am not going out of my way to appease her."

A few days later, we brought the baby back to Roger's father's house. The house seemed darker and dingier than it had before.

Since Roger's house was all the way out on the Islands, whatever friends I had left weren't always willing to drive a few hours for lunch or a visit. Roger Sr. gave us two bedrooms on the upstairs floor of his house. I felt like I was a prisoner. His father would project his distorted perceptions onto me. Once again, I was living with a narcissist who continually tried to gaslight me.

At that time, Roger's sister Christine and her boyfriend, Steven, had gotten thrown out of Aunt Naunie's house. Roger's grandmother said it was because they were smoking pot. It was obvious that Grandma just didn't like Steven.

Roger's grandmother had a habit of making people uncomfortable until they left or she found a way to get rid of them. She would even brag that she was Italian and knew certain people to call if she had to. I was happy Christine was moving back even though she was wild and much younger. At least I wouldn't be alone.

Roger was a mover. He was out of the house early. Then, when he got home, he needed his sleep, especially if we ever wanted to have our own place. So I would put the baby in the spare bedroom because I nursed him and would be up three to four times a night.

One early morning, Christine came into the bedroom to tell me that she had found my son on the floor, belly up, crying and trying to lift his head. We both knew that her father had taken the baby out of the crib and left him there. I was constantly catching him opening the door to where the baby stayed and letting his dog run all over the toys and blankets. What was worse was when I caught him, he would grin.

After much persuading and arguing, Roger and I finally found a house in Farmingdale, Long Island, when our son was eight months old. Roger had compromised as far as the area since I wanted to be near friends. Once we closed, I started to move whatever I could to the house.

Roger's father pretended to be happy about our house, but it was obvious he wasn't. He started finding things to complain about. As soon as he found out I was actually moving our stuff, he called Roger at work to curse him out and then threw us out.

I didn't know this had happened until Roger got to our house and started screaming at me, saying how selfish I was for upsetting his father. I knew at that point, even though we had only been married less than a year, I didn't want to stay married to Roger, though I tried anyway.

We had been living in the house in Farmingdale for a few months when I got pregnant again and Roger started in about getting an abortion again. It was a replay of what I had just gone through, only this time I had a baby to take care of. Also, the doctor had warned me my body wouldn't be able to handle another pregnancy.

But the thought of having an abortion made me feel sick. I had no one to talk to and no support. I prayed to God, asking him what I should do. A few days later, I was invited to a church with my girlfriend Mary, who lived next door. There was a special event going on. I hadn't shared everything I was going through with Mary, and I didn't know at the time what an *Annunciation* meant. I was just looking to get out of the house.

Once we got to the church, we saw a group of nuns. They were walking single file around the church before the mass started. The nun in front held up a picture as big as herself of the Annunciation to the Blessed Virgin.

The priest who led the mass spoke with a thick accent, so I didn't understand, never mind remember, what he said. Intuitively, I chalked it up to God realizing I didn't think he or Jesus understood what I was going through and how hard it was. He wanted me to know he did. Even if he didn't, Mary knew.

For a few days, I toyed with the idea of having the baby. After a solid week of fighting with Roger, I decided to abort because I realized the situation was only getting worse.

As soon as I was the required number of weeks along in order to abort, I made the appointment. As Roger pulled into the parking lot of the clinic, I saw the group of nuns that had been at the church. They were protesting with a bunch of other people.

As I got out of the car and started to make my way to the entrance doors, a group of protestors started running towards me, yelling, "Baby killers!" as they put pictures of dead fetuses in my face. Roger got out of the car and made sure I got safely into the building. Then he went home and came back a few hours later to get me.

For the next few months, I was in a depression. Roger didn't understand why I was crying all the time and why I no longer wanted to be intimate. I no longer could fake getting along with him.

He started to get spiteful because I wasn't having sex anymore, and he started going out, leaving me home alone with the baby.

Out of the blue, my older sister called me because she was visiting her in-laws with her husband. I thought it was odd that she was coming to my home for the first time. She would also be seeing my son for the first time. She came empty handed, but I didn't think anything about it in that moment.

Since Roger and I hadn't gotten our living room furniture yet, Andrea and I sat on the living room floor while my son napped in his crib in his bedroom. As soon as my sister and I started to talk, I could hear the animosity in her voice. She never said congratulations. Instead, she insinuated how she was the oldest and thought she should have had the first baby.

I felt as if I had to apologize and make excuses about how it had happened. I didn't normally confide in my sister, but she had caught me at a time of vulnerability. She knew Roger and I weren't getting along, but she had only learned about what was going on through my mother.

My mother assumed I was causing the problems. She had tried to end my relationship with Roger by calling his entire family and making up stories about me. Roger's grandmother and father had mentioned many times to me in disgust how my mother would try to convince them to help put an end to our relationship. But they would tell her there was nothing they could do because Roger loved me.

Once my sister knew I wanted a divorce, she gave me the number of her sister-in-law, Naureen, who was a lawyer. I knew my sister gave me the number, basically encouraging me to get the divorce, because she couldn't stand the fact that I had a baby and had a house before she did.

She had insinuated my mother had called her several times to let her know about everything that was going on in my life. I knew my sister was hurt by how inadequate my mother made her feel. It was an example of the way she got other people to emotionally manipulate and gaslight me. This was also a way to manipulate and gaslight Andrea.

But just then, I didn't care how or why Andrea gave me the number.

When Roger came home, he was cordial to my sister but left us alone until my sister left. Roger and I began to argue, and I told him I was going to call a lawyer. Roger looked at me and laughed.

He said, "Really. Where are you going to go? You have no money, no family, and a newborn baby."

"Watch me."

Within a few days, I got a job at a local cheap hair salon, working weekends. And although my lawyer didn't want me to move out of the house, after a month of fighting and spiteful behavior, I did anyway.

Roger's Baptism

It was always very important to me to make a big deal and celebrate the occasions of my son's life. Roger didn't see the need for a baby to have parties, but I really wanted to have my son baptized. It was hard to find a church that would, though, since I had gotten pregnant out of wedlock. Finally, after continuously looking for a few weeks, I had a meeting with a minister at a Lutheran church.

When I got to the church, a woman took me to Pastor Michael, who was sitting in his office. He stood up and stuck out his hand to greet me. Once we both took our seats, he began to ask me several questions, the first being, "Why do you want to baptize your son Lutheran?"

I really had no reason aside from wanting to have a party for my son. I obviously knew I couldn't say this, so I lied and said I was Lutheran. I said we had moved and needed a new church. After he asked the remainder of his questions, he nodded and agreed to baptize my son if I raised him Lutheran.

I felt that having a party wasn't just celebratory; it would also create nice memories and bring the family together. Since neither one of my sisters had taken an interest in the birth of my son, I decided to ask Roger's two cousins to be Roger III's godparents. I thought maybe it could start the beginning of extended family gatherings. I tried to create what I didn't have in my own family.

Unfortunately, my efforts were one sided.

How I Left—My First Apartment

No one wanted to rent an apartment to a single mother, it seemed. I found an apartment across town from where I was living with Roger. A Spanish woman named Carla took pity on me. She, too, at one time had been a single mother. She was married to a short, white-haired Jewish guy who had been the one to originally interview me for the apartment but wasn't interested in taking any single parents.

It wasn't my ideal because it was so near to Roger's house, but I just wanted out. I couldn't physically be with Roger after he made me abort. He treated me like an enemy more than a partner.

I didn't realize then it was the things I did that made Roger not trust me, such as starting projects I didn't finish, wasting money, and being all over the place, consumed in my own selfish needs. The years that we were together before I got pregnant had shown him I couldn't get a job because I never learned any skills. It was hard to stay present and focused when I was at work or in a class.

It was like I was driven by my addictions and compulsions. Roger gave and gave, but I wasn't satisfied. I consistently sabotaged myself and couldn't get out of my own way. I was constantly being triggered to the point where I couldn't control my emotions.

Before Roger, I was never angry; I was emotional and fearful. But once I entered my first live-in situation with someone, I became full of rage and even controlling. Everything from him sitting on the bed after I'd made it, to putting footprints in the carpet after I'd vacuumed, to questioning me about anything, infuriated me. Like his father and my mother, I was a walking time bomb, so he perceived.

As in most codependent relationships, our personalities are polar opposites. We had gone from a blissful relationship to it being very toxic within a matter of years. In many relationships like this, mistrust ruins intimacy, and soon after comes emotional abandonment, until finally the result is the demise of the relationship.

Roger and I had recreated the same karmic situations we each had run from. Roger had always been my rescuer, yet now he was rejecting me while still trying to control me because we lived so close. In the beginning, when I'd first moved out, he had come over often, trying to win me over. But I did not want to try to get back together, so within a few weeks, he began to date other people casually.

I was lonely in my dark basement apartment. I sat wondering many days if maybe I did deserve the treatment my mother gave because I acted out a lot. I wasn't conscious until years later that both my sisters were conditioned to believe that I was less than they were, that I was not capable or deserving due to my learning disability.

When she was eighteen, my little sister, Christine, came to visit me behind our mother's back. She wanted to help set up my dining room table. Christine, being very different from me, was book smart and great at putting things together.

I remember being in my parents' room when I was in first grade with a five-hundred-piece puzzle. The school psychologist had said puzzles would be good for me to do. Christine would be the only one in my family to come into the room for hours and hours. She would run into the room and jump on the bed, and I would grab her and kiss her.

Like all younger sisters, she stole my clothes and tried to emulate her older sisters. It bothered me when she took my things because I didn't have many things which I liked, but I always felt a need to try to protect her.

When I moved out of my parents' house the first time, when I was in the ninth grade, I had gone back to the house to try to visit her. I threw rocks at her second-floor bedroom window one early morning.

When I saw her swing open the window and look down at me, I expected her to be happy I was visiting her.

Instead, she just said, "You left me here. You left me here alone with her!" and slammed the window shut.

I was shocked. For years, my little sister had seen the vicious and cruel things my mother did to me, and yet she was upset I had moved out. My mother was abusive to all of us, but when I lived there, I took the brunt of the abuse.

I didn't realize that Christine knew down deep inside that my mother had to lash out at someone in order to feel okay about herself. She also knew my mother needed to latch on and use other people's energy and life force. Me not being there meant she would be the one my mother would suck that energy from.

Thankfully, Christine has always been very intelligent. She was able to escape that situation. Christine didn't visit me often because it would annoy her that I wasn't living at home. Even though I had then been living on my own for a few years, I was still suffering the consequences of living so emotionally, physically, and psychologically out of balance.

My energy was heavy. I couldn't stay present, and remembering anything was impossible. I was motivated by anything that could change my energy: foods that are salty and sweet, drugs, cigarettes, relationships, and whatever else I liked, regardless of the consequences. I was constantly causing inward and outward chaos for myself with my lifestyle habits.

This included what I felt about myself and what I was deserving of, to the point that it was reflected in my health.

I had horrific digestion issues. I had chronic asthma that forced me to regularly get IVs to open and clear my lungs. I had adrenal fatigue, sinusitis, kidney stones, and candida. If that wasn't bad enough, I flipped back and forth among having anxiety, having depression, and being manic.

After a few months of being in my apartment, I felt I would be better off living among people I didn't know, who didn't know my situation, than to live near people I knew who chose not to help.

I called the psychic hotlines in the back of the *Enquirer* to get advice and peace of mind, but whatever advice I got made me either obsessive or fearful. No psychic ever gave me solutions to any of my problems.

Farmingdale to Queens

Once I realized I needed to leave Roger, I got a job at a new hair salon. It was the first salon job where I was able to cut hair and not just be an assistant after graduating beauty school. Unfortunately, it lasted only a few months. I felt awkward as soon as I walked through the door. I was all thumbs, and even though I had gone to school to learn how to cut hair, I had never learned the correct, systematic way of doing it because I couldn't stay present long enough.

Once I got laid off from the hair salon, I began to look through the *Pennysaver* for odd jobs. Before long, just before I got my own apartment, I found a job babysitting for a young couple that lived a few blocks away from Roger and me. They had a baby boy named James. He was only a month old, and the wife, Kelly, was looking to go back to work within a month or so.

I met with the husband a few days later at my house. He asked me a series of questions, one being whether it would be okay if they brought James for me to babysit at my home. I agreed, but within a few months, watching the baby at the house became unbearable. I asked if I could watch James at their house, and they agreed.

After a few weeks, James had developed severe allergies to and asthma from the family cat. Kelly wound up staying home to nurse James back to health. After about three weeks, once James was better, I returned to babysitting him. On my first day back, Kelly had just finished giving James his breathing treatment with the nebulizer.

After about fifteen minutes, she started to feed James and mentioned to me that the doctors wanted baby James to get allergy tested. I said that would be a good idea and shared how I, too, had allergies and asthma. I had been tested and told her I was allergic to a lot of things, cats being one of them.

Kelly stopped feeding James, slammed the bottle down, looked me in the eye, and adamantly said, "I will not get rid of my cat. I love my cat!"

I was shocked. I couldn't believe what I was hearing from another person, that a cat's life was more important than a human life, never mind it being her own newborn. I was majorly triggered. She had just given her son a breathing treatment because he had been wheezing and having problems breathing a scant few minutes before.

I had thought there would be some empathy for her son. She had just placed a small plastic mask over her child's face so he could breathe. And yet she was worried about her freaking cat? It was mind blowing to me. I knew from that moment I wouldn't be babysitting long for little James' parents.

I became quite unhappy living on Long Island. Mary, my friend from next door in Farmingdale, offered for me to live in their apartment in Queens that was over forty-five minutes away from everyone. This was appealing because knew I needed to move away for my emotional, spiritual, and physical health.

One day after James' parents went to work, I searched their home for their phone book. I called a few salons that were located near that apartment in Queens to see whether anyone was hiring. Finally, after calling around for a while, I called a low-budget hair salon called The Lemon Tree located on Union Turnpike in Flushing. I spoke with the owner about my credentials, and after a bit, she agreed to set up an appointment for a personal interview a few weeks later when I would be visiting Mary.

The day I went to Mary's house, I had made plans to meet her and her husband, Gino, at their old house in Farmingdale. I then followed them back to Gino's mother's home in Queens, where they were staying during the remainder of Mary's pregnancy.

Gino's parents lived in a large home in which they had converted the entire downstairs into an apartment for the couple to live in. Once we got there, Mary showed me around the nursery, where the babies would be staying after she gave birth. Mary was expecting twins, and thankfully her complications had ceased once she and Gino had moved in with his parents.

After a short while, Mary asked me if I wanted to see the other apartment and decided to head over to the building. Gino and his father were barbers who had owned the barber shop downstairs. Over time, they had bought the building.

The apartment was located around the block from a main strip. Because convenience was a high priority for me, the Chinese takeout and deli across the street sold me on the area.

The apartment itself was perfect. The rooms were large with high ceilings. It had a big eat-in kitchen with a built-in table and bench made from tile. There were also a full bathroom, large living room, and one big bedroom. And the previous owner had made a built in kitchen table and bench you could see as soon as you walked through the front door and a short hallway.

Logically, it didn't make sense for me to move. I knew no one in the area except Mary. I had no real experience as a hairdresser. I was a single parent.

I told Mary I would take the apartment the beginning of November.

That evening, I drove back to my apartment in Farmingdale. I called Roger the following day to tell him I was going to move to Queens. He, of course, thought it was a horrible idea, telling me Queens was like a ghetto. "People moved away from the city, not closer," he said. He tried to persuade me to stay in Farmingdale by insulting everything from the town to my intelligence.

The following day, I got a phone call from Doreen's mother, Jackie, trying to talk me into staying with Roger. I tried to explain my reasoning to her, but it was obvious that no one understood or cared about what I was going through. I started to get defensive and eventually ended my friendships with both Doreen and Vicki because they weren't supportive of me wanting to move. They instead mocked me, saying I wanted to move because stores were closer and open later.

They had seen how I was treated, yet instead of being encouraging about the change I wanted to make, they downplayed my situation and acted as if I deserved the abuse. I soon saw that everyone from my parents to my friends had something negative to say about the move.

If that wasn't bad enough, I had to tell my current landlords I was moving. They were angry with me for moving in there only for a few months, but my intuition and inner knowing were aware I had to move. I knew Roger couldn't stop me from moving, so by the first of November, I had arranged for my things to be moved out of his house and into the apartment in Queens.

I had been living in the apartment for a week when there was a knock at the front door. It was Mary's older sister, Karen, and her daughter, Lisa. Lisa was supposed to watch my son when I went to work the following day.

Karen said, "Laura, I am sorry, but Lisa doesn't want to babysit. She was asked to be on the gymnastics team and wants to see her friends. It just wouldn't be fair."

What could I do but say I understood? After they left, I went into the bathroom, lit up a cigarette, and started talking to God.

"God, what am I going to do? I start work tomorrow, and my babysitter backed out on me, and I don't have time to put an ad in the *Pennysaver* to find another one."

I also reminded God how I thought he was the one that said I should follow through with having my son, Roger. I was pretty much waiting on some divine message. After a few minutes, my son waddled into the bathroom, swigging his bottle of Pepsi.

I put my cigarette out and let out a long sigh. A feeling of peace came over me. A few seconds later, I took Roger across the street to buy Chinese food. When I walked into the restaurant, I noticed two women, one older and one younger, sitting at a table, waiting for their takeout.

It was obvious by their looks and mannerisms they were related. I noticed straight away the older woman had a picture of Jesus on her coat. As I approached the counter, I heard a voice say, "Ask."

I thought I was imagining things, so I ignored the voice and kept looking at the menu.

I heard it again: "Ask."

I said to the counter help, "Can I get an egg roll with that?"

The voice got louder and sterner, so I turned around and said to both the women at the table, "Would you be interested in babysitting?"

The young woman's eyes widened with excitement, and she got up from her seat and exclaimed, "Yes, yes, yes!"

The mother of the younger woman said, "Jackie can babysit, but the baby must come to our house."

Before I walked out, Jackie handed me a piece of paper with her phone number on it, and I left.

As I walked across the street, I thanked God for bringing me someone, but then I said to him, "I don't know how much I can pay her. I don't even know how much I will make in this place. I never have made money consistently, nor am I good at budgeting money."

I heard God say, "Three dollars an hour."

I said, "Is that going to be enough?"

I heard in my head again, "Three dollars."

I called Jackie when I got home, and in my most confident voice, I told her the babysitting job would pay three dollars an hour. She was okay with that amount, and I was relieved.

The following day, I had to be at work at 5:00 p.m., so I drove over to Jackie's around 4:30 p.m. Roger was only a year and a few months old. I tried to explain to him even though I knew there was no way for him to really understand.

I had a good feeling about Jackie and her family, but I was overwhelmed with emotion. I had always seen myself as the babysitter, not as someone who would be dropping their child off to someone else.

When we got to Jackie's, there was a sticky note on the front door that read, *Please bring baby around to the back. Thank you.* So I took Roger around to the back of the house and knocked on the door. A small, older Spanish woman opened the door and held out her hands to take my son.

I handed her my baby. She patted my cheek, smiled, and said, "It's okay," and then shut the door. I started sobbing again as I walked to my car and drove off to the salon.

The night and weekend crew at The Lemon Tree was really laid back. Most of us were women who stayed home during the day with our kids. Thankfully, there were many walk-ins. Due to my limited experience, haircuts were a hit or miss. The women I worked with were kind and offered suggestions in cutting. After a while, I built up some of my own clientele.

In another week, it would be Thanksgiving. Roger III would be going to his father's house since as soon as I became divorced my mother stopped inviting us to holiday dinners. I never wanted my son to be deprived of the holidays and special occasions, so he always went with Roger Jr. because I was alone and had nothing to do.

It was the Saturday before Thanksgiving, and the energy in the salon was high with excitement for the upcoming holiday. The place was packed. I sat at my station and started to talk to God again.

"God, I have no plans for Thanksgiving. I am tired of spending every holiday alone."

I believe God brings earthly angels into our lives when we have hardships. I also believe we do not have to wait long periods of time to get answers. We get solutions to our answers in the perfect, divine time. The key is to be in the moment and be present for the guidance so you can apply it.

I learned this a few seconds later when I met Bobbie. Bobbie was a short Italian woman with a friendly and charismatic personality. Even though she was tiny, she gave off very dynamic and confident energy. I later found out she was principal of a school and had raised seven children of her own.

As she approached me, I noticed her dyed-black hair and an inch of grey regrowth.

In a very cheery voice, she said, "Hi! My name is Bobbie, and as you can see, I need my hair done."

We both laughed. Her cheeriness was contagious, and I felt comfortable in her presence right away.

I quickly got her a smock to change into, grabbed the color book to match up her color, and then went to mix her formula.

After a few minutes, I came back with her color and began to apply it.

I hated talking about the holidays because I either had to lie about them or admit I never had any plans—and then feel pity from the person I'd told. But I wanted to be polite, so I asked Bobbie what her Thanksgiving plans were.

She said she had a big Italian family she would be cooking for. Then she asked about my holiday plans. I lied and said Roger and I just moved to Queens from Long Island and still were settling in.

She replied, "But it is Thanksgiving!"

I then said my family lived out of state and couldn't get here in time, so my ex-husband would most likely be getting our son.

I think Bobbie had intuitively picked up on my uneasiness with the question and changed the subject. She shared she was the principal of a school located up the road.

She added, "The school does a soup kitchen for the people in the community who have nowhere to go."

I told her I'd always wanted to work in a soup kitchen for the holiday and asked her if volunteers donated anything for the meal. She said it wasn't mandatory but some people brought donations of cakes and different types of desserts. I thanked her, jotted down the address, and gave her a hug before she left.

Bobbie became one of my regular clients who stayed with me even after I'd left The Lemon Tree, and she helped me with school and transportation for Roger.

After Bobbie left, I thanked God for answering my prayers. I started to calculate how much money I would need for Roger's babysitter, gas, and my cigarettes. I started to get anxiety about not having enough money for a cake, so I prayed again and said, "God, I cannot walk into the soup kitchen with no dessert. My babysitter comes out to forty-five dollars for the week, my gas will cost me at least fifteen dollars, and I am sorry, Lord, I am not giving up my cigarettes."

A few moments later, I told Jennifer about the soup kitchen and asked if she would be interested in coming along with me. Jennifer, whose family was from Israel, was the owner of The Lemon Tree, and she was my age. Her father was a businessman who had bought her the salon when she'd come home from rehab a few months before I started working there. We hit it off right away. We both seemed to be in a place of uncertainty within our lives. Nevertheless, I was grateful that Jennifer hired me, knowing I didn't have any experience but wanting to pay it forward like someone had for her.

The salon was finally empty for the night. I always stayed late with Jennifer to lock up. While she was closing out the register, she asked me if I wanted to cash in my singles. I counted them out and handed her sixty dollars in singles. She handed me three twenty-dollar bills. I thought in my head about the soup kitchen and how I really didn't have enough for the cake. I thought to myself, *Maybe I will be able to scrounge up some change for it,* and then the thought left my mind.

As we were about to leave, a man came running into the salon, holding a large brown-paper bag. He asked if we could please accommodate him by giving him a beard trim. I assumed he'd gotten caught up shopping and thought we were already closed. Jennifer asked me if I wanted to do it, and I said I would, hoping I would get a few bucks for the cake.

The man sat and I quickly cleaned up his beard. Then he went to the bathroom to wash the excess hair off his face. When he came out of the bathroom, he asked, "What do I owe?"

Jennifer said, "Don't worry about it. Just tip Laura, the girl that cleaned you up."

A few seconds later, he handed me a five-dollar bill and the brown bag he came in with. He said, "Here. Take these pies as well."

I thanked him, at first not realizing what he had said to me. After he walked out, I pulled out three large, freshly made pies from the bag. They looked like they had just come from a bakery.

There were two apple pies and one pumpkin. God had listened to my concern of not wanting to go into the soup kitchen empty handed. I felt overwhelmed with gratitude for my new relationship with God, and I began to talk to him all the time.

Leaving the Lemon Tree

Jennifer and I went to the school Thanksgiving morning to work in the soup kitchen. I didn't really feel we were much help because they seemed to have a full staff, but we did what we could. The teachers and aides offered us dinner, which was good for me because I had nowhere to go and nowhere to be.

I saw Bobbie for a few minutes in passing at the school. She was there briefly to drop off some cookies she had made for the soup kitchen. She wished me a Happy Thanksgiving, and we chatted for a short while about how lovely the school was.

I mentioned that I wanted to get Roger into school early to see if he had any of the learning disabilities I had. I figured it would be good for him to get help if he needed it. He was only three, but Bobbie said if Roger was potty trained, I could use the school as my daycare so Roger could go to school, be observed, and learn.

Once I got my son potty trained, the concern became how he would get from school to Jackie's house, but Bobbie even figured that out for me. She told me there was a woman who drove a van every day from the school and dropped kids off in Bayside. She would talk to her about making arrangements for Roger to get dropped off at the babysitter's.

At one point, Jennifer started to have problems with her boyfriend. She didn't want to be alone at night. Many times after work, I would pick up my son and we would all go out together or Jennifer would come over. During the next few weeks, the salon was busy because of the holidays, which kept everyone's mind occupied.

Jennifer and another girl, named Vicki, had made plans to exchange gifts when we got off work. After picking Roger up from the babysitter's, I met the two women back at my apartment. When I opened the door to my apartment, I noticed a pillow had been moved slightly on my couch.

My intuition told me someone had been in my house. Jennifer quickly assured me I was being paranoid. She asked me to get her a Band-Aid from my bathroom. She said she had fallen. I didn't think anything of it.

I got her the Band-Aid and then went into the living room to find them both standing in front of a live six-foot evergreen Christmas tree with red bows decorating every branch. Jennifer and Vicki had bought it off the street for my son and me.

I was starting to feel as if I was getting my life back together. Unfortunately, the feeling didn't last. After the holidays, the salon slowed down. A few old-timers left, and Jennifer hired a few more girls. Diane was one of the new girls. She had known her previously because they'd worked together briefly.

Diane was nice but liked to go to the bar after work and drink. I didn't have the money, nor did I enjoy drinking. When Jennifer and her boyfriend broke up, she started to go out drinking, too, and left me by the wayside.

I started to have a hard time again making ends meet. I felt like I was lost again. I started to feel that my friend Mary, who had talked me into moving to Queens, only wanted me around when it was convenient for her. Generally, that was whenever she needed me to pick up cigarettes for her.

My parents, sisters, and old friends didn't call or come around at all. There was only an occasional bullying phone call from my mother. She loved to say, "Freedom, freedom. What good is it now that you have your freedom? You work like a dog and are alone."

You would figure she would be happy with me being alone. She had just spent the previous seven years doing everything in her power to break Roger and me up. It was so typical of my mother to make sure that no matter what choice I made, I would question it.

Right after the holiday, she called and asked me to check on my grandmother. I remember feeling irritated that she asked me for a favor. It's not like she or her mother had ever done anything for me. Just because my grandmother lived a few blocks away, I didn't feel the need to go and visit her.

After many phone calls and much pestering from my mother, I gave in and decided to go check up on my grandmother. My mother was concerned because my grandmother was alone. Her health was slipping, and my mother couldn't get out to Queens to see her often.

The following day, I drove to my grandmother's house. She invited me in and poured me a drink. As we sat at the kitchen table, she asked me why I had come to visit her.

I explained my mother wanted me to check on her. She nodded and said, "Oh, I thought maybe you moved here expecting me to help you."

I looked at her in disgust. I literally wanted to throw whatever I was drinking at her. Instead, I said, "No. I have plenty of friends and a job here in Queens."

She then invited me to stay and have something to eat. My intuition told me to leave, but I wanted to be polite. I declined the offer but still stayed seated at the kitchen table and chatted for a bit longer before I went home.

A few hours later, my mother called, screaming at me, asking what I'd said to my grandmother. I had purposely watched everything I'd said to my grandmother because I knew she loved to manipulate and antagonize my mother the way my mother did me. I tried to explain I hadn't said anything wrong, but as usual, it didn't really seem to matter.

I went into work that evening, and Jennifer wasn't there. I only had three clients all day. It had been slow all week, and now it was the end of the week. I needed to pay for my babysitter, and I was short. I didn't want to start owing Jackie money.

I didn't pay her a lot, so I had a weak moment and stole fifty dollars from the register. It seemed I got away with it, so I did it a few more times, but I always took exactly what I was short.

One day, Jennifer came to my apartment and asked me if I had taken any money from the register because a few times, she had noticed, they were short. I lied and said I hadn't, but I could tell she thought I was lying. She said her father was going to put in a camera to see who was dipping into the register.

Neither she nor I talked about it any further, but it started to eat away at me. When I was younger, I stole to fit in and be loved. Now I was stealing because I was afraid. I sat on the bed after Jennifer left, and I heard God as clear as day.

He said, "Come clean. You must come clean." I was afraid. I had no family, no saved money, and the future for myself and little Roger was very uncertain. A few minutes later, I got up from the bed. I decided to go visit Jennifer's father at the chocolate store he owned up the block from the salon.

Roger was in school, so I went by myself. When I walked into the store, Jennifer's mother recognized me right away. I asked if I could speak to her husband. She took me to his office to meet him.

I felt in my gut right away that Jen's father knew why I was there. He invited me to sit, and I did. I said, "I am here to apologize for the fifty dollars I stole from the register. I took it because I could not afford to pay my babysitter."

Jen's father accepted my apology. He said since he had to install a camera to monitor the register that I was going to pay for it. He said he would take twenty dollars out of my pay until it was paid off. I wound up working there for about another year, but things were never the same again. I wound up paying the camera off ten times over because Jen's father thought as long as he let me keep my job he would keep taking.

I ended up leaving there a year and a half later because they wouldn't change my hours. When I'd first started working there, Roger was a baby, so I worked nights and weekends. Now that I was looking to put Roger in day school, I needed to work different hours, but they wouldn't change my schedule.

I was forced to go up the block to another hair salon called International Haircutters. The staff was friendly, and the salon was close to the babysitter and to Roger's school, but the pay was horrible. Since the prices were a lot higher, my clients didn't follow me, aside from Bobbie from The Lemon Tree.

International Haircutters

While I was still working at The Lemon Tree, I had become friends with a woman named Bette. She lived downstairs from her parents with her husband, Phil, and their three kids. They lived in a mother-daughter home a few blocks from the salon.

I had mentioned to Bette how I didn't want to stay in Mary's apartment. I'd had a lot of things change since I had moved.

Bette told me her husband's friend Roy had an apartment in Richmond Hill. I didn't know where Richmond Hill was, but I was interested in seeing the apartment. Bette called Roy and planned for me to see the apartment on my day off.

The apartment was in a predominately Indian neighborhood, but I'd never had any prejudice towards any culture. If anything, the Indians I'd known always happened to take a liking to me, so I decided to sign a one-year lease.

Never having been anywhere aside from Long Island, I had never seen how other cultures lived, so for me, the neighborhood felt like I was in a different country, and that got me out of my head.

Behind the apartment was the train which took you to the Bronx and into Manhattan. Underneath the train, there was a very large strip of stores on both sides of the street that ran for a few miles. You could buy anything there, but it was especially known for the beautiful Indian clothing and jewelry. There was also a psychic on the strip who I frequently visited for advice—so often, in fact, I wound up bartering services when I went to her.

During holiday time, they would hang colorful Christmas lights from the street poles from one side of the street to the other. From the sky hung *Happy Duali* in gold and silver lights.

Roy, the landlord, and I became friends. He would see Roger and me every night when I got home from work as he tinkered around outside. After I got Roger settled in, I would sit and talk with Roy for hours. After a few months, we started to date.

I don't think Roy had had any serious girlfriends before me even though he was forty years old. He came from a large Italian family that had lost their father to a gunshot in the head. Roy and his older brother had found him in the basement. From that point on, he seemed angry, as if life had cut him a bad break

Every morning, I would wake up to prayer from the neighbor next door. The mosque, which was up the block, started prayers at around 6:00 a.m. I had been at Roy's apartment for a few months when I realized I just wasn't going to be able to work in Queens any longer because I needed more money.

When I went into work, Valeria, the manager, mentioned how Sal, the owner, was dropping the paychecks off to his salons in the city. When Sal came up to the salon, I asked him if I could pick up some hours at one of his salons in the city, so he had me work on Wall Street. After some time of getting extra hours at that location, he then asked me if I could fill in a day at his Upper West Side salon.

Out of all Sal's salons, this one was my favorite. It was located at 60 West 66th Street across from the New York City Opera, ABC, and The School of Performing Arts. The energy was amazing. I wanted to get transferred to this salon full time. Thankfully, Maggie, the manager, took a liking to me and convinced Sal to transfer me.

I hadn't been at the job long before my son started to get sick with ear infections. One morning, I went into his room to wake him up and I saw he had thrown up all over the comforter and floor. He had a fever and was hysterical, crying and holding his ears.

I cleaned Roger and his room up, stripped his bed, and put the sheets and comforter in the trunk of my car. I figured I would wash them at the Laundromat when I got home from work. I made an appointment with the pediatrician, who luckily saw us that morning for an emergency visit.

She prescribed antibiotics and a special diet for him. So after seeing the doctor, I went to the grocery store to pick up Roger's food then dropped him off at the babysitter's.

Every morning, it was a stressful hassle trying to find parking around the railroad station. Parking was limited, fines were high, and I was always trying to beat the clock, especially when Roger was sick. I was told by Sal that my problems weren't his problems when I missed the train because of a doctor's appointment for Roger.

I struggled with my own health, as well. I had chronic sinus and upper respiratory infections. Luckily, I met an allergist, who was located near the railroad, and went to his office one evening when I got off the train. I caught the doctor right before closing.

He wanted to send me to the emergency room, but I broke down, explaining how I couldn't go to the hospital because my son was at the babysitter's and I didn't have any help aside from them. He then gave me medicine intravenously, which thankfully opened my lungs, and I felt better.

The sinus infections got increasingly worse from smoking as well as poor diet and lifestyle habits. Any change in season or new stress and I would get sick. Many of my days off were spent at the allergist's getting breathing treatments and IVs, to keep my lungs open, while my son played with whatever toy or person happened to be there. My stomach was always distended to the point I looked a few months pregnant. All the antibiotics and steroids I was on gave me digestion issues and candida.

As I continued working on the Upper West Side of Manhattan, life started to get back on track. I loved the city and the people—not only those who worked with me but the clients that came in, too. I pretty much kept to myself, though. Every now and again, Sal would come up and insult my cutting skills, but fortunately, he at least gave me a chance,

Once I had been there for a few months, I became friends with a woman named Lisa. She was thirty-nine years old and had worked at that location for about ten years. One day, we exchanged numbers, and we started calling each other on the phone to chat.

Her family life was like mine. Her mother favored her brother and had ignored and abused her in her childhood. Her father was estranged. Lisa's grandmother was the only relative she considered to be her family.

She had been dating a guy named Jerrod, who she had met in Philadelphia when he was in the military. She had moved in with Jerrod and his father, but after six years, she moved out. They were still working on the relationship.

Thus, neither Lisa nor I really had family, so holidays were spent with each other, usually walking around in Manhattan and looking for psychics.

Lisa and I spoke every day, and I was grateful to have someone to hang out with. Luckily, we both had the same days off. Many times, Lisa would ask me to take her to doctors' appointments because she didn't have a car.

She also struggled with upper respiratory infections, and her dermatologist kept finding pre-cancerous moles that needed to be removed and also found a lump in her breast during one of the procedures. I scheduled all Roger's and my appointments around Lisa. I treated her like my sister. Because I knew what it felt like to be alone and not have anyone, I didn't want her to feel alone, too.

One day while we were at work, Lisa shared with me how she had practiced Santeria. She told me she had been dating a guy back home in Philly whose family were practitioners of the religion. The mother of the guy she was with didn't like her, and she said she had done spiritual work to try to get rid of her.

She said practicing a lot of their customs and rituals when she was younger had opened up her own psychic ability and she would sometimes get visions.

I thought it was odd that this whole time we were running around to psychics she had never shared about her gift. She said she didn't like to read for people but that she had just had a vision that her boyfriend was driving on Sunrise Blvd and he was stopped at a red light.

In the vision, Lisa had pulled up in her car right next time to him to see his arm around a Spanish-looking woman with dark hair.

She said to me, "I should have never moved out. I thought it would have brought us closer together. Instead, it pushed us further apart. Out of all the years we have been together, I never felt him stray. I know he is with someone else."

Sure enough, about two weeks later, Lisa was in the car with her chiropractor who had often bartered with Lisa for services. He was taking her home when they were stopped at a red light. As she looked out her car window, she saw her boyfriend, Jerrod, with his arm around a Spanish woman.

As soon as Lisa got home, she called Jerrod and left a message on his answering machine, saying, "Jerrod, this is not your lucky day. I just saw you in the car with someone else. We are now officially over." She was devastated.

The next day at work, she asked if we could go out because she didn't want to go home and think. It was Friday, and Roger's father had picked him up from the babysitter's, so I was free and agreed. We walked around on the Upper West Side for a bit then got a bite to eat. Then we went to 34th Street to catch the train.

I found I had just missed my train, and we had about forty-five minutes to kill, so we went into a bar in Penn Station called Charley O's. Lisa ordered a beer, and we both sat down in a booth. wenty minutes later, a good-looking Israeli man came up to the booth and started talking to us.

Lisa was exceptionally flirty, and for whatever reason, after only a short while, she mentioned how she'd helped a friend out a long time ago and married him so he could get his green card and stay in the country.

I don't know if Lisa had intuitively picked up on it or just got lucky that the man, whose name was Avi, was an illegal and needed his green card. I stayed at the bar for a bit longer until my train came and said goodbye to them both.

The next day at work, Lisa told me she was now dating Avi and the dynamic of our friendship changed. She only wanted to hang out with me to chauffeur her around to all her doctors' appointments. She became more and more distant, but when she called, she expected me to drop everything. I tried to set boundaries with her, but the more I did, the more bullying she became. I started to see a lot of resemblance between Lisa and my mother.

When I had taken her to get one of her moles removed, she had asked the doctor whether he could remove scars. When Lisa was younger, she had gotten a tattoo removed from her forearm, which had left her arm looking like it had been burned in a fire.

Lisa was insecure about her body and was trying to do whatever she could afford cosmetically to enhance herself. The doctor said he would be able to do the procedure but call it something else so he could bill the insurance and she wouldn't have to pay for it. He said as soon as her insurance company cleared it, he could do it.

She looked at me and said, "You're going to take me."

At this point, I was tired of spending my days driving her around. I hated who she was becoming. She was obsessed with fixing her body and making Avi happy. I told her she would have to ask me in advance, and she agreed.

At that point, I didn't talk to Lisa outside of work for some time. Out of the blue about a month later, she called me one evening while I was on the phone. I put my other conversation on hold to tell her I'd call her back, but she expected me to hang up with who I was speaking to. I didn't, and she tried to quickly tell me what time she would need to be picked up.

I said I would talk to her about it after I got off the phone. She intuitively knew I was going to tell her I wasn't taking her, so she refused to pick up the phone when I tried to call her back. I left her a message, but the next day she called me, pretending she never got the message.

She called me from the doctor's office and left another message on my land line that I heard once I got home from dropping off my son. I was livid and called her doctor while she was in surgery. I asked the receptionist to tell Lisa I would not be able to pick her up because I had to take my son somewhere and I wasn't feeling well.

About seven hours later, I got a phone call at home from Avi, who Lisa had since married, asking where Lisa was. I told him I had never agreed to pick her up, that she kept trying to stick me with being her chauffeur, and now that they were married, it was his obligation. And then I hung up on him.

The following day, I went into work and Lisa started to bully and intimidate me by telling the entire salon how I'd left her stranded after promising to pick her up from her surgery. I sat in my station, reading a magazine, and mumbled under my breath how I'd never promised her.

I said out loud to her, "The agreement was you were supposed to give me some advanced notice. You didn't."

Livid and in shock that I was defending my actions, Lisa came over to where I was sitting and grabbed me by my ear off the chair and onto the floor then started punching me as I laid there. The entire salon watched. No one wanted to get involved because they had seen this ugly part of Lisa before.

Once I got up from the floor, I called Sal to tell him what Lisa had done and waited outside until he came up. Two of my coworkers came outside and apologized, saying they knew they should have done something. But no one wanted to deal with her.

It was the same scenario that had played out over and over and over. Everyone saw how my mother had abused me, and no one ever got involved. Now, no one wanted to confront Lisa because they would have to deal with her.

When Sal arrived at the salon, he fired me mainly because Lisa had worked there longer and was a better hairdresser.

As I emptied out my station, I couldn't figure out why this had happened to me. I asked God to show me the reason. Not until a few months later, when I went to my old psychic Zena, did it come up in a reading that Lisa was jealous of my new apartment and my increase in clientele at work. She was used to seeing herself as someone who mentored me and was better than me, but my life was showing her that her perception was off, and she didn't like it.

I went back to my apartment in Queens and sat wondering what I should do about work. It was a only few weeks after the terrorist attacks of 9/11, and my friend Eddie had come by to check on me. She was still in shock from having to walk over the bridge to get home the day of the attack.

She asked me how I was doing. I shared with her about what had happened with Lisa. She asked me if I would be interested in moving into the apartment she had for rent. She sold me on the fact that she lived nearby and we would do things together. I was afraid to stay where I was because the rent was $1,300 a month, and moving into her apartment the rent would only be $1,000 a month. I tried to cut back any way I could.

A few weeks after I had met with Eddie, I moved into her apartment. As soon as I did, I realized it was a mistake. They said they were going to put a kitchen in. They never did. The washer and dryer they said I could use, Eddie's mother reneged on. And the apartment had bugs.

It seemed they wanted a good tenant who they knew would pay the rent and not have parties, but they didn't want to keep their end of the bargain. At this point, I was ready to play hardball with whoever messed with me and my son. I threatened to call the HPD (the Housing Preservation and Development Agency). They thought I was bluffing until an HPD rep came knocking at their front door and left a note.

I came home from work to find my door was locked. I had mail in my car with the apartment's address on it, showing I actually lived there, so I called the police, who met me at my landlords' house and started banging on their front door.

They denied I lived in the apartment, but the cop had my mail and said to open the door immediately and that they knew I lived there. Eddie's mother came to the door and started making up lies, saying I was crazy.

The cops told her to shut up with her nonsense and to let me in. Then, once they saw my apartment was packed up, the police screamed at Eddie and her family. They told me that I should sue them for breaking and entering and damaging my property since they broke my son's bed.

That evening, I stayed in a hotel room, and the following day I subpoenaed Eddie and her mother to go to court. The morning of our court date, my car had a flat tire and I noticed colored paint all over my car.

Eddie's mother's boyfriend painted houses for a living, and I had remembered him wearing pants that had the same colors splattered on them. Thankfully, I was able to get the tire plugged up and get to the courthouse on time. I walked into the court room, and Eddie and her mother were sitting there.

I looked over and smiled and said, "Sorry I'm late. Someone gave me a flat."

Eddie looked down. I knew she knew what she had done was wrong. The judge said I would be able to sue, but I said I didn't want to. I think part of me didn't want to lose Eddie's friendship and thought if I didn't sue that maybe we could make amends. We never did, though, and shortly after the court date, Eddie and her husband put the house up for sale and moved to Montauk.

For a delusional moment, I thought maybe my family would be different because I had been away for a while. I would soon find out the only difference transpiring with my family was a different day on the calendar. They still acted nonexistent in my and Roger's life.

I decided to look for a salon to work in out on Long Island again. I had called the salon I'd worked with before I went into the city. The owner, James, gave me my job back. But building clientele there was not only brutal but nearly impossible, and the clients were rude. It was a high-end salon, and it was the dead of winter. I made no money. Many days, I couldn't afford to eat because any money I made went towards babysitting and gas money.

Things went from bad to worse when my car broke down.

Once my mother knew I was working at that salon again, she would invite herself to get services done for free and never offered to give anything. One day, she came to the salon and invited me to dinner. I made the mistake of saying I appreciated it.

When I got off work and called her to tell her I was on my way over, she uninvited me, denying she'd ever offered. I said, "Can I come over anyway and make a peanut butter and jelly sandwich? I am starving and broke."

After a long pause, she told me she was out of peanut butter and jelly and that I should drive to Queens to rent a car. I could then drive back the hour to make myself a sandwich, she added.

This was not the first time my mother denied me any help. In fact, she did everything in her power to isolate me from the family so I couldn't get help from anyone else, either. I tried asking my mother to put other members on the phone to ask for their help, but she would always lie and say no one else was there or they were busy.

I learned very fast that my family only knew how to take and use me. They enjoyed treating me like I was beneath them because of my learning disability and the way my mother had always treated me.

When I went back to Long Island, my ex-husband offered to buy me a house out on the island that my son and I could live in. He tried selling me on the fact that we all could help each other. I could help his girlfriend and her kids, and they could help with Roger. I declined the offer and decided to take the next day off and hit the pavement back in the city.

I wound up walking into a salon on 34th Street called Dramatics NYC. It was one of ten salons of that chain in New York City. I walked in and asked for an application. They gave me the phone number of the main office, where the owners interviewed every

Wednesday. It was relatively early in the day, so I walked down to the office and knocked on the door.

The receptionist came to open the door and said, "Can I help you?"

I said, "Yes, I am looking to apply for work to be a hairdresser."

"Interviews are done for the day." She began to close the door.

I put my foot in the door and said, "But I am here now, and no one else is here now."

A second later, I heard a man's voice saying, "Let her in."

I walked into the office. A short bald man with glasses said, "Please take a seat."

His name was Rock, and he was one of the owners. He asked me how much experience I had, where I'd worked last, and why I'd left. I answered most of the questions honestly, except for the reason I'd left. I said I'd outgrown the place.

He said that Dramatics was more of an upscale salon than those that I'd worked at, but he was willing to give me a chance. After my interview, he shook my hand and told me to go down to the training center on 23rd Street to do the practical part of the interview.

I walked down to the training center and sat outside, smoking a cigarette. It was already 3:00 p.m., and Roger would need to be picked up by 6:00 p.m. I went inside and saw a bunch of students working on mannequin heads. From the office came an attractive Italian-looking man smoking a cigarette.

He said, "Who are you?"

"My name is Laura. I just saw Rock, and he asked me to come down here to do the practical part of the interview."

"Madison is out on lunch. She should be back shortly. Take a seat."

After an hour and a half, Madison came walking in, holding a bunch of shopping bags. Ace, the Italian-looking man, pointed to me and said, "This woman has been waiting over an hour," then gave me a mannequin and asked me to wet the mannequin's hair and to do a haircut that I enjoyed doing.

Thankfully, no one was really watching or checking the technical part my haircut. Ace left before I was finished. From what Madison saw from the other room, it looked good. I had a knack for styling uneven and technically-off haircuts and making them look good.

It was now 4:30 p.m., and Madison tell me to hurry up and foil the entire mannequin's head because she wanted to leave. I didn't want to risk the opportunity to finish the interview, so I did it as fast as I could. When I was finished, I didn't feel bad to say I had to hurry to get to my son by 6:00. She quickly looked from across the room at the foils and she said, "Your haircut was good but your foils were sloppy, so we will put you on the floor. You will need to go to color classes."

I quickly cleaned up and thanked her and ran as fast as I could to the train.

Dramatics and Meeting Ace Miami

I liked working on 34th Street, but my coworkers were competitive. They could tell I wasn't confident in my technical ability. Nobody there ever complained about my work, though, until I started making more money than they did. I loved the part of the job which allowed me to connect on a deeper and more intimate level with my clients. It made me feel as if I wasn't alone and that I had some people who cared about me.

Rock allowed me to keep my job because I was making money for the salon. A lot of money. I was the number-one salesperson, so they kept me on the floor. I also had to go through their haircutting training course, which took about year, which meant I had no days off.

I didn't mind because I never had any plans aside from running errands and chores, anyway. Everyone I knew worked during the time I was off, but I was able to still pick up Roger from school and have our quality time.

Every week, I had to be at the training center by 9:45 a.m. I got an hour for lunch, and we were finished by 6:00 or 6:30 p.m. On Mondays, it was all classroom time and learning the technical aspects of cutting. On Wednesdays, we worked on clients who had seen the advertisement for discounted services and had walked in off the street.

Every Wednesday, the training center was busy. On Wednesday mornings, we learned how to give a proper consultation by practicing on each other up on stage while Rock critiqued us.

Most of us dreaded going to consultation because Rock would yell and carry on in frustration that we weren't doing it properly.

His anger transported me back to when my mother tried to teach me division with egg noodles. She had gotten so frustrated she threw the noodles at me and then made me eat them off the floor. Both she and Rock were able to make me feel as if I was defective because I could not think when I was around either of them. It gave me the same sick, paralyzed feeling.

The receptionist of the salon announced there were tickets to a Hair Expo in Las Vegas. I had never flown on a plane or traveled anywhere, and I was determined to take the opportunity to experience somewhere new.

I had become friends with and worked next to a girl named CoCo at the hair salon, who also was interested in going to the Hair Expo. She told me she had traveled to many places by herself and that she loved to travel. She asked me if I wanted to go with her and offered that we could share the expenses. She said she would call me that evening to set everything up.

After the receptionist made the announcement about Las Vegas and the Hair Expo, Ace walked in to pick up the payroll. Having overheard CoCo and me talking about booking our reservations, he said he was going to be there as well, mentioned it would be fun to meet up, and asked me for my phone number.

I didn't think anything of it, being he was one of the owners. I chalked it up to him being nice and wanting to make sure that we saw everything once we got there.

At one point, Ace had run and managed the salons. Rock was more of the silent partner. Over time, the staff was doing whatever they wanted to do, and in order to run the business properly, Rock had to take control. Before Dramatics, Ace had owned salons all over the United States, and in his youth, he had been a platform hair designer. He didn't just have a knack for doing hair; he had a great sense with people, too.

He had heard about my gift for sales and thought he would be able to teach me, but I found it difficult and confusing because he was asking me to unlearn everything I knew, from the way I held my scissors to how I interacted with the clients. But everyone loved Ace. He was considered the "good boss." He was charismatic, fun, and always made everyone laugh. Working with him made the day go by faster.

Ace and I became friends. We had a lot in common. We both had a son around the same age. Ace had been separated for over eighteen years and divorced for ten when I met him, and he had two children from a previous marriage. Even though his ex-wife, Debra, was dating someone else, I still felt as if she could control and manipulate him. She didn't feel that Ace should be able move forward.

Ace said as soon as he put the ring on Debra's finger, he knew it was a mistake. He told me how she had hidden her thirteen-year-old daughter she had from a previous relationship until a few days before their wedding. During their marriage, she cheated several times on him and stolen money from him. In the end, it was if she'd only married him for his money.

In the beginning of our relationship, Ace and I would prepare dinner and watch movies. He would ask me if I wanted to go out, but I very rarely did. I was physically and emotionally exhausted all the time because of the long hours at work, raising a child on my own, dealing with abusive family members when they decided to be in my life, and never feeling good enough or that I had enough. I was grateful to just sit and have something to eat, somewhere warm, with someone who cared about me. After some time, Ace's son, Anthony, met me and wanted to be over when I was there because we did things as a family. We would play board games, cook, and watch movies.

Debra soon realized I was the reason Anthony was suddenly wanting to stay at his father's house every night, and it made her jealous.

We would be hanging out in Ace's apartment, and his land line would ring and ring until the answering machine would pick up. Debra would then leave lengthy, nasty messages, talking down to and degrading Ace.

She would say, "Ace, pick up the phone, you useless man. You owe me your life. What kind of father are you? You better believe that most fathers are up at their children's school making sure their children are being taken care of. What kind of man are you? You owe me your life!" She would call two and three times in a row until Ace took the phone off the hook.

Debra was always using her children as pawns to manipulate and control Ace. Early in my relationship with him, Debra wasn't threatened in the least. She thought I would be short-lived like all the other women he'd dated. She believed she was above the hairdressers and the other working women Ace had gone out with.

He had given her a comfortable life on the Upper East Side of Manhattan. While they were married, they lived in a penthouse apartment. She had shopped at Saks 5th Avenue and Bergdorf Goodman, buying the newest fashions. More than loving Ace, she loved the lifestyle he provided and couldn't bear to lose it.

She could tell Ace didn't treat me as well as he had treated her, which gave her a false sense of security. She believed they would reconcile. If she couldn't convince him, it appeared, she would manipulate their children to do it.

Roger was about to go into fifth grade, and he didn't want to go to the after-school program at YMCA anymore. He asked me if he could stay with the babysitter, but the babysitter didn't get off work until 6:00 p.m. Thankfully, he enjoyed spending time with his friend Henry at his house.

Henry was Asian and had a large family. Four brothers and sisters, parents, and grandparents lived with him. I felt more than comfortable that Roger would be taken care of. I offered to pay his parents in order for Roger to stay there, but they agreed to let him stay without payment because the boys got along so well.

Roger's father didn't like Roger spending so much time at his friend's house. He thought Roger was running the streets unsupervised. He didn't believe me or Roger that he was in good hands. He would question me about what I was planning on doing the following year when Roger went into middle school.

I told him that I would let our son make the choice of who he wanted to stay with. I couldn't help but think if Roger stayed with me he would get gypped out of big Christmases, family gatherings, and Thanksgiving dinner. My mother's words echoed in my mind, "Freedom, freedom. What freedom do you have when you are a slave to work? Your son is going to want the things money could buy."

Trying not to pressure him, I would ask Roger what he wanted to do. I knew he felt uneasy for having to choose, but after he contemplated it, he said, "Mommy, you had your turn. Now it's Daddy's turn."

Secretly, I wanted Roger to not want to go even though I knew it would be better for him.

Christmas Eve was very busy at the salon, so I was grateful to be invited to my friend Noel's house in Staten Island. I'd met Noel in the salon when I first started working on 34th Street. She worked down the block from the salon. Many times before, during, and after work, we would see each other.

She came from a big Italian family who went all out for Christmas. Everyone was friendly and kind, but I always felt out of place. I started to think about my Roger not being there and how he would no longer be living with me. I couldn't help but get emotional.

During dinner, I don't know why or how I started to think about what it felt like. I didn't mean to lose it. It was almost as if I forgot that it was Christmas and I was a guest. Noel sat with me, trying to make me feel better. As I found my way out of myself, I noticed a few of Noel's family members glancing over at me with annoyed looks.

One of her aunts said to me, "We are here for you," but I felt pitied and embarrassed. Their gestures were nice, but I knew no one cared about what I was going through. I knew down deep inside this was the moment my mother had waited for.

When I had gotten pregnant, my parents and little sister went away to Antigua. On the plane, my sister told me later, they met a woman who had just had a baby. She was sitting with her mother. My sister and mother started a conversation with her as the plane took off.

The woman asked my mother how many children she had and whether she had any grandchildren. My mother said, "No, not yet," while knowing I was eight months pregnant.

My mother first pretended my pregnancy was nonexistent. She tortured me throughout it then isolated me and her grandson from the family. Aside from seeing my sisters a handful of times, we didn't see my family.

After three years of dating him, I moved into Ace's apartment. When I moved in, Ace had to go to California to visit his friend Dominick who was dying of liver cancer. Debra obviously thought she would try to take the opportunity to get rid of me, so she kept calling me the day Ace left, but I wouldn't pick up.

She left a message on the land-line answering machine, saying, "Laura, you'd better get used to taking care of Ace's kids, because I am not taking care of them. They are not worth the measly two thousand dollars a month I get for them. You guys can move your bed over and make room for them. While you're at it, you can come by my apartment and pick up Anthony's filthy birds. I am not cleaning up after them. Since you want to be with him, you can take care of the kids, also."

I didn't pick up the phone at first, but then she started calling my cell phone. I picked up the phone and told her I was on my way to work and I would not be picking up Anthony or his birds. The conversation ended with me hanging up the phone on her.

We had to wear certain colors on certain days at the salon, so the staff all matched. When I got into work, I was wearing all black because that was the option if you didn't want to wear or didn't have that day's color. My manager asked me to please get an orange shirt, though, because we were taking a group photo.

I asked the front desk when my first appointment would be there, and she said not until noon. So I decided to take my lunch early and walked from the salon on 47th and 2nd to the Express on Lexington and 47th Street, which was only a ten-minute walk. I wasn't in Express longer than twenty minutes when my cell phone rang. It was the receptionist at work saying I needed to come back because I had a client waiting for me. I guessed the other receptionist had forgotten to write her appointment down.

I walked back to the salon and found Debra sitting in the waiting area, wearing sunglasses and pretending to read the paper. I walked into the salon and said, "You guys did not call me back here for this lady, did you?"

Debra dropped the newspaper and jumped up from the bench she was sitting on. She started yelling and getting in my face, telling me to go outside. The manager tried to calm her down, but she wasn't having it. I agreed to go outside, where we then had a heated argument.

She tried to convince me Ace didn't really care about me, that she was his wife and still being taken care of, and that I was only the girlfriend.

That's when I flashed my engagement ring at her. She gasped and took a step back.

I said, "That's right, you old hag. He got rid of you a long time ago."

I knew she was so vain about her looks it killed her that he was with someone twenty years younger than him. Her boyfriend, Fernando, was ten years younger than her, and for years she had been trying to make Ace jealous with him, but Fernando had never had any intention of marrying her and had actually made that clear in the beginning of their relationship.

Debra lived upstairs from the Dramatics on Third Avenue, and she would often go into the salon and get her hair done as if she were still married to Ace, which annoyed me. She treated everyone horribly, but because Ace's daughter would do all Debra's negotiating for her, working with her as a team to manipulate him to get what they wanted, Ace felt bad.

While Ace was away, he called me, and I told him Debra had come to my job and caused a scene. He replied, "She always does this." Then he started to get upset, making me promise that she would not be able to break us up.

He said, "This is why I used to hide you from them in the beginning. My ex-wife and daughter are vultures. They are so afraid that I am going to give something to someone; that's all they care about."

I agreed to not let Debra break us up.

The next evening Natasha, Ace's daughter, came over with a suitcase. She said her mother kicked her out of the house. She said her mother woke her up out of a sound sleep and yanked her off the bed. At first, I believed her—until Ace called later.

Natasha happened to be out when he called, so I was able to talk freely about what had been transpiring. Ace told me not to listen to his daughter. That his daughter and ex-wife liked to play games to try to manipulate him. He told me to first ask Natasha when she got in if what she said was true about her mother, and next, ask her if she would be willing to repeat it in court. He guaranteed she wouldn't.

When Natasha came in, I told her what her father said. She looked at me with a blank stare. It broke my heart. I knew Ace was telling the truth. The next day after I got home, Debra sent Anthony over.

She thought I would be angry. I wasn't. I wound up ordering dinner, and we watched TV. The following day, Debra tried to call Anthony. He didn't want to get on the phone. She realized her plan of pushing her kids onto me wouldn't push me away. Instead, I embraced it, which made her livid.

The night before Ace came home from California, he called and I said I wanted to get married by the justice of the peace. My intuition had told me earlier that day that if Ace and I waited to get married, Debra and Natasha would find a way to stop it. Ace agreed, and the day after he got home, we went downtown and got married.

Later that day, Natasha came over to visit her father. He broke the news to her. She didn't realize I was in the back room. I heard her questioning Ace, asking him how he could get married without telling her. Her back was facing towards me as I approached the living room.

I said, "Natasha, I told you."

Taken off guard, she almost fell off her seat. She turned around to look at me, and I saw the stream of tears rolling down her face. She started to get nasty, so Ace threw her out of the apartment. A few hours later, Anthony came over after school and we shared the news with him, and he was happy.

I told Ace he should tell Debra; otherwise, I felt certain she would cause problems at work. Ace tried to call Debra several times, but Natasha kept picking up the phone and then hanging up. She was afraid of what her mother might do. Finally, Debra called Ace, realizing Natasha must be hiding something, and Ace told her we'd gotten married.

She tried to act happy for him and said her congratulations, but that night she brought all of Anthony's toys over and dumped them in the lobby of Ace's building. After days of being harassed, Ace I went down to the court buildings to get an order of protection.

Ace's lease was up, and we decided to move into a larger apartment. Anthony was sleeping over every night, and Debra was abusing him, saying he wasn't honoring her by being nice to me, and reminding him that she was his mother.

Sometimes Anthony would sit in the corner and say, "I must honor her…she's ugly, she's ugly. I must honor her." One day, after he started saying, "She's ugly, she's ugly," he stopped himself and said, "No, she's not."

I started to grow such a strong bond with Anthony. I knew what it was like to be raised by an abusive parent that looked at you as nothing more than their property and at what they could get from you. Even if I was in another room, I could feel if Anthony had anxiety or was upset.

The night before we moved, I asked him if he wanted to come along with us. He did, but he was confused and scared and didn't know whether Debra was lying about me. She had said,

"She didn't want her own son, so why would she want to raise you?"

It wasn't until Ace and I played a message she had left, saying she didn't want to raise her children that Anthony began to understand. From the moment he heard her message, he knew his mother was lying and he decided to come live with us.

Once Anthony started living with us, Debra started to act like a concerned parent when it came to Anthony's schooling. She would yell at Ace and me, telling us we didn't know what we were doing. And yet, Anthony had gotten held back a grade in school because she was too lazy to take him.

She had also convinced him he was stupid. He was so emotionally abused that he was close to seventy-five pounds overweight when he came to live with us. Debra reminded me so much of my mother.

I had taken a little time off from work at the salon for moving and running back and forth to court so we could get the order of protection against Debra and custody of Anthony. Before I went back, the receptionist and manager had told me how all my clients were waiting for me and asking when I was coming back.

When I finally did go back, they were giving my clients to other people. It wasn't worth it to argue with Ace over how I was getting treated. Ace had never been able to be assertive enough to set appropriate boundaries with Rock about how unfair he was when it came to Ace's family as opposed to his own.

Rock had his entire family working for Dramatics and getting high-paid salaries. They worked when they felt like it, and their pay was way over what they deserved, but when Natasha wanted to be a receptionist for a few days a week when she was in college, Rock denied her the position, claiming she couldn't work enough hours and they needed someone full time. On the other hand, Rock always had his own daughter as the spokesperson for Dramatics when it came to doing parties and events but acted like Ace's kids were nonexistent.

I sat there at my station, wondering what to do. I felt victimized and knew I really couldn't explain because Ace and his partner did not have equal respect for each other, especially when it came to each other's family.

My intuition told me I had to leave, but I suddenly felt panic. Logically, I couldn't figure out why I was jumping out of my skin.

When I told my friend Charm I was leaving, that I needed to go, she tried to convince me to stay. But I called Rock at the end of the evening, thanked him for the opportunity, and told him I felt it was time for me to move on. When I returned home, I told Ace I was not going back to Dramatics.

Later, a friend I had worked with told me the manager didn't want an owner's wife supervising and collecting commissions and pay, which explained why they had been giving my clients away.

I had thought originally I would get a job as hairdresser someplace else. But to be a successful hairdresser in NYC, you must have real talent, and I knew my work wasn't polished.

My lack of focus and effort along with my inability to stay present were how the spiritual diseases manifested in me. I had no energy, I had OCD, I was compulsive, and I was navigating by emotional desires which changed from moment to moment.

But God had gotten me through it all. No matter the situation and no matter what I did or who I was, God had gotten me through it.

The night before we moved, the apartment was in shambles. We had boxes everywhere. Ace insisted on doing all the packing yet waited until the last minute to actually pack.

Anthony had his bed in a portion of the living room. We were down the hall in the bedroom.

As I laid down to go to sleep, anxiety hit me. I had no reason to have anxiety. My internal knowing sensed Anthony, so I went into the living room.

I saw Anthony sitting at the kitchen table. He had chocolate ice cream all over his face. As I approached him, I could feel him trembling with anxiety. My intuition told me that Debra must have made him worry he was never going to see his father again, that we weren't really going to take him with us.

I assured Anthony that we would never leave him behind. The next day, I said we were all ready to go to our new apartment. Ace asked if Anthony was coming with us.

I said, "Yes," and from that moment we became a family.

Living with Ace on the Upper East Side of Manhattan was a magical experience for me. The smell of the city, the unconventional living, and the constant flow of people made me feel alive. Unconsciously, I had even decorated our apartment in the chakra colors.

Our leather sectional was a bright orange that lifted your spirits when you looked at it. All three of us, without knowing it, started our own healing journey, as well. Over the next nine years, we would all grow together as well as individually.

The healing for Ace wasn't just that he was giving love another chance after having two failed marriages and after being betrayed. He became a proactive and hands-on parent to the point the president of the PTA asked him to become the new president when she retired. Anthony flourished. He became a top student in Food and Finance in high school and landed himself a position on the set of Bobby Flay's TV show.

Ace had friends that were great hairdressers all over the city. One day, he came home and asked me if I wanted to take hairdressing lessons with a guy named Jose. Jose had worked as an educator as well as a hairdresser for Dramatics years earlier.

I didn't have anything else to do and felt as if I should, so I went down to his salon on the Lower East Side. I realized I had no true desire to learn hairdressing or be a hairdresser, so I only went a few times. I didn't know what I was going to do for work, but I wasn't worried about it, either, because Ace didn't care one way or another.

Shortly after we got married, I started to feel sensations in my tail bone, like an aching. It brought back memories from when I was a kid and my mother was screaming at me or in one of her manic moments. I would feel pins and needles run up and down my spine.

I started to look on the internet for some information. I came across a lot of kundalini yoga spiritual awakening websites. After clicking on many sites, one led to an online psychic radio show called *Ask 1*.

I noticed they had a show about to air called *Spirit Animals* with a psychic named Reverend Theresa Shilley. I called into the show, and my phone clicked over to a man named Marc, who managed the radio show. He told me there would be about an eight-minute hold time before I got to talk to the psychic.

Marc made small talk at first, then I started to talk about the symptoms in my body and my own psychic phenomena, and before I knew it, it was time to speak with the psychic, Theresa. There was nothing about her reading that was helpful or stood out except that she said one of my power animals was a dolphin.

Dolphins are known in animal medicine to be intuitive and are said to carry the dead to the next reality on a symbolic level. That means rebirth and renewal. I thanked Theresa for my reading and said I would make it to one of her sermons at the Church for Spiritual Living.

The following Sunday, I went to the church and heard her speak. After the sermon, Theresa invited everyone upstairs to her mediumship circles. I approached Theresa to introduce myself, and as I did, she looked me up and down.

I had always been conscious about how I looked, but I had never considered downplaying my wardrobe from my hairdresser days. It was obvious, just in our appearances, how different she and I were. I had bleach-streaked hair, a face full of makeup, and wore jewelry and fake fur. Theresa wore her hair long and straight, dressed in overalls, and wore no makeup. I could tell immediately that she didn't like me, but she was polite and asked me to stay for the circle.

I'd never participated in a mediumship circle before, but I was curious. Theresa started the circle in prayer and then left it open. She told everyone if they got any messages just to blurt them out to the whole circle, telling who the message was for and what the message was. We sat there for a few minutes, then Theresa gave a few messages to some of the people.

Suddenly, I had the urge to raise my hand. Theresa nodded at me, inviting me to share my message. I pointed to a girl about thirty years old who was sitting in the corner and said to her that she had recently lost her grandmother, that her grandmother was in the room, and that she wanted her to continue their family traditions during the holidays.

I felt that the grandmother and granddaughter both feared that the remainder of their family would drift apart. The woman's grandmother had come to assure her granddaughter if she continued the family traditions, the family would not only stay together but they would grow and be blessed.

After I gave the woman her message, she thanked me, and Theresa closed the circle. As I got up to leave, Theresa complimented me on my accuracy on the reading I had given. I could feel her compliment was not genuine, though, which made me not want to return to her circle.

I decided to put more effort into building my own business. Through the years, I had done paranormal investigations and had dealt with spirits, ghosts, and incarnates who were stuck in *bardo*—being stuck between death and rebirth—and couldn't cross over. The work lead me to working on phone and chat lines where I got a lot of experience and gained confidence doing mediumistic and psychic readings. It took me a total of working twenty-five years to cultivate my own style and the niche I would be known for, healing the effects of psychic trauma.

I hired someone to help me put together my first website, and *Pure Energy Healer* was born. Living in Manhattan, I had a constant flow of new clients every week, but I got bored with never going out, so it wasn't long before I found work at all the healing centers in NYC. The centers didn't pay high, but they advertised and gave me plenty of exposure.

A few weeks later, I found out I was correct about Theresa not liking me. In order to learn a new healing modality and to train my nervous system, I wanted to enroll in a "birthing breathing" class taught by a woman I presumed Theresa had mentored whose name was Peace. Peace said I needed to ask Theresa if I could take her class because Theresa oversaw enrollment. I tried to explain to Peace that I didn't think Theresa would let me, but Peace assured me Theresa was a nice lady.

I called Theresa that day and left a message on her answering machine about wanting to enroll in Peace's birthing class. Theresa called me back a few days later while I was on the beach with my sister Christine. As soon as she told me who she was, I immediately thanked her for calling me back.

She abruptly let me know that she was not going to enroll me in Peace's class. She said Peace was a nice lady who was starting up her own business as a birthing coach to help individuals overcome anxiety. She didn't want me going to one of her classes and then going home and putting the service on my own website.

I said I wouldn't and didn't understand why she would think that. She said because I only went to one of her classes and then went home and put up a website. I said I didn't know I had to ask her permission about what I do with my time, but I didn't want to argue with her. In fact, a part of me wanted for us to get along, but it was clear that wasn't going to happen.

After I had been on the phone with Theresa for a few minutes, my sister threw sand at me to get my attention and mouthed "Hang up already!" I didn't know what to do for a few seconds, but finally I had the nerve to hang up.

My sister said, "Why must you explain to her why you set up a business? You don't have to. You seem weak when you explain. Can't you see she is threatened?"

For so long, I was used to people not liking me and to feeling inadequate and like a failure. I couldn't fathom anyone thinking I was threatening. All I knew for sure was the familiar feeling of being hated for just being.

Even though I was giving accurate readings to others, I was getting readings from friends and hotlines for myself when I got emotionally triggered. After Theresa had shut me out of the class, I called a hotline during my lunch break at work. I remember God saying to me, "So, you're going to pay four dollars a minute to call a psychic line while you are at work giving psychic readings and only making two dollars an hour? Does this mean you trust the other person more than you trust yourself?

I said out loud, as if God was sitting across the room, "Apparently, since I have to make sure Theresa will not try to sabotage me. If you really cared anyway, you would stop making people hate me for no reason."

I called the hotline and asked for a straightforward psychic that used no tools. They transferred me to a psychic named Maria. I introduced myself and quickly blurted out the scenario and my fear. Maria assured me Theresa wasn't going to be able to do anything to me or my business. She told me it was a spiritual test.

The test was to see whether I would give up or whether I would get up. I realized at that moment how many times I had been emotionally manipulated to give up things I wanted and to do things I didn't want. I was determined to never allow anyone to make me feel that way ever again.

Finally, I had a sense of individuality that not only made me feel purposeful but made me feel that I belonged. I took Theresa's behavior as a compliment to my skills.

My Spiritual Gifts

I was born with all the spiritual senses, but my strongest psychic gift is clairsentience, which means "clear feeling and clear sensing." As long as I could remember, I had been able to receive physical and emotional sensations projected from Spirit as well as from people in the physical realm.

When I was younger, it was very much like a curse more than a gift. I thought everything I felt was my own, and I was easily gaslighted and manipulated by my surroundings until I trained my nervous system to not react to everything I felt. I also needed to learn to love myself enough to create boundaries.

It also took me some time to differentiate between physical sense and spiritual sense. Physical sense works simultaneously with all our senses, while spiritual sense tends to work by giving one piece of information at a time.

The most important thing which really helped open my abilities was healing my psychic traumas and learning to recondition my body and mind through the constant trial and error of different holistic and spiritual practices. In healing myself, it inevitably brought me to my soul's path.

Radio Show

A few days after I had called in to the radio show, I received an email from Marc, the owner of *Ask 1 Psychic Radio*. He asked me if I would be interested in hosting my own radio show. I thought he had made a mistake, so I deleted the email. A few days later another came.

I deleted it again, and by the end of the week, I received another. This time it said in big bold letters across the top of the email: "I don't think you understand what I am offering you here. I am offering you your own psychic radio show to host for only $179.00 a month."

I went to the *ASK 1 Psychic Radio* website and saw about ten different spiritual shows and their host of psychics. I recognized a few of the names from participating in some of the New Jersey and New York holistic and spiritual fairs and expos as a psychic reader.

I finally responded to Marc's email after much contemplation. I would give it a go. I was scheduled every Thursday at 8:00 p.m., EST, and my show was called *Psychic Surgery with Laura, the Voice of Truth*.

Until my show, I had only done readings in person, where I saw the person's face, so I was a bit nervous at first. After I introduced the show's first caller, I had a clear connection to her and the information started flowing. The woman's name was Jean Marie, and she was in a toxic codependent relationship in which she was being treated with disrespect and taken for granted.

She had been with her boyfriend for over five years, and the relationship had progressed from bad to worse. Jean Marie wanted to know whether her relationship was worth salvaging.

Spirit began by telling her that she didn't realize he never treated her with respect because he never put in any effort and would only verbally express the way he felt about her. Spirit said she didn't recognize her boyfriend's lack of effort because of the way she was used to having been treated, starting way back with her parents. Her own anxiety was related to her own confidence issues in that she was always trying to be perfect. She didn't realize she was teaching the men who came into her life that they didn't need to give her respect.

The message resonated with her, and she thanked me.

I worked on *Ask 1* for about a year. It was a good beginning even though it didn't pay. *Ask 1* gave me confidence in seeing I was able to communicate with Spirit. When I was then invited to work at an event in New Jersey, however, I had so far only worked online, on the telephone, and doing one-on-one readings in person. This would be my first time at an event.

I had finally been able to be in a place called home without feeling uncomfortable, but I had rarely left the apartment since Ace and I had gotten married. I told Ace about the event, and he encouraged me to go. I was concerned about the drive since I tended to always get lost, so Ace offered to drive me and keep himself occupied while I worked.

Some of the other psychics from *Ask 1* were also working at the expo, which was called The Gala, and I was happy to meet them in person. I was especially looking forward to meeting Allison May, the Crystal Girl. I grabbed her hand in excitement, but before I had the "Hello" out of my mouth, she whisked her hand out of my grasp.

She glared at me and said in a loud voice that increased as she repeated three times, "Do I know you? Do I know you? Do I know you?"

In hopes she would change her tone, I replied in a friendly manner, "We are on the same radio show."

She then looked at me with a mixture of being puzzled and disgusted. After an uncomfortable few minutes, she shrugged her shoulders as if to say, "Who cares?" and I walked away.

They were still setting up, so I couldn't go into the readers' room. I decided to walk around in the venders' room, where I found Ace, who had just finished getting a massage. I must have had a puzzled look on my face, because he asked me what the matter was.

I said, "This is a spiritual community, but some of the people do not act spiritual." I told him what had just happened with the Crystal Girl, and I asked him what he thought that meant and why she had done that to me.

Ace said he thought she might have been trying to act as if she were superior to me since she had been known in the industry a little longer.

After a short while, the readers started to file into the reading room where there were twenty-five tables covered in burgundy tablecloths. In the center of each table was a number.

I was assigned to table five in between a girl named JD, who did all types of readings using different divination tools, and Jackie Horn, the Angel Card reader. Both girls had worked many expos and were very down to earth and friendly.

They shared that although the Crystal Girl was nasty to everyone she worked with, she was compassionate while she gave readings. Most of the other psychics who participated in any event they did with her, I learned, experienced the same type of behavior from her as I had.

For about ten years, I participated in healing fairs until I started to work at a healing center called Namaste in NYC.

I actually found it while looking for another center called East West that I had first heard about from Ace. He passed it every day in making his way downtown to the Dramatics headquarters.

I had called East West several times, but I was never able to get a manager on the phone to book an appointment for an interview. I decided to jump on the subway downtown to the center, but when I arrived, I saw they had closed.

After walking around aimlessly for a bit, I had decided to do a little shopping to not make the trip a waste when I came across Namaste Healing Center. I walked in and was greeted by a friendly Indian man named Rakesh. As I extended my hand in introduction, I asked if they were looking for psychic readers. He bent down and grabbed a clip board and asked me to fill out a form. When I was finished, I handed it back and we both exchanged thank-yous.

Since Namaste took some time to get back to me, I decided to hit the pavement around the city and wound up applying to three other healing centers. Eventually, I got called for my first interview. In order to work at Namaste, you had to read for three different employees and all three had to like your reading.

For a few years, I worked at four different centers during the week as well as taking appointments at home. The centers didn't pay much because the readings were discounted and offered in intervals of fifteen minutes, thirty minutes, and an hour. They were not only priced at one third of my normal price, but half of what I made was shared with the center, as well. Nevertheless, every reader wanted to work at Namaste because there was no other place like it.

I worked at Namaste from noon to 8:00 p.m. on the weekends for over three years. Though I loved it and met some of my best friends to date there, I wasn't as busy as I would have liked.

The bookshop where patrons bought spiritual tools and booked their appointments was always jam-packed. Also, its staff didn't have the time to educate the clients about each reader, and clients very rarely read our bios.

One day, while I was working by myself, I started to talk to God: "God, you said I was going to work in a healing center where I would be helping people. What's up with that? I don't know if you see what's going on, but all I'm doing is sitting in a room they call a healing center."

A few moments later, God replied, "A building is not what makes a healing center; people are."

I pondered that thought for a few moments. I took out my cell phone and called the owner, Chino, to ask for a meeting, and we set something up for the following week.

The day of the meeting, I met Chino and Rekesh at a Thai restaurant across the street from Namaste. Over lunch, I proposed an idea to them, but I got the feeling they weren't going to move forward with it.

A few weeks later, I reached out to Chino again, and he said they were still thinking it over. About a month after that, I was in the center again by myself when I said to God, "So, you tell me to ask the owners about putting on a psychic healing fair to promote healing work and to stir up more business for myself. Well, I hate to tell you, but they aren't interested."

A few moments later, God said to me, "Why do you need their permission to promote your work or educate the community?"

I sat and thought for a few moments and realized I didn't need Namaste in order to be a healer, to share my knowledge, or to throw an event. What I did need were good psychics and healers as well as space to hold the event.

I decided to call around town to price spaces. By the end of the day, I had decided on a large room in a building called TRS a few blocks away from Namaste.

The space often was used by holistic and spiritual practitioners. I had asked a few close friends of mine who worked at Namaste to participate. They agreed and also offered to extend my invitation to their close friends who were psychics and practitioners, as well.

On December 20, 2013, I put on my first psychic healing fair. I had a total of fifteen psychics, two healers, and one artist who painted auras. The day was busy from the time the doors opened at 10:30 a.m. until we had to kick people out at 6:00 p.m. because we only had the room until 5:00 p.m. and didn't want to get charged extra.

I was ecstatic with the good turnout, and the participants were pleased with the amount of money and new clients they acquired from it. Later that evening, as I retired for bed, I thanked God for allowing me to be a vehicle for him to work through.

I admitted I had been skeptical and even nervous about the idea of having to ask my coworkers for money to participate so we could evenly split the room. I had been afraid the participants wouldn't make their money back, but due to my faith, God not only matched my efforts tenfold but got the owners of Namaste to appreciate me more, too. And better yet, I appreciated myself more.

I put on several fairs after that. They increased in size for many years until Ace and I moved.

Ace's Accident

After Theresa's mediumship class, I decided to see what other places I could connect with. Within a day, without really looking, I was contacted by a psychic via Facebook who asked me if I wanted to do *Oranum,* an online psychic web chat. She said it was a great place to start and that the founders of the site invested a lot of time and money into the readers by marketing them.

It wasn't the easiest work because you had to entertain people in a chat room and hope they were interested enough to buy a session. Otherwise, you were stuck behind the computer all day without getting compensated.

I had worked on the site for a little over a year before I began working for the Namaste Healing Center and also received an email from Constant Contact about building my own website. I called Constant Contact and explained I wasn't tech savvy and that I didn't mind paying someone to help me.

A woman named Sheila Brown offered to do it, and within a few days, it was up and running. Since I lived in New York City, my phone always rang.

Having a website in NYC opened me up to new opportunities—everything from being a guest speaker on radio and online web summits to landing a part on a psychic reality show that got canceled after a year of taping.

During the taping of that show, I met a girl named Emily. She was a clairsentient psychic who used the gift of telekinesis, through which she was able to tap into a person's energy by holding one of their possessions. She had seen me give a few readings on set, and she had just ended a long-term relationship. She was further along in her career than I was, I had admired her work, and I had concerns about my own business, so I agreed to do an exchange reading.

On the day of the exchange reading, Emily only wanted me to answer questions about her love life, which I did. She was happy with the message. I chose to not direct Emily and see whether Spirit would be able to convey my concerns.

Within two minutes, Emily started to get flooded with information from Spirit about my business. Emily had opened my reading by saying I was right where I was supposed to be, regardless of the discombobulated feelings of being scattered within my craft. The fact I did not resonate with any of the online platforms was fine, as well. Emily then said Spirit wanted me to start teaching meetup groups and to begin teaching classes. I signed up to be an organizer of my own club, Holistic and Spiritual Transitions.

All these experiences gave me the confidence I needed to seek out healing centers in Manhattan. Before I knew it, I was working at all the healing centers in Manhattan, doing psychic readings. During my time at the centers, I met most of my closest friends and learned a lot of different healing modalities.

For a while, life was predictable until the morning of my thirty-fifth birthday. I was working at Namaste Healing Center when I got a phone call from Anthony that the police had just been at our house. Ace had just gotten hit by a cab.

Anthony said his father was at Cornell Hospital, which was about twenty minutes away by subway. As soon as I hung up the phone, I ran downstairs to where the manager was and explained what had happened.

Within a few minutes, I was on my way to the hospital. My son, Roger, went with Anthony, and Natasha met me at the hospital. We were all sitting in the waiting area when a doctor came and introduced himself as Dr. Green, the physician who was assigned to my husband.

The doctor said Ace was in bad shape. The car had run over his leg and shattered the bone. While the leg was bad, the doctor was more concerned about the blood on his brain. I could tell the doctor was carefully choosing every word he uttered, purposely making sure we all knew the severity of Ace's condition.

The boys sat there in shock while Natasha sobbed. I couldn't believe Ace was hurt that badly. I needed to see him. I didn't believe he was as bad as they were saying.

When Ace got out of surgery, he was conscious but in the ICU, where only close family members could visit. When Ace recognized me and the kids, I knew in my heart he would be okay. He was conscious but disoriented. He didn't know why he was in the hospital or what his injuries were and just kept trying to get me to take him home.

While Ace was recovering, I never stopped working. My job kept me grounded. Aside from keeping me on my path, my job taught me how to maintain balance within myself by making sure I didn't lose myself. For most of my marriage, Ace and I were always together.

We were comfortably in a codependent relationship, but both of us were oblivious. Ace had always taken care of anything having to do with the house. Now I was expected to pick up where he couldn't. I probably should have been scared, but I wasn't. I welcomed the responsibilities and feeling purposeful for the first time in my life. I felt like an adult. I was needed, and I enjoyed being needed.

Ace had been in the hospital for two months when he was transferred to Lennox Hill for rehabilitation. He stayed there for about a month until he was sent home to continue his rehab. Ace had always worked out and had a very muscular body, but being in the hospital for over three months had caused him to lose a lot of his strength and he had become very thin.

Our lease was up shortly after he got home. If we renewed the lease, we would pay an astronomical increase. Ace kept saying he would look around for an apartment, but he was exhausted. I made my mistake of being too afraid to assert myself to look. I was too afraid I would make Ace mad by paying over ten thousand dollars to move.

Ace's daughter was living with Debra in the apartment that Ace had gotten when they were married. They had a hard time affording the rent, and Debra still wasn't doing anything except threatening to abandon Natasha and the responsibilities of paying rent.

A lot of time had passed since Ace and I had gotten married. At that point, Debra was splitting her time between staying with her brother in Florida and her sister in Las Vegas, so we figured if Debra stayed away, we would move in to that apartment and take over the rent.

Natasha could then focus on her career and Ace on his healing. But as soon as we moved in, Debra started having Natasha bring her into the apartment to stay over. Of course, Ace and I started to fight because we had previously agreed that if Debra started in on us, we would move immediately.

When push came to shove, Ace felt guilty about setting boundaries and making Debra follow the agreement of her not being in the apartment while we were living there. Once Debra and Natasha saw I did not approve of the situation and yet my wishes were not being respected, they hoped I would see that Ace was not capable of having appropriate boundaries and I would move out.

One day, a girlfriend of mine, Pardis, who I also worked with at Namaste Healing Center, called to tell me that while she had been taking a shower, Spirit told her I had to move Ace and myself out of the apartment. This was due to Debra and Natasha stopping at nothing to get rid of me.

I continued to beg Ace to move out, but now he was comfortable living there and felt guilty about having to tell his daughter he and I would be moving out. I realized then I had compromised myself by marrying a man who never really treated me with the respect I deserved. I'd never been shown respect, nor did I even know what respect looked like. Throughout my entire relationship, I had taught him he didn't have to respect me, and Debra and Natasha knew it.

Ace and I decided to take a mini-vacation down to St. Augustine. We had bought a house there and closed on it the day before Ace's accident. The first day we arrived in St. Augustine, we went downtown to a coffee shop called Conscious Coffee, a hip little place that doesn't just sell coffee and cakes but novelties as well. I sipped my coffee while talking to God in my head, asking for some divine guidance about what I should do about the apartment situation. I suddenly noticed a magnet that was hanging on a metal shelf right in front of my face. The magnet read, *If you want greatness, get up and take it. Don't wait for someone to give it.*

I realized right then and there that Spirit was waiting for me to step into my power and to do what I needed to for my own well-being and to finally stop asking other people to take care of me.

Ace had done so much for me that it was now my time to take care of him.

In an odd way, I was thankful for the opportunity to not only give back to him but to see myself differently. Someone who was needed, important, and capable. Though our relationship was dramatically changed by Ace's accident, I learned the important spiritual lesson of unconditional love. Ace had always displayed this with ease. I, on the other hand, needed the experience to transcend my beliefs.

Healing Begins with Awareness and Proactive, Positive Steps

While Ace's accident cannot be categorized as abuse, growing up, he had suffered from the same type of abuse with his own father as I had with my mother. Psychic and emotional trauma has the power to play out as physical trauma and undesirable life experiences that affect health. This does not mean Ace is not a good man; it simply is a reflection of latent, pent-up negative energy within the body manifesting as accidents and health issues.

Ace's accident happening on my birthday is one tie-in to past psychic trauma with me. My mother, as you read earlier in this book, never celebrated my birthday and manifested in this accident for me. The other instances of trauma throughout the first section of this book manifested in similar ways in my life, and I've had to learn how to heal them. In fact, I still learn every single day.

Trauma caused by psychological, emotional, and physical abuse keeps good people who have done great things asleep to participating in everyday life with their family and loved ones. Fragmented pieces of the soul can damage a person's energetic body, distorting thoughts and behaviors manifesting as abusive behaviors, lack of empathy, betrayal, victimization, abandonment, feelings of defectiveness, and feelings of unworthiness. These then keep the person trapped in their internal toxic limiting beliefs manifesting as addictions, poverty, bad relationships, and all other undesirable life experiences.

Make no mistake about what I've written to this point. I'm not bashing my family and other people who've brought me all these life experiences of psychic trauma. These issues were passed on through the generations of my family, and that is true of yours as well. I am presenting this information as a basis for understanding what I've learned about healing and how I can teach you to do the same.

Now that you see where I've come from with all the emotional, psychological, and spiritual issues, let's learn the steps of healing!

Let's Heal!

This book is not intended as a substitute for the medical advice of physicians. The reader should regularly consult a physician in matters relating to his/her health, and particularly with respect to any symptoms that may require diagnosis or medical attention. For a more detailed disclaimer, please go to the copyright page in the front of the book.

Healing Spiritual Disease Patterns

There are a lot of inherited factors that affect our health aside from inherited genes. Until recently, a human being's health was thought to be predicted, controlled, and determined according to our inherited genetics. Science now uses the analogy that our genes are only receptors, much like a radio receiving signals from the environment.

These signals are not just physical energy but also are thought and emotional energy. In many ways, we become what we eat, feel, and think. Biology has finally accepted that we can inherit certain characteristics that are not connected to our genes, that we are much more than what is known from strictly a scientific and physical point of view.

Our health is a complete process, primarily a reflection of our inner strength. Illness and other health troubles come from not being in touch with our deepest reality. Our true nature is to be healthy.

In my blog, *Spiritual Disease Patterns*, I refer to psychological, emotional, and mental thought patterns brought about by unresolved or deeply consuming spiritual stresses. The stress can be either due to long-running patterns from childhood, such as feeling rejected and inadequate, or from a recent perceived traumatic incident. These stresses over time become emotional imprints, psychic wounds also known as *soul wounds*.

The emotions which hold the highest frequencies of energy, such as love, joy, passion, and excitement, hold the same vibrational frequencies as wellness and self-love. Within these higher emotions, diseases aren't capable of existing. Imbalances are already in the body, but only until they are activated by a discorded thought pattern can they physically manifest.

An experience which causes a soul wound doesn't need to be traumatic or perceived as threatening to anyone outside of the person experiencing it in order for it to create imbalances. Soul wounds cause spiritual blocks. Spiritual blocks are negative beliefs about oneself and/or one's environment—negative beliefs which affect an individual's reality. What an individual feels as true concerning life, God, and other people plays a large role in how they live.

What we believe also affects how we feel physically and emotionally. Our emotions consciously and unconsciously determine our actions. Addictions are formed from unconscious feelings, thoughts, and emotions which are stagnant within us and affecting all layers of our being.

Individuals who are ill tend to have belief patterns that are disempowering. Individuals with the inability to give or receive love because of trust and intimacy issues in childhood most times are immune-compromised in their adult lives. This is because our lives are supposed to evolve around love, and we are in physical form, living in a physical world, in order to express love. We co-create with God and the universe by giving love to the world through our own unique purpose.

Individuals who do not feel they have a purpose are lost souls. The physical feelings which come from not knowing one's purpose include feeling empty and disconnected from the world and the physical body.

How effectively an individual exercises their power of choice over their own affairs is a good indication of how spiritually balanced they are. This doesn't mean you shouldn't compromise; it means to not allow yourself to become victimized or to turn over your power.

People hand over their power for many reasons. Fear is the number one reason, whether it is psychological or emotional fear. Fear keeps us spiritually blocked, locked into believing disempowering and sabotaging thinking patterns: fear of not trusting or believing in yourself and others; neither knowing nor understanding who you are and what your purpose is; denial, which is the inability to face areas in your life that aren't working.

The basic premises of spiritual and holistic health are: 1) that illness does not just happen randomly and by chance, 2) that our genes are only responsible for one third of our sickness and diseases, and 3) that every illness, imbalance, or dysfunction an individual develops is an indication of an emotional, spiritual, or psychological stress.

The body's capability to heal or resist disease depends on its ability to draw energy into the body through the intelligence of the cosmic source otherwise known as universal or God energy. Cosmic energy can transform chemistry in the body. Our bodies are not physical objects. Our bodies are multi-dimensional, holding patterns of energy, and these patterns can be changed. Changing negative or unsupportive patterns creates instantaneous healing.

In my opinion, the success of an individual's healing is dependent upon two factors. The first is the courage to evaluate one's life honestly, and the second is to make empowering choices that honor and feed the inner spirit.

Some techniques for healing negative disease patterns are to:

1. Meditate

2. Pray

3. Do positive affirmations

4. STOP!! all-or-nothing thinking

5. Stop overgeneralizing

6. Not have a negative mind filter, i.e., only seeing the negative

7. Not jump to conclusions; stop being paranoid

8. Stop trying to read minds or foretell the future

9. Not respond emotionally

10. Get rid of "should" statements

11. Stop labeling

12. Stop blame/self-blame

13. Stop comparing unfairly

Healing Psychic Trauma

(Healing Emotional, Physical, and Psychological Abuse)

Psychic trauma is a type of damage to the psyche that occurs as a result of a traumatic event or recurring traumatic events. The word *trauma* is derived from the Greek word for *wound*. Psychic trauma is a combination of psychological and emotional reactions caused by stressful situations that shatter a person's sense of security, making them feel helpless and vulnerable.

There are several situations and events which can lead to someone experiencing psychic trauma—anything from living in poverty to witnessing or being a victim of physical, emotional, or mental abuse, witnessing or being a victim of interpersonal violence, natural disasters, and/or any accident which causes physical pain and/or trauma.

It is important to know that even less severe situations can trigger traumatic reactions, and the situations do not have to be traumatic to anyone other than the person who experiences the trauma. But a few things are the same.

While psychic trauma is caused by an event, soul wounds are an accumulation of experiences that have a karmic theme: abandonment, betrayal, feeling defective, etc. The psychic trauma causes unconscious behaviorisms, while the soul wounds make us a magnet for experiences that have the same karmic lesson.

Soul wounds are personal and deeply painful. Also, if a soul's wound isn't healed, it can affect everyone the same externally within their outer world.

There are strong physical reactions for people who have suffered psychic trauma. As I said earlier, each person is different and responds differently to psychic trauma. However, some common manifestations are paranoia, becoming overly concerned about survival, insomnia, fatigue, exhaustion, addiction of any kind, brain fog, learning issues, and memory loss. Emotional reactions to psychic trauma are numbness and detachment, depression, guilt, anxiety, anger, and irritability.

Because psychic trauma causes a lot of negative physical, psychological, and emotional imbalances which make it impossible to live a normal life, healing is imperative! Otherwise, many people who were victims of psychic trauma isolate themselves and withdraw socially due to trust and intimacy issues, which in turn lead to depression and other emotional issues.

Many people confuse stress with psychological trauma, but they are not the same thing. Stress disregulates the nervous system, and in a few days or weeks, the nervous system reverts back to its normal equilibrium. This normal state of balance is not possible when we have suffered psychological trauma because victims of psychic trauma no longer trust themselves, which causes them to have fear. The emotion *fear,* if prolonged, causes physical, emotional, and psychological damage to the body, mind, and spirit.

Traumatic stress can be distinguished from routine stress by reviewing a number of details. For instance, how frequently the victim remembers aspects of the incident, how intensely threatening the source of upset was or is, how long the upset lasted, and how long it takes for the victim to calm down.

Traumatic stress in childhood influences brain development and unconsciously causes children who suffered psychic trauma to develop personal and behavior disorders and imbalances, which lead to future experiences of trauma. Everything from substance abuse, compulsive and self-destructive impulses, negative thought patterns, and feelings of being permanently damaged are all manifestations of psychic trauma.

A traumatic experience which affects the psyche can cause emotionally devastating results in the psyche for many reasons. There is no one clear answer, but we can look at a few repeating factors that are usually involved, such as the severity of the experience; an individual's personal history, coping skills, and valued beliefs; and the relations with and support from family.

Symptoms of psychic trauma should be taken seriously, and steps to healing the spirit need to be incorporated the same way steps to healing a physical ailment would be. There is no norm as to how fast the healing of psychological trauma will occur. The time and assistance required to recover varies from person to person, but incorporating daily healing rituals (to recondition the mind), spiritual counseling, soul healing, and clearings are all very helpful for seeing results not only quickly but also for transforming the damage into empowerment and tools for your success!

Healing begins with investing in yourself!

Codependency and Trauma

(Healing Trauma that Manifests as Codependency; Finding Balance; Healing Trust Issues; and Establishing One's Own True Individuality)

You can overcome codependency in all areas of your life by developing new attitudes, skills, and behavior. People can become dependent on anything, not just relationships. The root of addiction is codependency. Sometimes a deeper recovery may involve healing many layers of trauma that usually began in childhood. Themes of victimization, betrayal, feelings of shame and doubt—these themes play out through our everyday lives as experiences.

Trauma is not just physical. In fact, psychic trauma is psychological and emotional. The bully gets away with the abuse because gaslighting can't be monitored. This causes additional trauma because the individual is perceived as crazy because they are being emotionally gaslighted, thus making them question their own reality.

Childhood events had more impact on us in the past than they would today because we didn't have any support or coping skills. As a consequence of growing up in a dysfunctional family environment, codependents often suffer further trauma due to relationships with other people who may be abandoning, abusive, addicted, or have mental illness—all because they do not recognize the warning signs and because they were taught to neglect their needs for their own emotional, psychological, and often physical well-being.

When we are fixated on our primary survival needs, we subconsciously create thought patterns which lead our neurological pathways to mirror out into automatic behaviorisms and habits. These behaviorisms determine our physical DNA, turning genes on and off. Of the factors which lead to disease occurring in our bodies, only one third are inherited factors; the remaining two thirds are reliant upon whether you have the same thoughts, habits, and behaviorisms creating the same living situations and stresses as your ancestors had.

Childhood Trauma

Childhood itself may be traumatic when it's not safe to be spontaneous, vulnerable, and authentic. It's emotionally damaging if you were ignored, shamed, or punished for expressing your thoughts and feelings. Children are not supposed to be perfect, and they have needs. But when parents have their own trauma, they are stuck in their own limitations and personal hell of feeling imperfect and unworthy, reliving their own neglected emotionally or physically abandoned issues. The parent teaches the child unconsciously to hide their real, child self and play an adult role before they're ready.

Divorce, illness, or loss of a parent or sibling also can be traumatic, depending upon the way in which parents handle it. Occurrences become harmful when they're either chronic or severe to the extent that they overwhelm a child's limited ability to cope with what was happening.

Most everyone manages to grow up, but the scars remain and account for problems in relationships and coping with reality. Deeper healing requires reopening those wounds, cleaning them, and applying the medicine of compassion.

Symptoms of Trauma

Trauma is an abstract experience and differs from person to person. Each child in a family will react differently to the same experience and to trauma. Symptoms may come and go and may not show up until years after the event. You needn't have all the following symptoms to have experienced trauma:

- Overreacting to triggers that are reminders of the trauma.
- Avoiding thinking, experiencing, or talking about triggers for the trauma.
- Experiencing depression and detachment. Avoiding activities you once enjoyed.
- Feeling hopeless about the future.
- Experiencing memory loss or inability to recall parts of trauma.
- Having brain fog and difficulty focusing and concentrating.
- Not trusting; being paranoid. Having difficulty maintaining close relationships.
- Feeling irritable or angry.
- Feeling overwhelming guilt or shame.
- Having addictions and being self-destructive.
- Being easily frightened and startled.
- Being hypervigilant (excessively fearful).
- Feeling numb, emotionally flat, or detached from emotions, other people, or events.
- Feeling depersonalized; a loss of self or cut off from your body and environment—like you're going through the motions.
- Having flashbacks of scenes or reliving the past event.
- Having nightmares about the past.

- Experiencing insomnia.
- Experiencing anxiety and anxiety attacks.

Post-Traumatic Stress Disorder

Post-traumatic symptoms are ongoing for days and can start long after the triggered event. Core symptoms include:

- Abusive self-talk, OCD behavior, waking flashbacks, recurring negative thoughts.
- Avoidance and forgetting: detachment, numbness, and emotional ups and downs.
- Hypersensitivity: putting your nervous system in overdrive from constant arousal; creating mood swings, paranoia, irritability, exhaustion, and sleep issues; and many times leading to addictive behavior.

There is a direct connection between adult poor health and childhood trauma. Psychological trauma is played out dozens and dozens of ways. Some are:

- Physical abuse
- Psychological abuse (gaslighting, bullying)
- Emotional abuse
- Sexual abuse
- Substance abuse
- Parental death, separation, or abandonment
- Incarcerated household member

Treatment of Trauma

Healing trauma requires going back in time and feeling what was unexpressed, re-evaluating unhealthy beliefs and decisions, and getting familiar with detached and missing parts of yourself. Awareness of what happened is the first step in healing. Many people are detached and in denial of trauma they experienced in childhood, especially if parents weren't physically abusive but were emotionally detached, in which case the feelings and thoughts are manifested the same as someone who was abused. They experience loneliness, rejection, and shame about themselves.

Re-experiencing, feeling, and talking about what happened are significant parts of the healing process. Another step in recovery is grieving what you've lost. Stages of grief include anger, denial, depression, guilt, and finally acceptance. Acceptance doesn't mean you approve of what happened; it is that you're more objective about it without resentment or strong emotions.

We release stagnant emotional energy by integrating the spiritual lesson with movement of the physical body. Integrating means learning and grounding the spiritual lesson into your life. Movement is done to help blood and energy move through tension in the body. Once you do these two things, you will have more energy and motivation to invest in yourself.

In this process, it's essential—and too often omitted—that you discern false beliefs you may have learned as a result of the trauma and substitute healthier ones. Usually, these are shame-based beliefs stemming from childhood shaming messages and experiences. Recovery also entails identifying and changing the ways you relate and talk to yourself that lead to undesirable outcomes and behavior.

PTSD and trauma do not go away on their own. It's important to get treatment as soon as possible so they don't escalate into other issues. There are literally hundreds of treatment modalities recommended for healing trauma. But it's imperative to know that everyone responds differently to different modalities and that healing is a three-part system. First, there is awareness of the spiritual/psychological cause, then there's the integrating of the spiritual lesson, and lastly there is a physical regimen which includes body/mind work, daily reconditioning through habits and lifestyle practices that can include yoga, spiritual response technique, energy psychology, past-life regression, soul retrieval, and many different forms of shamanic and holistic healing combined with meditation and reconditioning.

Meditation

(Reconditioning the Nervous System to Get Out of Fight-or-Flight Response; Tapping into the Divine Inside)

Meditation and Attunement with the Divine

There is very little preparation for meditation and creating a sacred space. Incorporating just a few tips can make meditation even more beneficial.

Meditation opens the door to the spirit world. Doing meditation at least once a day is fuel for mediumship. Meditation increases awareness of and sensitivity to the subtle energies of the spiritual realm, and daily meditation leads to greater focus and self-understanding. A daily practice of meditation provides a person with more understanding and greater levels of spiritual awareness and compassion not just for ourselves but others as well.

How to Prepare Yourself for Meditation

Find a room, a quiet space where you will not be interrupted. Banish all distractions. Shut off the TV and cell phone.

Spend ten to fifteen minutes decluttering. Clearing clutter has proven to create bigger changes within our life, therapy studies have shown. Use natural cleaning products whenever possible by combining water, essential oils, vinegar, and baking soda.

Use the power of intention for cleaning, clearing, protection, and blessings.

Create an altar with things you love to honor your space.

Write out any grocery or to-do lists beforehand so your mind will be clear.

Wear comfortable clothes.

Adjust lighting accordingly. The choice of lighting will set the mood for your space. Dimming lights triggers relaxation and is calming.

Sit in a firm seat that has a straight back. Sit upright. Put both feet on the floor, legs uncrossed. Let your hands relax in your lap with your palms upward and open to receive. Good posture promotes an energy flow that is most conducive to spirit communications.

Avoid alcohol and recreational drugs before meditation. They interfere with spirit communications and alter perceptions. They may also attract lower vibrational entities, spiritual as well as earthbound.

Specific Colors for Your Meditation Space

Using specific colors can bring you back into balance naturally.

Blue promotes peace, calm, relaxation, self-expression, honesty, and truth.

Indigo promotes wisdom, spirituality, and peace.

Orange stimulates the body and mind, self-esteem, creativity, and self-expression. Great for anyone fighting depression.

Gold promotes enthusiasm and helps balance thoughts and feelings.

Yellow is uplifting and good for depression, fatigue, and despair.

Green promotes balance, harmony, compassion for self and others. Good for stress, anxiety, and confusion.

Red promotes energy, strength, motivation, confidence, and willpower.

Fragrances to Soothe Senses

Sandalwood is one of the best essential oils for meditation. It is extremely cleansing and can break up negative thoughts that cloud your mind. It's also a hypotensive which helps lower blood pressure and helps promote relaxation.

Clary sage can clear the room of any negative energies that can distract the mind from focusing.

Frankincense is the most powerful essential oil for the spirit. Frankincense helps stabilize the root chakra so the energy can flow freely through your chakras. Frankincense also has numerous healing benefits like relieving stress, pain, and inflammation, all things which distract during meditation.

Lavender is one of the best oils to use to get you in the right frame of mind to achieve clarity and enlightenment. Lavender is an antianxiety oil, an antidepressant, and a relaxant.

Sound that Brings You Back into Harmony

The Root Chakra–LAM

The Sacral chakra–VAM

The Solar Plexus–RAM

The Heart Chakra–YAM

The Throat Chakra–HAM

The Third Eye–OM

Crown Chakra–OM

Other Helpful Things to Remember

Once your body is relaxed, continue breathing slowly and evenly. Begin to count backward from one hundred. Imagine seeing the number in your mind's eye.

Spend time daily in nature. Nature is an extension of God. Spending time in nature allows us to easily get into the right frame of mind and be more open to Spirit.

Try to meditate at the same time and in the same place daily because the spiritual energies build up in that spot. After a while, your meditation will become automatic. If you are someone who has trouble sitting still, don't give up. Instead, do a walking mantra meditation. Go for a walk on the beach or in nature and speak a mantra. A mantra is a word or sound that is repeated to aid concentration. Any word, affirmation, prayer, or verse from a Psalm can be used as a mantra. Many use the mantra OM.

Become aware of the divine spark that animates you and gives you life. Notice how your chest rises and falls with each breath. Visualize your chest as a magnificent flame of God within you. Merge with the energies all around you. Just like a piano can be tuned with a tuning fork, attune yourself to the energy of the Divine by visualizing and feeling the emotions and sensations of the Divine.

The Importance of Prayer

(Gratitude Heals and Allows More Abundance and Blessings to Come into Your Life)

Having a regular prayer practice brings us into alignment with God and his energy, which permeates through all life. The profound mystery of God's Infinite Intelligence is love. When we create a daily practice of praying, the infinite energy begins to flow through us, expanding our capacity to give and receive love and be more compassionate towards others as well as ourselves.

I personally used to struggle with praying. It brought back memories of rigid Sunday school and dogmatic religious practices. Unless you have a connection to certain traditional prayers, you do not need to use them. I have friends who start their prayers off with calling on many angels that have different and colorful names. Another friend sings various Psalms.

From my personal experience, prayer works best when we use our own words. You do not need to know every angel or use flowery words. It doesn't have to be lengthy. What matters is that you're sincere.

Prayer is not always about creating a mental monologue. Sometimes prayer is getting lost in an activity that requires deep introspection that is felt spontaneously. Anyone can purposefully engage in activities that touch the spirit and allow us to connect with God in everyday life.

If you are confused or don't know where to begin, start by practicing gratitude for all the big and small blessings in your life.

Pray in Nature

On a day you have free time and are alone, bring whatever you need to be comfortable when sitting outside. Find a comfortable spot where you will be able to watch the sun setting until it completely sets. Thank God for all the gifts earth gives us. Feel your prayers deep within you, and let them well up in whatever way you desire. Imagine the remaining light rays taking your prayers through the dusk and up to God.

There are certain situations in life that consume us to the point of obsession. Try writing your prayers in a journal. Set a timer for twenty minutes, and start writing. Don't worry about grammar. Just write as fast as you can, and allow your heart to pour out. Don't stop writing until the timer goes off. After you have written it out, release it from your heart and mind and know that it is now in God's hands and help will reveal itself.

Practice praying for everyone, including your enemies. Pray for anyone and any given situation. When we pray for everyone, we see that situations heal and transform more quickly and with more healing benefit because everyone receives what they need.

Don't pray for people to change to suit your wants, needs, or desires. Pray for the person's highest good and for their well-being. Praying for everyone allows us to be the light for others, softens attitudes, and is a wonderful way of expressing unconditional love.

As a psychic medium, I work with the spirit world with prayer to ensure the highest and best spirit communications are going to connect with me and that the messages serve my clients' highest good and purpose. Some mediums like to specify protection before and within their prayer. I personally believe if you need protection, you are focusing on what you don't want and have a greater chance of attracting it. Also, I feel by invoking God within your prayer, one already has protection.

Here is a short prayer you can say before doing psychic or mediumship work.

"Infinite and Divine Spirit, surround us with your love and light. Uplift our minds and hearts so we can see and act with your discernment, patience, and compassion. May we be cognizant with your loving presence and wisdom."

We ask for information for the clients' highest good. If we are using prayer for mediumship, you may say, "We miss our ancestors, friends, and loved ones who have crossed over and would like to visit them. We ask that they bring abundance of proof that there is a continuation of life as well as messages of comfort, guidance, encouragement, and inspiration. Thank you, Divine Spirit. Amen."

Endocrine System

(Healing Psychic Trauma that Has Manifested as Sickness, Disease, and Imbalances in the Physical Body)

What Is the Endocrine System?

The foundations of the endocrine system are the hormones and glands. As the body's chemical messengers, hormones transfer information and instructions from one set of cells to another. Although many different hormones circulate throughout the bloodstream, each one affects only the cells that are genetically programmed to receive and respond to its message. Hormone levels can be influenced by factors such as stress, infection, and changes in the balance of fluid and minerals in the blood.

A gland is a group of cells that produces and secretes, or gives off, chemicals. A gland selects and removes materials from the blood, processes them, and secretes the finished chemical product for use somewhere in the body. Some types of glands release their secretions in specific areas. For instance, exocrine glands, such as the sweat and salivary glands, release secretions inside the mouth and through the skin, respectively.

Endocrine glands, on the other hand, release more than twenty major hormones directly into the bloodstream, where they can be transported to cells in other parts of the body.

The major glands that make up the human endocrine system are:

Hypothalamus

Pituitary

Pineal

Thyroid and Parathyroid

Pancreas

Adrenal

Reproductive, including the ovaries and testes

The root cause of disease and all imbalances are the psychological and spiritual imbalances that trigger too much hormone secretion or not enough.

Endocrine System—Chakras

The human body contains vortexes of concentrated energy between our physical and spiritual bodies. These energy centers are called the *chakras*. The levels of life force (Chi or prana) in our bodies have an impact on our inherent healing ability as our life force helps to nourish organs and systems of the body.

Root Chakra–Base of the spine

Gives vitality to the physical body; life force, vitality, survival

Endocrine System: Spine/glandular system, adrenals, kidneys, spinal column, colon

Body: Excretory system function; survival issues and base instincts

Spiritual Blocks: Fear, physical safety, feelings of defectiveness, unworthiness, and not having enough; abandonment, betrayal, lost, love unreceived

Spiritual Lessons: Matters related to the physical world; individuality, security, stability, health, courage, and patience

Affirmation for Healing: "I am not here by mistake but by God's design. No one can take better care of me more than I can. I am worthy of love. I am grounded in my body."

Emotional: Fear, rage, anger, shame

Mental/Emotional Strengths: Safety, actions, needs, security, and grounding

Sacral Chakra–Lower abdomen

Governs the hips, large intestine, pelvic area, sexual organs, and urinary area

Endocrine System: Ovaries and testes, prostate, genitals, spleen, womb, and bladder

Body: Reproductive system

Function: Center of sexual energy, feelings, and emotions

Spiritual Imbalances: Blaming self, fear of change, sexual problems, guilt, relationship issues, poor ethics, poor social kills, codependency, excessive mood swings, and finance problems

Spiritual Lessons: Giving and receiving emotions, desires, pleasure, love, change, movement, assimilation of new ideas, health, family, tolerance, working with others

Mantra for Healing: "I accept myself and others."

Mental/Emotional Strengths: Feelings, trust, warmth, intimacy, letting go

Solar Plexus

Endocrine system: Adrenals, pancreas, stomach, liver, gallbladder, nervous system, muscles

Body: Digestive system

Function: Power and wisdom center; to vitalize the sympathetic nervous system; digestion processes, metabolism, emotions.

Spiritual Lessons: Personal power, self-control, transformation

Mantra for Healing: "I am confident and in control of my life."

Mental/Emotional Strengths: Self-critique, willpower, personal power

Heart Chakra

Endocrine System: Thymus

Body: Circulatory system, arms, hands, lungs

Function: Unconditional love, self-love

Spiritual Lessons: Forgiveness, compassion, group consciousness, acceptance, peace, contentment

Heart Functions: Anchors life force from the higher self; Energizes blood in the physical body

Mantra for Healing: "I love myself and others."

Mental/Emotional Strengths: Trust, lovingness, gentle with self and others, growth, coping, balance

Throat Chakra

Endocrine System: Thyroid/parathyroid, hypothalamus

Body: Respiratory system, throat, mouth

Function: Communication, self-expression, speech, sound, vibration

Spiritual Lessons: Power of communication, creative expression; integrating truth, knowledge, wisdom, loyalty kindness, reliability

Mantra for Healing: "I speak my truth. I can ask for everything I need."

Mental/Emotional Strengths: Open and clear communication, feelings, thoughts, speaking up, releasing, life force

Third Eye

Vitalizes the lower brain, cerebellum, and central nervous system

Endocrine System: Pituitary gland

Body: Autonomic nervous system,

Function: Intuitive center of will and psychic abilities

Spiritual Lessons: Soul realization, intuition, insight, concentration, clairvoyance, peace of mind, wisdom and perception beyond duality

Mantra for Healing: "If I can imagine it, I can create it."

Mental/Emotional Strengths: Visualizing psychic and subtle awareness of other's addictions healed and service to others

Crown Chakra–Pineal

Endocrine System: Pineal gland

Body: Cerebral cortex, central nervous system

Function: Connects us with our spiritual self, vitalizes the upper brain, the cerebrum

Spiritual Lessons: Unification of the higher self with ego/human personality; oneness with God, spiritual will, unity, and divine wisdom

Mantra for Healing: "I am connected to God and all beings in the universe."

Mental/Emotional Strengths: Compassion, seeing self in others, harmony, nonattached, non-reactive, and loving

How Emotions Affect the Meridian System

Too much anger injures the liver.

Too much fear injures the kidneys.

Too much sadness injures the lungs.

Too much thinking or worrying injures the spleen.

Too much joy or excitement injures the heart.

Too much emotion injures the heart.

Some Healing Modalities to Dig Out Emotions

- Using aromatherapy oils, chrome essence
- Journaling your thoughts and dreams
- Identifying all your "unimportant hurts"
- Observing your behavior
- Praying
- Meditating
- Utilizing crystals: Crystal healing is an alternative medicine technique that employs stones and crystals as healing tools. The practitioner places crystals on different parts of the body, often corresponding to chakras, or places crystals around the body in an attempt to construct an *energy grid*, which is purported to surround the client with energy.

Core Beliefs

a. What are some core beliefs about yourself?

b. What are your core beliefs about others and the world?

c. What recent events caused negative reactions?

d. What is your automatic negative thought about an experience, and what does the negative thought mean to you?

Your relationships with your parents or whoever raised you have a great influence on your core beliefs. Siblings, parents, neighbors, educators, and society all shape your beliefs, which determine your life experiences.

- Who were the significant people in your life during childhood and young adult years?

- What were the recurring themes of those experiences, and what beliefs did you subconsciously learn through them?

Taking Control over Your Negative Self-Talk

To change what you feel, change your internal dialogue. Most triggers come from internal thoughts and beliefs about how we perceive and interpret a situation or event. Make an effort to focus on your internal thought process going on inside your head. Negative and upsetting words need to be reframed to allow you to stay physically and emotionally balanced.

Some other tips:

Watch consumption of junk food, sugar, drugs, alcohol and caffeine.

Take time to meditate on your problems. Search for options and solutions.

Cultivate more positive emotions by being around uplifting people and setting time aside to do the things you love.

Actively seek ways to use positive emotions to cope with negative moods.

Trigger positive feelings by meditating on the positive triggers in your life: a child, a job, a pet, etc.

What places, situations, or people prompt positive emotions?

What activities, passions, and goals help you stay present?

Exploring Your Triggers

Externally: Anything which occurs within your environment and outside of you

Internally: Anything we tell ourselves; our internal dialogue and thinking process

We can trigger positive emotions by savoring pleasures, writing a gratitude list, showing kindness towards others, and by having a passion, interests, and hobbies.

How to Gain Greater Self-Awareness

1. Feel your emotions physically. What sensations do you feel? Is there tightness anywhere?

2. Know your triggers. Pay attention to what pushes your buttons—people, places, situations, etc.

3. Keep a daily emotional journal. Write down thoughts, triggers, and emotions.

4. Pay attention to when you are stressed. Being aware of when your feelings of stress occur is the best way to see how your emotions manifest.

5. Get feedback from friends, coworkers, and family. Many times, we do not see how or when our emotions dictate our actions and behaviors

6. Regulate your feelings by setting goals after you have developed the skill of having awareness without reacting.

7. Use peaceful imagery. Having a focal point stops the mind from racing and helps us stay grounded.

8. Deep belly breaths reset the nervous system and get one into full body consciousness.

Things I've learned about Hypersensitivity Caused by Trauma

Self-care is important for hypersensitive people (HSP). Because of their different nervous system, HSP are more prone to illnesses and imbalances if they do not honor their own sensitive constitution.

Reframing your life: Rethink all your perceived failures in light of now knowing your unique trait.

Healing your past: HSP who have lived traumatic childhoods (abuse, neglect, etc.) are more prone to anxiety and depression.

Some Facts about Sensitivity

Overstimulation means being over-aroused; overwhelmed and exhausted in the total body; can't coordinate; can't relax; fried-out.

Physical Manifestations include pounding heart, churning stomach, headache, shallow breathing, hot flashes, cold skin, damp skin.

When an individual is over-aroused, they aren't capable of performing to the best of their capabilities.

HSP have more memories and experiences of failing due to their sensitivity.

Sensitivity is not our society's ideal. Countries like China and Japan value sensitivity, while cultures which are aggressive and expansive don't (USA and Canada).

HSP who have experienced emotional abuse are more prone to anxiety and depression, whereas HSP who weren't abused handle stress better than non-HSP.

Lifestyle and Diet to Support the Nervous System for Trauma Victims and Highly Sensitive People

While I do have some suggestions about food choices that can help support nervous-system activity, I also want to point out that no amount of supportive food can completely offset a lifestyle that features high levels of stress or the lack of good sleep, two factors that can affect the nervous system. For those who experience challenges in these areas, working on stress reduction and sleep improvement through other strategies besides dietary interventions is critical.

It's also important to keep in mind that our bodies work as a whole, not as isolated parts. As convenient as it is to talk about foods that support the nervous system or foods that support the cardiovascular system, the more lasting way to supporting health is by supporting all body systems through a meal plan that takes into account not only the nervous system but also the way the nervous system interacts with the endocrine system, the immune system, and other body tissues and systems. A balanced, plant-based, whole-foods diet is the best way we know of to accomplish that goal.

Nutrients for the Nervous System

Omega-3 Fatty Acids: The structure of the nervous system is unique in terms of many nutrients. Many of the nerves are wrapped in sheaths called myelin sheaths. Omega-3 fatty acids—especially DHA (docosahexaenoic acid)—are particularly important within the sheath structures surrounding many nerves. Wild-caught cold-water fish (like salmon), seeds (like pumpkin seeds or flaxseeds), nuts (like walnuts), and some oils (like canola oils) are important food sources of omega-3 fatty acids.

Protein/Amino Acids: Our neurotransmitters (special messaging molecules) transmit neurologic information from one nerve cell to another. In some cases, these molecules are simple amino acids or derivatives of amino acids, the basic building blocks of protein. Therefore, optimal protein intake and balanced intake of the amino acids within it can also be very helpful in supporting the nervous system.

B-Complex Vitamins: B-complex vitamins are essential for the nervous system to be able to properly synthesize and circulate neurotransmitters. Vitamins B6, B12, and folic acid especially are critical for nerve metabolism. Green leafy vegetables are good sources of many B vitamins.

Clearing Exercises to Do When You Are by Yourself to Deal with Overstimulation

1. Repeat affirmations.
2. Regulate your breathing and heart rate.
3. Release body stress through yoga and other healing exercises.
4. Become the witness while you are in your sacred space.
5. Honor all emotions.
6. Surrender—see your emotions as sacred.
7. See challenges or problems as opportunities to connect with your inner knowing.
8. Shift your attention—your choice of focus is your strongest tool.
9. Meditation and imagination can ground you in the feeling that your intention is stronger than your reaction.
10. Develop healthy boundaries. Take care of yourself first! Refuse to go against your own values. Do not be afraid to say no. Personal boundaries are the way we set limits in our relationships. Having boundaries helps us create emotional stability.

Psychological and Metaphysical Meanings and Healing Solutions for the Systems of the Body

(Healing the Body, Mind, and Spirit)

Chi (life force) supports the vital functions of the body's organs and systems and contributes to the healthy growth and renewal of cells. However, the amount of Chi isn't always sufficiently replenished, and there are many impurities which can block the nadis (energy channels).

Blocks and imbalances consist of energy forms we've created from our own behavior. Spiritual imbalances of self-limiting thoughts and motives make up most of these energy blocks. The subtle and physical bodies are linked together by etheric matter, so virtually anything that affects one automatically affects the other. Thus, physical impurities such as body toxins caused by unhealthy diet, drugs, tobacco, alcohol, nervous tension, etc., cause corresponding blocks in the subtle body as well.

Over time, if these blocks are constant, the energy body will be depleted. The person's Chi will be low and not circulating effectively through the body. This is when we become weaker and even more susceptible to illness, disease, premature aging, and even physical death. As the primal source of all energy forms, this energy manifests itself in various frequencies, and your level of consciousness (awareness) determines the frequencies of Chi you can receive and store.

Every imbalance, disease, or disorder a person manifests feeds on negative thoughts and feelings. The more density there is in your mind, the more fuel your body must degenerate. The first step towards healing is to set the intention that you are ready to get better.

The next step is learning to understand your blocks and the behaviorisms which manifest from them. Healing should encompass every aspect of your being, including your physical health and fitness, emotional well-being, mental attitude, energetic welfare, and spiritual strength. It is important to understand that your body is self-healing. With the right knowledge and conscious action, you can heal not just your physical body but your life.

Healing means internal transformation. To heal, you need to change your thoughts, feelings, and actions from sabotaging and non-serving to fruitful and empowering. Whatever part of the body is experiencing a problem, it needs to be looked at as a metaphorical representation of the challenges you are dealing with in your life.

As a Master Psychic Healer, I see a lot of clients who change their lives and let go of problems when they begin to understand the interconnection between their ways of living and the problem they are experiencing.

Your body is your teacher. It gives you opportunities to learn and expand. Once you have learned your lessons, it heals because there is no need to keep holding on to the pain any longer. Our bodies teach us spiritual lessons to evolve our consciousness into Christ consciousness. Personally, we learn through intimate experiences of love, compassion, forgiveness, courage and much more.

Healing takes you through many different stages and layers of discovering who you are. Sometimes change happens quickly; at other times, more slowly. Healing occurs on many levels physically, mentally, emotionally, and energetically so be patient with your process.

Psychological Spiritual Meanings of the Systems and Metaphysically Healing

The Nervous System

The nervous system helps us to create a link between our external and internal worlds. It teaches us that what we experience within is also reflected on the outside. The nervous system begins to break down when we experience internal and external conflict, stress, and fear.

To work with the nervous system, create a daily practice that includes body/mind medicine, yoga, or weight training to recondition how the body deals with stress.

Here are some other suggestions to aid healing and reconditioning of the nervous system:

- Breath work
- Ayurvedic detox work
- Energy psychology
- Nutrition

The Circulatory System

The circulatory system provides sustenance and nurturing to our bodies. It teaches us about relationships with other people and with ourselves. The circulatory system starts to break down when we blame others for our experiences or hold on to anger, fear, and self-loathing. To regenerate the circulatory system, we need to be willing to take risks and open our hearts to love.

The Lymphatic System

The lymphatic system helps to cleanse our bodies and destroys germs. It teaches us how to stand up for ourselves and fight for what we believe in. The lymphatic system begins to break down when we allow fear, guilt, and doubts to rule our lives.

To restore the lymphatic system, we need to develop self-esteem, self-appreciation, and creativity. We need to allow ourselves to play and be spontaneous.

The Respiratory System

The respiratory system keeps us alive by supplying oxygen to the blood and releasing waste products. It gives us energy and helps us grow and move. It teaches us how to recognize what works and is helpful in our lives and what we need to let go of. The respiratory system begins to break down when we carry feelings of resentment, bitterness, judgment, and anger.

The Digestive System

Our digestive system breaks down food for energy to maintain and repair the body. Our digestion begins to break down when we sabotage our progress, buy into fear, hold on to guilt, and act like victims. To improve the digestive system, we need to start nourishing, loving, and honoring ourselves by listening to our intuition, practicing patience, and using our creative talents and abilities.

The Muscular System

The muscular system gives us strength, support, and the ability to move. It helps us to see things from different points of view and have flexibility in our bodies and lives. The muscular system begins to break down when we stress, carry too much responsibility on our shoulders, and become stuck. To heal the muscular system, we need to relax, build our confidence, and express our feelings.

The Reproductive System

The reproductive system allows us to experience sexual connection, nourishment, and life. It helps us to express love, experience pleasure, and give birth. The reproductive system begins to break down when we hold on to guilt, shame, and humiliation from past relationships. To heal the reproductive system, we need to learn how to value ourselves, forgive others, and enjoy our sensuality.

The Urinary System

The urinary system removes waste from the body. The urinary system starts to break down when we feel irritated, angry, and bitter or "pissed off." To heal the urinary system, we need to take responsibility for our actions, recognize that we always have a choice, and increase our self-worth.

The Skeletal System

The skeletal system provides support, protection, and structure for the body. It helps us to protect the other body systems from our external environment and teaches us about boundaries. When we judge ourselves and others harshly or feel betrayed, resentful, and bitter, the skeletal system begins to break down. To strengthen the skeletal system, we need to become flexible, become self-sufficient, and learn to look for blessings in challenging situations.

The Endocrine System

The endocrine system produces and releases hormones into the blood which act as messengers that influence almost every part of the body. It helps us to regulate our emotions, behaviors, and metabolism. The endocrine system starts to break down when we experience stress, confusion, and frustration. Include meditation in your schedule twice a day to help create a more balanced, healthy, and happy lifestyle.

The Immune System

The immune system protects us against viruses, harmful bacteria, diseases, and other imbalances. But when we feel insecure, experience inner conflict, and feel stressed, the immune system begins to break down. To strengthen it, we need to focus within and allow the innate wisdom of the body to heal any imbalance and to maintain overall wellness. We need to stay true to ourselves and have the courage to stand up for what we believe in.

The Anatomy of Your Energy System and How It Relates to Your Health

The chakras are seven spiritual centers in the human body. The word *chakra* is a Sanskrit word meaning *wheel* or *vortex*. Each chakra is related to a layer in the aura. These energies represent what and who you are, and they are affected by your surroundings and lifestyle. They reflect your health, character, mental activity, and emotional state.

The chakras are energy transducers in the aura, in which they receive, process, and transmit universal life-force energies known as Chi or prana. The chakras circulate Chi throughout the body, bringing oxygen and nutrients to cells, organs, muscles, and other tissues. The *aura* is made up of a complex combination of atoms, molecules, and energy cells which generate a large magnetic energy field that can be sensed, felt, and even seen.

Our chakras serve to integrate the physical, emotional, psychological, and spiritual character traits of human consciousness into Christ consciousness. The chakras interact with specific aspects of our consciousness and have individual characteristics and functions, each corresponding to various major organs and glands in the body's endocrine system.

The human aura is a reflection of one's chakras. The aura is often referred to as the subtle energy bodies and auric field. The seven layers of our aura are known as the etheric layer, emotional layer, mental layer, astral layer, etheric template, celestial layer, and ketheric template.

The first layer of your aura is the *etheric layer*. It is closest to the physical body and represents all physical aspects of the world as well as the physical body (muscle, tissue, bones, etc.). It also represents all major systems of the physical body such as the endocrine system, immune system, and skeletal system. The first layer represents the root chakra.

The second layer is the *emotional layer*. It represents our emotions and feelings. This second layer represents the sacral chakra.

The third layer is known as the *mental layer*. It represents thought, cognitive processes, and states of mind. This layer represents the third chakra, the solar plexus.

The fourth layer is the *astral layer*. It represents where we form astral cords with others. This layer represents the fourth chakra, known as the heart chakra.

The fifth layer is the *etheric template*. It represents the entire blueprint of the body and everything you create on this physical plane, such as identity, personality, and overall energy. This layer represents the fifth chakra, known as the throat chakra.

The sixth layer is the *celestial layer*. This layer represents the connection to the Divine and all other beings. This layer reflects the sixth chakra, known as the third eye.

The seventh and last layer of the aura is known as the *ketheric template*. This layer reflects your crown chakra. It holds all the information about your soul and previous lifetimes, and it represents oneness with the Divine and all energies of the universe.

Your energy level, environment, emotional state, and the way you use any particular part of your energy greatly influences the size of your aura. Imbalances and diseases are caused by depletion, congestion, or blockage of Chi in a person's energy body. In fact, stress, trauma, and emotional pain usually show imbalances in our magnetic energy field long before they manifest as disease in the physical body.

It is a good idea to protect and balance your aura from time to time. This clears out any negative thought patterns and emotional blocks and sets a shield of protection around yourself, helping your body retain Chi.

Your energy body, more than any other single human trait, manifests the sum and substance of your existence as an endless life force in the universe. Your whole energy system can uncover important resources that would prolong life, help avoid sickness and disease, and enrich your life with new insights. Having a clear understanding of the anatomy of the energy system known as your chakras and auric field will enable you to take control of your overall well-being.

The Connection between Spiritual Imbalances and Imbalances in the Endocrine System

Our chakras function like pumps and valves, regulating the flow of energy through our energy system. We open and close these valves by the thoughts we think, what we feel, and through our perception filters. The chakras, which are denser than the aura but not as dense as the physical body, interact with the physical body through the endocrine system and the nervous system.

Each of our seven chakras is associated with one of the seven primary endocrine glands and with a group of nerves called plexuses.

The endocrine system is one of the body's primary structures for communicating, along with controlling and coordinating the body's functioning. This vital system works in alignment with the nervous system, immune system, reproductive system, and the kidneys, gut, liver, pancreas, and fatty tissues to help maintain and control the following:

- Body energy levels
- Reproduction
- Growth and development
- Internal balance of body systems, called homeostasis
- Responses to surroundings, stress, and injury (known as the fight-or-flight response).

Each chakra is not only associated with a particular part of the body and function within the body; it also reflects different aspects of consciousness.

Karmic Clearings

Spiritual issues are intertwined with emotional and psychological health. Spirituality is something that allows us to transcend the limitations of the day-to-day routine and become aware that we are all inextricably connected. Unlike any other social structure or establishment, spirituality cannot be understood fully by psychology and the normal social processes. Spirituality focuses on the sacredness of being deeply connected to one ultimate truth, as it forms the truths of humanity.

Successful healing is not effectively gained through outside establishments, groups, religions, or people. The journey of healing is found by going within the heart. Spiritual healing involves qualities of the mind such as love, compassion, forgiveness, and gratitude—characteristics which create awareness that transcends the mind to see new and supportive realities individually as well as globally.

Karma in Hinduism and Buddhism is the sum of a person's actions in this and previous states of existence, viewed as deciding their fate in future existences.

Karma has nothing to do with punishment. It is based on the idea of cause and effect. Every person has karmic patterns that create negative experiences and negative emotional energy. Contrary to popular belief, negative emotional energy is not a natural response in most situations. It is, instead, a habitual, self-destructive response which causes us to be out of alignment with our truest sense of self and our creator.

The Maya, back in 2012, referred to the new paradigm and new consciousness as the "end of the world." During the current global transition, everyone on the planet is ascending spiritually. This means individuals are noticing more things are out of balance, personally as well as globally, and they are experiencing more emotional triggers as a result.

There are many names for and many types of karmic clearings:

1. Clearing past-life programs, contracts, and cords

2. Clearing blocks to empowerment and self-esteem

3. Clearing blocks of self-punishment and victimization

4. Clearing self-sabotaging behavior, self-destruction, and a desire to suffer

5. Clearing family and ancestral karma

6. Clearing blocks of feeling undeserving and unworthy

7. Clearing blocks of guilt and shame

8. Clearing blocks of lacking, limitation, and poverty consciousness

9. Clearing blocks of codependency and addiction

10. Clearing blocks self-disempowerment

Karmic clearings and past-life clearings are often referring to the same thing. Regardless of the name, a karmic clearing is a process where limiting and sabotaging core beliefs and judgements are identified and cleared by integrating the knowledge.

Some indications of needing a karmic clearing are: health problems, addictions, imbalanced relationships, financial problems, brain fog, memory loss, learning issues, unexplained and intense negative emotions, anxiety, depression, not feeling connected to the world, and not being able to stay present.

Many psychologists as well as spiritualists teach different forms of it, but the important steps to karmic clearing are gaining awareness of the spiritual/psychological block, awareness of what caused the block, and learning how to integrate the new awareness. This can be done through a psychic reading, past-life-regression reading, or clinical psychological testing. As a Master Psychic Healer who specializes in karmic clearings, I integrate both spiritual and psychological practices into my clearing methods.

Eckhart Tolle, spiritualist and author of the *The Power of Now,* states that "There is such a thing as old emotional pain living inside you." It is an accumulation of painful life experience that was not fully faced and accepted in the moment it arose. It leaves behind an energy form of emotional pain. The energy from the emotional pain comes together with other energy forms from other instances, and so after some years you have a *pain-body*, an energy entity consisting of old emotion. A pain-body is an accumulation of stagnant negative emotions caused by experiences that were not faced, accepted, and eventually integrated with the victim's energy field.

My work primarily consists of channeling into my client's unconscious and sabotaging habits, conditions, and reflexes (pain-body) that block them from manifesting their own desires. I psychically connect with one's soul in order to advise them in their specific needs and guide them to their soul's path and purpose. Through a step-by-step and individualized program, I provide life coaching and design strategies to ensure success for my clients in order to holistically improve their well-being spiritually, mentally, emotionally, and physically.

Individuals who experience the following can benefit from my services:

- Anxiety, depression, extreme anger/rage, and any other negative emotions
- Recovery from addiction(s)
- ADD/ADHD, OCD, and PTSD

- Psychic trauma
- Recovery from an accident
- Difficulty moving past a breakup or death of a loved one
- Emotional, physical, and spiritual suffering
- Recovery from chronic or acute illness
- Living or working in (past or present) toxic environments

Toxic Relationships/Psychic Trauma

Whether they are between families, spouses, co-workers, or, so-called friends, bad relationships contribute to adrenal fatigue as much as, if not more than, lifestyle and diet.

Symptoms of a Toxic Relationship

- Anyone trying to isolate and separate you from your family, friends, work, hobbies, and interests
- Anyone keeping watch on you or not allowing you to have alone time and personal boundaries
- Anyone verbally abusing you
- A toxic person being overpowering and overly possessive
- Anyone dominating you, not leaving any space for your preferences
- You losing your self-identity as you depend more on the toxic relationship, not knowing how to survive without him/her
- You being afraid of telling the truth for fear of upsetting your spouse, family, or whoever is toxic
- Your self-esteem being always at a low level as the person makes you feel worthless and unattractive
- Your thoughts, words, opinions, and accomplishments having no value

Feelings that Define the Characteristics of a Toxic Relationship

- Unsupported
- Dissatisfied
- Fearful
- Depleted
- Drained
- Unaccepted
- Judged
- Frazzled
- Guilty
- Tired
- Angry
- Untrusting
- Unequal
- Stifled
- Shameful

Though most of us want to find love and intimacy, we also find ourselves fearful of being hurt, worrying about commitment, and dreading abandonment—also known as anxiety. Our relationship comfort zone is often determined by behavioral patterns that are neither too close to trigger fusion anxiety nor too distant to trigger separation anxiety.

These boundaries have been formed in early childhood and rarely change without gaining awareness of your trauma and forming a daily protocol to recondition your behaviorisms. Working with a spiritualist to create conscious awareness is sometimes the route to go in the beginning of your healing process.

In a toxic relationship cycle, power struggles arise many times without resolution. Intimacy turns into conflicts which lead to anxiety. These anxieties then lead to arguments, hurt feelings, withdrawal, and detachment.

Detachment and withdrawal may bring temporary relief but ultimately become feelings of isolation and loneliness, thus setting off fear of abandonment, which triggers the fight-flight-or-freeze response, which causes the adrenals to go into overdrive.

Getting out of a toxic relationship

- **Take responsibility. Don't be a victim anymore.** Know that you contribute to the abuse by not leaving. Ask yourself why you are willing to allow the behaviors to continue. What can you learn from this?

- **Set Boundaries.** Let the abusive person know they need to change their behavior. Describe what you are looking for and what your expectations are for the future if they are going to remain in your life. Also, be aware that individuals who are used to being abusive usually do not want to change, so really hold to your boundaries. Obviously, some people's boundaries have to be stricter.

- **Forgive.** People are not usually toxic at birth. The environment and circumstances over time mold us into who we are. Learn to see the good in a person beneath the toxicity on the surface. Learn to forgive and return love, which is our primary purpose on earth. Use love to heal one another. This doesn't mean remaining in the person's life. It means forgiving from a healthy distance.

- **Get a new perspective from a neutral party** who has no bias against your relationship—for example a counselor, coach, neighbor, or co-worker. The key is not to vent to the person or create someone to pity you. The point is for the other person to help you focus on the situation, the part you have played, and what you are willing to do to move forward.

- **End the relationship/Drop who or what no longer serves or supports you.** If nothing changes after you have tried all the above, walk away from your relationship with your head held high.

Unless you remove the negative toxic relationships from your life, the constant negative energy flow needed to sustain the toxicity prevents adrenal fatigue healing. To channel the toxic negative energy into positive constructive energy is key to the healing process.

Healing Adrenal Fatigue with Ayurvedic and Traditional Chinese Medicine

The fundamental principle of health and healing in Traditional Chinese Medicine (TCM) theory is the concept of balance. Your body contains both yin and yang (opposing yet counterbalancing) Chi, and in health, the relaxed yin state balances the adrenal yang state.

The problem arises when you have an excess of either yin or yang influences in your life. In Chinese medicine, the adrenal glands are part of the water element and relate to kidney energy. The kidneys are the single most important organ affecting the length and quality of your life. They control your internal Chi, your yin/yang balance, and house your Jing, which is your aliveness, your creative power, and your essence.

Abundant kidney Chi correlates to a strong physical constitution as well as a strong innate sense of purpose and will. Since the adrenals relate to kidney Chi, adrenal fatigue is considered to be a kidney yang deficiency. However, if the condition continues without treatment, it can also result in a kidney yin deficiency.

Kidney yang relates to the reactive, sympathetic nervous system and the secretion of epinephrine and norepinephrine. In contrast, kidney yin is the parasympathetic nervous system relating to the secretion of cortisol. Just as the body requires some degree of yang adrenaline hormone to create motivation to react both to normal as well as life-threatening stimuli, it also has a continual need for the yin hormone, cortisol, to buffer the effects of stress. In the early stages of stress, the body increases its production of cortisol, while in the later stages its secretion of this hormone is severely diminished. This lack of cortisol, then, is diagnosed as kidney yin deficiency.

The clinical manifestations of kidney yang deficiency are: soreness of the back, cold knees, sensation of cold in the back, aversion to cold, weak legs, bright-white complexion, weak knees, impotence, premature ejaculation, lassitude, abundant-clear urination, scanty-clear urination, apathy, edema of the legs, infertility in women, poor appetite, and loose stools.

The tongue is pale, swollen, and wet, and the pulse is deep and weak. In TCM theory, when there is kidney yang deficiency, the body fails to transform the essence, leading to a decline in endocrine and physiological functions.

The way to treat kidney yang deficiency is to warm the kidneys. This means reducing your intake of cold foods/beverages (i.e., ice cream and other frozen foods or iced drinks), raw foods, and antibiotics, as these inhibit your body's warming function, eventually depleting yang. In addition, the use of sugar can overstimulate the sympathetic reflex and deplete kidney yang.

Deficient kidney yin, on the other hand, is manifested with symptoms of aching, soreness of the lumbar region of the back, weakness of the legs and knees, tinnitus, dizziness, vertigo, constipation, night sweats, insomnia, dry throat, feverish sensation in the soles and palms, nocturnal emission, and in women, scanty menstrual flow and amenorrhea, flushed complexion, heat, nervousness, anxiety, insomnia, dryness, and chronic signs of inflammation and wasting. A deficiency of yin suggests that the maintaining and repairing function of the body is depleted or lacking.

From an Ayurvedic standpoint, the adrenals are not addressed in the classical texts, nor is cortisol level testing a part of the *ashtavidha pariksha,* the eight traditional diagnostic methods.

Three vital essences—*prana, tejas, and ojas*—are the positive forms of the corresponding three doshas (*vata, pitta,* and *kapha*) which together promote and sustain our physical vitality, mental clarity, and overall health and immunity. The doshas circulate in the body and govern our psychological activity.

When ojas, the essential energy for vitality, strength, and well-being, is diminished, the person feels fatigued, fearful, and worried, experiences problems with their sensory organs, has deranged luster and mental ability, is rough and emaciated. This depletion can be brought about by things like anger, hunger, worry, grief, and overexertion.

If you have adrenal fatigue, Ayurvedic practitioners discourage their patients from using adrenal extracts that may have been purchased online or from another practitioner. These products act exactly like corticosteroids in impairing adrenal function and causing adrenal insufficiency.

Instead, it is important for those with these symptoms to make lifestyle changes by eliminating the following: toxins such as white sugar, parasites, and heavy metals; excess alcohol consumption; and poisons, especially caffeine, nicotine, and uppers. Also, the amount of fish in the diet should be examined carefully as a potential source of heavy-metal poisoning.

Staying awake at night is extremely stressful to the adrenals, which operate on a diurnal cycle designed for days of activity and nights of rest. Similarly, *prajagara* (always wakeful) is an important cause of *ojokshay* (loss of energy). Wherever possible, the schedule should be adjusted to permit night sleep rather than day sleep. Ongoing traumatic or stressful situations should also be addressed.

It is essential in Ayurvedic Medicine to understand one's unique physical constitution by doing a *prakruti* (primal matter/substance) test, which involves answering various survey questions to determine which doshas are out of balance.

In place of an adrenally exhausting diet high in refined-flour products and sugary baked goods, an Ayurvedic diet emphasizing whole grains, legumes, and vegetables will support both ojas and the adrenals. Also, since our vata dosha governs all movement in the mind and body, controlling blood flow, breathing, moving through the mind, and waste elimination, this diet is likely to have a vata-soothing emphasis. However, adjustments would have to be made based on individual *prakruti*.

Ayurvedic stress-management strategies may be helpful, as well. One of these is gentle yoga with emphasis on calming *shivasana pranayamas* like *Nadi Shodhan*, a nostril-breathing technique that lowers heart rate, reduces anxiety, and synchronizes the left and right hemispheres of the brain, thus clearing the channels of circulation. Other helpful practices include meditation and daily self-massage with ashwagandha bala oil or other appropriate dosha-specific massage oil to help relieve stress, balance vata, and strengthen ojas.

Adaptogenic herbs with an affinity for the adrenals include ashwagandha, tulsi, and licorice, which is endowed with aldosterone-like qualities.

Ashwagandha is among the most outstanding of the *jivaniya* (life prolonging) herbs and forms the foundation of treatments aimed at restoring ojas and enhancing adrenal function. Certain stress-easing or calming teas, for example, are blends containing ashwagandha and designed to address many of the symptoms associated with adrenal fatigue. Tulsi tea, or a tea of tulsi and licorice, will also be valuable (avoid licorice if you have elevated blood pressure).

A non-dairy ojas drink can be made for those with sensitivities to cow's milk. Non-vegetarian patients can take chicken soup as a jivaniya food, and vegetarians can take urad dal and mung dal soups for the same purpose.

Ojas Almond Restorative Drink

To restore adrenal function. You can buy most of the ingredients at a natural foods market or Indian grocery or spice store.

Drink this on an empty stomach in the morning. Do not wait longer than one hour after waking to drink. It is compatible with the sattvic diet, which is soothing, nourishing, and incorporates foods that are fresh, juicy, light, and tasty to give the body optimal balance.

Serves 1:

Soak together overnight: 10 raw almonds & 1 cup pure water. In the morning, drain off the water. Rub the skins off the almonds.
Bring to a boil: 1 cup milk (unhomogenized if possible; milk is highly rejuvenative when digested)
Pour the milk in the blender with the drained & peeled almonds and add:

1 Tbs organic rose (rejuvenative)
1 tsp ghee (rejuvenative)
1/8 tsp organic cardamom (increases digestion)
pinch of pippali (prevents kapha provocation)
1/2 tsp of sweetener (increases lactose digestion)

Blend until smooth.

Non-Dairy Almond Drink

Soak together overnight: 10 raw almonds & 1 cup pure water. In a separate container, soak 20 raisins in 1 cup pure water overnight or for several hours.
In the morning, drain off the water. Rub the skins off the

almonds.
Put the raisins AND their soak-water in the blender with the drained & peeled almonds and add:

1 Tbs organic rose (rejuvenative)
1 tsp ghee (rejuvenative)
1/8 tsp organic cardamom (increases digestion)
Pinch of pippali, (prevents kapha provocation)

Blend until smooth.

In the Ayurvedic paradigm, sufficient and healthy ojas is the key to immunity, strength, and resilience. In the biomedical paradigm, adequate cortisol levels similarly support immunity and stress resilience.

Holistic Diet: Avoid These Dietary Stressors for Good Adrenal Health

- Refined sugar or artificial sugar substitutes that contain aspartame.

- Foods rich in potassium like bananas, melons, dried figs, raisins, dates, grapes, oranges, and grapefruit as they may make your adrenal fatigue worse.

- Simple or refined carbohydrates like pasta, white bread, crackers, cakes, cookies, etc.

- Caffeine, alcohol, sweetened fruit juices, and carbonated soft drinks.

- Processed foods that use sodium nitrates as a preservative such as hot dogs, lunch meats, and bacon.

- Gluten-containing grain products found in breads, crackers, pastas, etc.

- All fermented foods such as wine and cheese.

- Monosodium glutamate (MSG) used in many processed foods.

- Stimulant drugs and nicotine

Endocrine System: Understanding Adrenal Fatigue

The endocrine system is responsible for hormonal functions in the body and produces over sixty distinct hormones, each of which has a very specific job to do. This system controls your physical growth, mood, stress response, reproduction, mental functionality, and immune system.

When it is not working properly, you become more susceptible to disease and your ability to fight off infection is weakened. Endocrine glands and their function impact every area of your health. The keystone of Energy Medicine has always been awakening the body's natural intelligence to heal itself and restore balance to all nine energy systems.

The *acupuncture meridians* are energy pathways that crisscross the body, communicating with organs and endocrine glands. When your body's energies become depleted, you can suffer from fatigue, hot flashes, environmental sensitivities, anxiety, weight gain, joint pain, irritability, depression, digestive problems, dizziness upon rising, poor concentration, infertility, insomnia, and much more.

Optimizing Your Adrenals

The endocrine system provides regulation of the body through hormonal secretions. Cultivating your endocrine health, combined with proper nutrition and diet, can boost energy, reduce insomnia, relieve depression, improve circulation, improve appetite, relieve muscle aches, and assist in recovering from endocrine disorders. One of the easiest ways to create a healthy endocrine system is to eat nutritious meals and have a well-balanced diet.

Lifestyle tips to improve your overall adrenal health:

Meals—When you eat is just as important as how you eat. Eating a nutritious, protein-rich breakfast within an hour of waking, whether you feel hungry or not, will provide energetic benefits throughout your day. Eat slowly and don't rush through your meals. Allowing your body time to properly digest food reduces after-meal fatigue, boosts your immune system, and enables your endocrine system to properly process nutritional intake. Eating regular meals and snacks throughout your day will support your adrenal glands and will balance your blood sugar and cortisol levels, too.

Exercise—Regular exercise boosts the immune system, improves cardiovascular health and muscle mass, and prevents bone loss. Stress-reducing exercises such as a daily Energy Medicine routine, yoga, qigong, or tai chi can also be beneficial for stress reduction. Enjoying a walk in nature or along the beach helps us to stay healthy and happy. See the beauty of nature all around you. Watch a sunset, listen to the wind blow, smell the flowers, enjoy the birds.

Manage Your Stress—Another important part of maintaining a healthy endocrine system is stress management. Having a lot of stress in your life can cause overproduction of hormones, especially cortisol, which can lead to hormonal imbalances.

Rest—Take a day out of the week for rest and rejuvenation, allowing your mind and body recovery time. You will be more productive the rest of the week. Enjoying an afternoon siesta is also a great way to restore your adrenals.

Sleep—After 11:00 p.m., the body begins to run on adrenal reserves, so it is important to be asleep before that time. Also, *triple warmer energy* is at its peak between 9:00 p.m. and 11:00 p.m. The triple warmer meridian is the one that controls our fight-flight-or-freeze response. It has the power to influence our immune system and is interconnected with our stress response.

Allow six to eight hours of sleep per night in order to reduce stress and keep hormones balanced. The combination of stress and a lack of sleep may cause some of the glands to malfunction. If you are experiencing difficulties sleeping, aromatherapy, Energy Medicine, and acupuncture are excellent for treating a variety of sleep problems.

Gratitude—Having a daily practice of gratitude, forgiveness, deep breathing, prayer, or meditation will reduce stress, balance hormones, and bring more joy into your life. Surround yourself with loving and supportive people!

Nutritional Support for Adrenal Health

Eating meals and snacks made of fresh whole foods, preferably organic or locally grown, without colors, dyes, chemicals, preservatives, or added hormones, is best. Including protein in all your meals and snacks is part of any healthy diet. To directly affect your endocrine system, make sure your diet includes these foods:

- **Salmon**—provides your body with omega-3 essential fatty acids as does ground flax. Both directly affect cognitive function, cellular function, and kidney function.
- **Protein**—Eating lightly cooked animal and vegetable proteins like meat, fish, poultry, eggs, and legumes is important three to five times a day.
- **Vegetables**—Drink vegetable juices and eat plenty of vegetables like spinach, chard, other dark leafy greens, celery, zucchini, peppers, kelp, sprouts, and green and black olives. Put a little zing in your cooking, and eat all the brightly colored vegetables as well (green, red, orange, yellow, and purple).
- **Fruits**—papaya, mango, plums, pears, kiwi, apples, cherries, and berries are preferred. If you are dealing with adrenal fatigue and blood-sugar problems, it is best to avoid fruits in the morning.
- **Sprouted Nuts and Seeds**

- **Low-glycemic carbohydrates**—brown rice, sprouted grains, and winter squash.

- **Extra Virgin Organic Coconut Oil**—is a beneficial saturated fat that can help stabilize blood-sugar levels.

- **Salts**—many people with adrenal imbalances often crave salt and will tend to have low blood pressure. Electrical function of the heartbeat requires salt to make hydrochloric acid in the stomach and for fluid around the cells. Sodium is the main substance outside of a cell and is important in proper function of all cells, including nerve cells of the brain, which impact all of our emotions, too. Don't deny your craving; adding a good-quality sea salt or pink salt to your diet will help.

- **Garlic**—boosts your immunity, thus increasing your ability to fight off infection. It also helps regulate blood-sugar levels. Cooking with one or two cloves of garlic a day is recommended.

- **Calcium**—keeps nerves healthy and ensures their ability to communicate effectively. Organic milk, almond milk, cottage cheese, cheese, leafy greens, dried beans, and yogurt are all rich in calcium.

- **Vitamin Bs**—directly influence the nervous system's proper functioning and health and one's physical and mental performance concerning the nervous system. Found in chicken, fish, eggs, whole grains, beans, and nuts.

- **Vitamin C**—Adrenal glands have a very high content of ascorbic acid (vitamin C). This vitamin helps stimulate adrenal glands to produce more of the disease-fighting hormone *cortin*. A continued stressful environment depletes vitamin C reserves and increases the tendency for infection and disease. Good sources of vitamin C include apricots, strawberries, other berries, green veggies, sweet peppers, and tomatoes.

- **Water**—Drink one half your body weight in ounces per day of good-quality filtered water.

Additional results of adrenal fatigue include hair loss, hot flashes, reduced insulin sensitivity (that can lead to diabetes), osteoporosis, infections such as viral, yeast (candida) overgrowth, and herpes. It also causes an increased fat accumulation around the waist and protein breakdown that leads to muscle wasting and the inability to reduce weight. And it creates high blood pressure and estrogen dominance.

Kinesiology—which studies the movement of the body in terms of biomechanical, physiological, and even psychological dynamics—can identify an adrenal health problem at its beginning stages, whereas blood tests for diagnosis may be misleading. For example, your body could continue in the progression until Addison's Disease can be fully diagnosed with complete failure of your adrenal glands.

Uncovering the Spiritual Gift of Adrenal Fatigue

The main difference in those who were born with endocrine imbalances and those who acquired them later in life is that those who came in with these challenges tend to carry a specific archetypal signature, which can be called that of the "wounded healer." They may find the study of the mythology and astrological placement of the comet Chiron in their natal charts to be extremely insightful. If and once they step into their true power, they often become servers of their community in some way. Having experienced so much illness and trauma firsthand, we instinctively know how to help others.

Modalities to Heal Adrenal Fatigue

Oils to heal adrenal fatigue:

Chamomile, moroccan, birch, black pepper, ginger, mandarin, petitgrain

Crystals to heal adrenal fatigue:

Aventurine–heals adrenals

Kyanite–treats adrenals

Rose quartz–heals adrenals

If you or someone you know suffers from adrenal fatigue, I strongly suggest hiring a lifestyle and holistic health coach! Results when working with a certified holistic counselor are amazing, and it does not take long to see those results physically, mentally, emotionally, or/and spiritually!

The Spiritual Message behind Candida
(Healing First-, Second-, and Third-Chakra Issues)

It is my belief that the manifestation of unresolved emotional trauma and negative mental toxicity play a large role in the overgrowth of harmful bacteria as a result of *candida albicans* infection (thrush).

Emotional and psychological trauma are considered anything which is perceived as traumatic to the spirit. Anything from natural disasters, accidents, physical pain, and sickness to anything else which brings psychological, physical, or emotional pain.

Anyone who is familiar with candida albicans, a form of pathogenic yeast that lives in the human gut, knows to avoid sugar, yeast, and antibiotics because they contribute to the overgrowth of the candida itself (candidiasis), which in turn promotes the growth of harmful bacteria and the suppression of beneficial bacteria, especially in the intestinal tract. Individuals who suffer from candidiasis manifest physical ailments such as bloating, fatigue, mind fog, spaciness, headaches, irritable bowel syndrome, thrush, and muscle and joint aches, among other things.

Having effectively treated myself and others with candidiasis, I believe all major imbalances and chronic diseases stem from candida (fungal) overgrowth and the resulting overabundance of bad bacteria allowed to thrive in the digestive tract. It is important to realize that the diseases and imbalances caused by candida differ from person to person. Everything from depression to chronic fatigue syndrome to cancer can manifest in people who suffer from candidiasis. The reason is because candida suffocates the immune system and deteriorates the digestive tract.

Candida grows through the intestinal wall, causing a condition known as leaky gut syndrome. This is where undigested food particles enter the blood stream. Candida also produces biotoxins which have their own negative side effects aside from leaky gut. However, to cut to the chase, the overall digestive and immune systems are compromised, causing the individual to become more susceptible to nutritional deficiencies and infections.

The reason there is a correlation between candida and healing the spirit is because any situation which makes us question ourselves and look to ourselves begins with a situation that triggers our survival instinct. The freeze response of our survival instinct is a spiritual factor. When the freeze response is triggered, an individual is unable to psychologically "integrate" the traumatic event because the situation was overwhelming. When this happens, we feel frozen and stuck The stagnant energy stays within our energy body and etheric level of our aura until it is revisited, integrated, and released.

If the negative psychological or/and emotional energy isn't released, later experiences can re-trigger the unresolved trauma. Unresolved trauma is seen as energy blockages and/or spiritual blocks. These blocks cause the body to become over-reactionary, causing an overactive immune system. The physical and psychological manifestations of candida cause the individual to unconsciously form habits, conditions, and patterns of behavior that are sabotaging to their overall well-being.

Unresolved emotional trauma affects not only the endocrine system but the limbic system, which over time causes abnormal impulses affecting the central nervous system, cells, and organ tissue.

Detoxifying and releasing unresolved emotional trauma by healing the spirit is just as important as diet, lifestyle, and other biochemical approaches. There are many holistic and spiritual programs and rituals to heal candida. I personally offer spiritual response therapy (SRT), energy healing, and psychic healing combined with nutritional and lifestyle recommendations. If you suspect you have candidiasis, it is best to begin a daily healing regimen as soon as possible.

If you are unsure whether you have a candida overgrowth, stool testing along with adrenal stress testing is the most accurate and best way to go.

Some recommendations for healing candidiasis are to avoid heavy metals and consider working with a certified holistic health coach to do a metal cleanse. Metals such as aluminum come from antacids and food additives, while wood preservatives, antiperspirants, water supplies, pesticides, and paint, contain arsenic. Some sources of cadmium are cigarette smoke, refined grains, shellfish, tuna, organ meats, soft drinks, batteries, tea, and coffee.

Metal cleanses also include lead and mercury cleanses. Lead is contained in cosmetics, hair coloring, old plumbing, and glazed pottery. Mercury buildup is caused by consuming non-organic fruit, vegetables, and grains because they are treated with mercury-based fungicides. Also, avoid vaccines, atmospheric pollutants, and seafood because they, too, have mercury.

A general diet with nutritional supplementation for treating candida overgrowth can be followed, but for best results, work with a certified holistic health coach because every individual is uniquely different. However, some suggestions are: follow the nutritional balancing diet, eat a lot of dietary fiber, follow a diet low in sugar (both natural and refined), incorporate enzymes and probiotics, incorporate a daily antifungal like Bragg's apple cider vinegar.

The nutritional balancing diet consists of: 20% high-protein foods, such as fish, chicken, duck, seeds, and eggs; 10% complex carbohydrates, such as rice, beans, and oats; 5% fresh fruits; and 65% vegetables.

The ideal diet for those who suffer from candida is one that is high in fiber and protein. Some acceptable foods are:

Grains: whole amaranth, whole barley, buckwheat, under-germinated corn meal, popcorn, millet, brown basmati rice, Texmati brown rice, Wehani brown rice, rye flour, spelt, whole teff and teff flour, wheat berries, unprocessed wheat bran, Japanese soba or rice noodles

Legumes: black-eyed peas, chick peas, garbanzo beans, lentils, soybeans, soy flakes, split peas

Dairy: plain yogurt and acidophilus culture

Nuts and seeds: almonds, Brazil nuts, cashews, hazelnuts, macadamia nuts, pecans, pine nuts, poppy seeds, pumpkin seeds, sesame seeds, sunflower seeds and tahini

Fruit: fresh lemon, lime, tomato, and eggplant

Vegetables: beans, broccoli, Brussels sprouts, cabbage, cauliflower, celery, cucumbers, green peppers, kale, lettuce, onions, radishes, parsley, peas, salad rocket or arugula, spinach, tomatoes

Beverages: unsweetened almond, soy, or other plant-protein milk, toasted-whole-barley coffee substitute (without malt), pau d'arco tea, plain or carbonated water

Condiments and seasonings: chicken broth without sweetener or yeast, fresh garlic, fresh ginger, fresh herbs, fresh onion, cilantro, pepper, pink or sea salt, raw apple cider

Meats: Antibiotics in meats that are not organic can make candida worse. When you cannot get organic meats, choose wild game meats such as antelope, bear, buffalo, duck, caribou, venison, elk, frog, quail, moose, and turkey.

These foods, when taken in recommended portions, will foster healthy levels of candida, a healthy immune system, and a strong physical body.

Supplements to kill candida: oregano, Pau d'arco, garlic, propolis, neem, golden seal, echinacea, clove, olive leaf, colloidal silver, castor bean oil, grapefruit seed extract, and oregano oil

Anti-parasitic herbs: black walnut, Blastocystis, hominis C

Vitamins and minerals: biotin (3 to 6 times per day); copper and zinc (work together to heal IBS caused by candida)

Antioxidants: vitamins A, B, E, and C help with infection from fungi micro-punctures

More herbs: chlorophyll, bitters, and phellostatin

Anti-inflammatories: cayenne, marshmallow root, slippery elm bark, comfrey leaf and root, aloe vera, chaparral, thyme, ginger, moringa

Electrolytes: to balance pH levels

Incorporating intestinal hydrotherapies and coffee colonics is also helpful.

The Sacral Chakra

All-around wellness is not just the absence of diseases; it is being physically and emotionally able to joyfully be in alignment with our deepest and truest selves. The sacral chakra provides the "oomph" to living human experience because it represents our emotional center.

The sacral, or second, chakra rules our vital sensual body. It is the mammalian portion of our brain where the limbic system controls memories and emotions. It also contributes to our creativity and learning processes because it is where memories and emotions combine. Our endocrine system is also associated with the sacral chakra because of its location (right below the navel and above the pubic bone).

Since the brain's centers for emotions and memories are intimately related, unhealed and repressed emotions from past experiences reflect in present situations, manifesting the same undesirable feelings until healed.

How balanced our second chakra is not only dictates our emotional responses but also represents themes in the karmic lessons we will experience throughout our lifetime. The sacral chakra holds energetic patterns of any addictions as well as repeating relationship patterns.

Our emotional areas of life are embodied by the second chakra. Psychologically, the second chakra translates to our sensuality, intimacy, self-acceptance, and all relationships.

A healthy understanding of the nature and meaning of relationships is having a happy attitude towards others and having a strong sense of security in oneself. Individuals who have second-chakra imbalances have abandonment issues, have trust issues, and tend to lose themselves in their relationships.

The second chakra is the chakra which helps us achieve and sustain attachments to other people, beginning with the vital maternal cord known as the umbilical cord.

Weakness and imbalances within the second chakra lead to extreme empathy, which causes one to be guided by the emotions of others. Failing to heal imbalances can also manifest in a complete an utter lack of emotions.

The second chakra deals with dualities, such as yin and yang, male and female, light and dark. When we have blocks within the second chakra, we become imbalanced. Spiritual imbalances manifest as emotional and physical imbalances which affect physical life experiences and physical health.

The areas of the physical body governed by the sacral chakra include: genitals, reproductive organs, the sacrum and lumbar vertebrae (lower spine), stomach, liver, gall bladder, pancreas, kidneys, spleen, upper intestines.

The second chakra is formed between the ages of two and four, when an individual learns to live beyond basic survival consciousness. It is a time when children are not only determining their place in the family but their own unique individuality.

A balanced second chakra manifests as easygoing, expressive, compassionate, emotionally sound, balanced, warm, and joyful. Whereas an imbalanced sacral chakra's symptoms are being addictive, obsessive, controlling, guilty, depressed, creativity-blocked, overly sensitive, frigid, angry, and fearful.

Healing the Sacral Chakra—Facts, Techniques, and Tips

1. Food therapy: Eat orange foods, such as oranges, mangos, sweet potatoes, curry, orange pepper, etc.

2. Movement: hula hoop, yoga poses (angel forward bend, pigeon pose, and bound ankle pose)

3. Essential oils: sandalwood, rose, vanilla, orange peel, jasmine

4. Mantra: VAM

5. Vowel: O

6. Music note: D

7. Chakra element: water

8. Sense: taste (represents the sweetness of life)

9. Crystal healing: carnelian, coral, gold, calcite, amber, citrine, gold topaz, moonstone

10. Symbols: the crescent moon and the six-petal lotus (represents responsibilities and harmony in your environment and the people you share your environment with)

11. Sweet foods

12. Bach flower essences: oak, olive, pine

13. The second chakra name in Sanskrit: Svadisthana (meaning *sweetness*)

14. Affirmations: "I enjoy life, I accept myself, I trust I am loved, and I deserve happiness."

Cosmic Laws

Cosmic laws are also known as nature's laws. These laws explain how the universe works. Cosmic laws function on many different planes and in many different dimensions. They encompass the physical, mental, and spiritual. Everything is governed and controlled by cosmic laws, whether we are conscious or not.

By knowing and understanding cosmic laws, we automatically promote our own spiritual growth and evolution. All laws are interrelated. Cosmic laws are an integral part of nature. We apply and operate those laws to co-create successfully with the universe. The principles are guidelines concerning the nature of the law. Cosmic laws come from one universal mind. Some call that universal mind *God*.

The Law of Karma: "What we sow, we will reap." Our thoughts, deeds, and whatever we put our energy toward all have consequences, and they always reflect back to us through our physical world experiences. The law of karma doesn't go by moral code or judgments; it is neutral. Karma's only purpose is to help us learn and evolve into a higher state of consciousness. This higher state of conscious is one of God consciousness (Christ consciousness, universal consciousness).

The Law of Grace and Mercy: This can neutralize an individual's karma. The neutralizing energy lessens the consequences of karma. When a person takes responsibility for their behaviors and actions which caused the negative karma, it activates the law of grace and mercy. Forgiveness is a sub-law of grace.

The Law of Motion: Everything is in motion in the physical universe, and motion is found in every atom within the galaxy. Motion is the manifestation of life. Nothing is absolutely still, regardless of perspective. When we do not move, our energy becomes stagnant. Stagnant energy causes energy blockages which manifest as sickness and disease in the physical body. Energy moves in all different directions and realms. Energy which is considered time is linear and is divided into the past, present, and future—chronological time in the physical realm. In the spiritual realm, time doesn't exist.

The Law of Becoming: Motion that results in transformation—a change in position, magnitude, quality, nature, etc. Inertia doesn't exist in God's creation. Inertia is a violation of the cosmic law of "progress." Death does not exist; in reality, it relates to transition and transformation. Humans have the capability to will and direct their energy and free will to be what they choose.

The Law of Evolution. Becoming more God-like: evolving into oneness and becoming more awakened. Evolution expands consciousness and improves the quality of life. Reincarnation is the periodical incarnation of God into the physical realm, for the purpose of his evolution. We learn from spiritual lessons and soul relationships. Unfortunately, the karma we incarnate with binds us to karmic debt, the reason why souls forget their true purpose.

The Law of Correspondence, also known as The Law of Reflection: This cosmic law helps us understand the higher dimensions by carefully examining and analyzing our physical world. Understanding what we feel and perceive on the inside allows us to see how we manifest things on the outside, in the physical world.

This also helps us understand that what we think about consciously and unconsciously creates our energy vibration and frequencies. These frequencies make us a magnet for matching vibrational frequencies (like goes to like). This psychic energy manifests in your life unconsciously.

The Law of One: This refers to everything being connected. Everything that is manifested in the universe is an expression of God and God's expression. The law of one can also be called the law of unity, the blending of the mind with all minds of life.

The Law of Duality: Any force or concept can be divided into two opposite forces, each containing an essence of the other. Opposites can only be defined in relation to each other. Duality is a sense of perception of one's universe other than *them*, *you*, and *I*. Duality is an illusion of the senses. The absolute state only knows one. The law of opposites relates to the law of duality and the law of polarity.

The Law of Trinity, also known as the Law of the Triangle: The law of trinity is an expression of the law of creation within all creating energies in the universe. These energies give birth to the law of formation. An example of trinity would be the Father, Son, and Holy Ghost. The law of trinity functions as two parts, as a marriage to create union and birth.

Healing Spiritual Blocks to Restore Spiritual Equilibrium

Spiritual blocks are another way of saying negative core beliefs. Our core beliefs are the very essence of how we see ourselves.

Spiritual blocks stop us from living as our true and authentic selves. Spiritual blocks are made of thought energy, otherwise known as astral energy, and emotional energy.

Spiritual blocks can be felt within the physical body as tension and stress and felt within the emotional body as anxiety and depression. Our negative core beliefs are rigid and inflexible and are maintained by focusing on information which supports these beliefs and ignoring evidence which contradicts them. This is usually done unconsciously.

Spiritual blocks have the power to bleed into every area of a person's life because they affect the mind. The subconscious mind is the part of our mind which relates to the ego and survival. When we are blocked from perceived traumas, we become disconnected, detached, and unconscious of how we have contributed to our undesirable experience. This causes us to become emotionally imbalanced because the negative emotions do not dissipate until integrated.

Equilibrium is a state in which opposing forces or actions balance; one is not greater than the other. Spirituality is about self. Spiritual equilibrium means to balance the shadow aspects of self with the light aspects of self to create overall wellness in the body, mind, and spirit.

In order to restore spiritual equilibrium, one must clear negative beliefs and incorporate empowering and supportive beliefs. Understand that beliefs are not caused; they are created, and many times created from past experiences or past perceptions of experiences. Our environment, society, peers, and media can all trigger a person to become spiritually blocked. Many times, our blocks become activated in emotionally charged situations.

Our beliefs affect our thoughts, feelings, attitudes, and judgments, consciously and unconsciously. It is imperative to heal spiritual blocks in order to experience the life and life experiences we want to have.

The first step to healing is understanding that your beliefs dictate your life, and in order to manifest the life experiences you want to have, your beliefs have to be congruent with the outcomes you seek. Identifying your limiting beliefs is done by allowing yourself to be the witness, without judgment, to what you feel.

Many blocks are around money, worth, love, and success. Understanding that our outer world mirrors our internal world gives us big clues to what needs healing within our own lives. Letting our own thoughts and emotions guide us in the healing process allows us to go at our own pace.

Judging ourselves in how we heal or where we are in our healing blocks the process. The steps to healing are accepting, experiencing, and letting go. And no one step is more important than another. Each step in the healing process must be honored. Becoming the witness allows us to become aware, but not until we feel the emotion do we experience how the situation has affected us.

Letting go is usually the hardest stage in the healing process because it means we have worked through all the raw emotions and have fully integrated the lessons we have learned.

Tips for Healing Spiritual Blocks

Be mindful of your thoughts.

Restate judgments you have in terms of consequences.

Look at your entire situation; look for what is being left out instead of focusing on the aspects which support your negative belief.

When overwhelmed by emotion, remember to breathe, relax, feel, watch, allow, and let go.

Spiritual equilibrium comes from balancing the light aspects of ourselves, which is considered the spirit part of self, with the human ego part of ourselves.

When we are balanced, we can receive spiritual guidance and ground that knowledge into the physical realm. This is how we consciously co-create with the universe to manifest.

To determine your spiritual blocks, book a psychic soul reading or karmic and spiritual block clearing, please go to http://www.pureenergyhealer.com.

Channel Building for Psychic/Spiritual Healing

When doing energy work for healing or any other self-transformation, it is important to increase and balance one's energy. To raise your vibrational frequency, there are many different types of exercises to build, strengthen, and expand your ability to channel energy for healing.

Chi, *mana*, *prana* and *ki* are all words that refer to life-force energy. Tai chi, chi gong, yoga, and dance are a few physical activities that help in increasing this life force, while meditation and toning raise frequency and increase energy on a vibrational and energetic level. Alternating between physical, mental, and spiritual techniques ensures the channeler balance and helps them to avoid getting drained.

Channel Building

The purpose of channel building is to strengthen the flow of energy for healing.

All human beings have meridians (energy pathways) which govern all systems—immune, digestive, endocrine, etc.—in the physical body. How well an individual's energy flows distinguishes their wellness. Stagnant energy, known as spiritual blocks or energy blockages, causes many different types of imbalances which lead to disease.

There are as many channel-building exercises as there are healers. No method is better than another. It is strictly the healer's preference. I personally like to use the microcosmic orbit also known as the self-winding wheel of the law and the circulation of light.

The home practice for the microcosmic orbit is twenty minutes long and is a sitting or lying-down meditation.

1. The first steps are to still the body, calm the mind, and regulate the breath. If you are sitting, make sure that your spine is upright.

2. Focus your attention below your solar plexus center (navel) and visualize a ball of energy while keeping your focus on your solar plexus until you can feel the energy from the ball. This can come in the form of heat, vibration, and/or a sensation. Remember—everyone experiences energy differently.

3. Begin abdominal breathing. This breathing method starts by inhaling through the nose so your abdominal area expands (not your chest) Exhale through a slightly opened mouth, keeping your tongue behind your upper teeth so it is lightly touching the palate. Exhale so abdominal muscles contract and air expels gently.

4. Inhale and visualize an energy ball moving through your navel chakra past the *Hui Yin* (the center of the perineum gland). This is our center which controls balance. Then visualize the energy moving up through the coccyx and visualize the energy going up to the *Ming Men*, a center which is located between the kidneys and second lumbar. This center is considered a very powerful energy center in Chinese medicine. Then see the energy ball where your ribs meet the spine, continuing through this area, and right up to the back of the head, where it joins the neck.

5. Visualize the energy ball in the center of your brain, taking in energy through the crown chakra.

6. Next, focus your attention on your third eye, draw in energy from the kidneys and liver, then feel the energy go through the roof of your mouth (this can cause tingling or throbbing). This is the end of the inhalation.

The microcosmic orbit is good for all forms of running and channeling energy. Even though the microcosmic orbit is a Taoist meditation, it can be combined with other energy work derived from different cultures. For instance, many people use this Taoist method before doing a Japanese Usui Reiki healing. The microcosmic is just one technique for circulating and refining energy.

I use this method of channel building before I begin any psychic readings or do any type of healing practice or ritual. Doing spiritual/psychic work requires a lot of energy. Doing psychic readings and spiritual work for a living can easily drain or imbalance my energy if I do not channel build prior to work.

It is important to remember that our life-force energy circulates around the body in the network of meridians. Our life force nourishes and supports all our organs and body systems. The microcosmic meditation allows us to dissolve energy blockages before they turn into physical imbalances that cause disease.

Spiritual Integration of the Shadow Self

Psychologists and spiritualists alike have studied the shadow aspects of man since the beginning of time. The shadow is the ego part of self, the dust of man. This part of man perceives himself and his outer world from the experiences he has had and his environment. Individuals who have suffered from psychological and emotional abuse manifest many soul wounds (also known as *samskaras*).

Samskaras are a combination of astral energy and emotional energy. The energy of a samskara is held in the physical body as stress. It is where our energy vibration comes from. Individuals who vibrate at a lower frequency have more samskaras, which means more ego, and less love and light, which are of one's true self.

Samskaras cause unconscious conditions which are habitual behaviors. Conditions become neurological pathways within the mind. The ego mind's main concern is survival. Whether it's emotional, physical, psychological, or spiritual, the mind doesn't know the difference. Conditions caused by psychological trauma, depersonalization disorder, and feelings of detachment from the physical body make it difficult to stay present and more likely to repeat unconscious sabotaging behaviors.

Spiritual integration is spiritual healing at the deepest level. Integrating the shadow aspects of self makes us feel whole and brings us back to our truth and divinity. Society's greatest pain is caused from the illusion that we are separate from our creator.

If you experience anger, resentment, fear, and any lower vibrational energy after being triggered emotionally, you need to integrate an aspect of yourself. It is important to note that often there isn't a memory to go along with a sensation or feeling. The body holds on to memories, sensations, and feelings in the pain body. Many times, babies have traumatic experiences before their logical thinking is developed, and this would be one example of how an individual may not remembering mentally yet physically have sensations and feelings related to an unconscious trauma.

Severe trauma that is physical, psychological, and/or emotional becomes stagnant in the pain body. Over time, stagnant energy affects all major systems of the body—the endocrine system, digestive system, immune system, and nervous system.

The first step of spiritual integration is to surrender. The spiritual law of resistance tells us what we resist persists. To surrender is to look at yourself, the situation, and/or person without judgment.

Judgment keeps us locked into feeling victimized and powerless. To begin to surrender is to look at yourself from a spiritual perspective, to realize we are in physical form to learn and manifest. To know all experiences, good and bad, will lead to the greatest spiritual gifts, once integrated.

To be without judgment is to love yourself in the process of spiritual integration. By understanding the meaning of our negative emotions, we allow ourselves to see different realities and dimensions of ourselves, which then brings us closer to oneness.

Acceptance means accepting your emotions, uncovering unconscious feelings which cause sabotaging behaviors. During integration, you must have full self-acceptance. This does not mean you approve of an event or person which has harmed you but rather, you have an acceptance of the experience.

Experiences happen on a feeling level, where we are most unconscious/unaware. To completely heal, one must allow themselves to feel deeply without resistance. The purpose of life is to awaken our sleeping creative intelligence so we can return back to universal oneness.

All resistance causes pain. To integrate our shadow, we must come into the moment by activating witness consciousness. Be sure to remember self-rejection prevents negative energy from dissolving. It also amplifies the negative feeling. One must come into a space of surrender and acceptance; acceptance eventually leads to forgiveness.

The mental processing steps for shadow integration are:

1) Awareness

2) Acceptance

3) Feeling the direct experience emotionally and physically

4) Transformation, which leads to spiritual transcendence

Awareness of the event includes owning one's behavior, becoming conscious of how one has contributed to their undesirable life experiences. When we come into a space of acceptance, it means mentally, we cease resistance.

One becomes blocked by various self-rejecting ways of thinking. The act of acceptance allows us to become conscious, which brings us into the direct experience related to the physical body, and the body brings us into the moment, thereby allowing us to dissolve the energy with awareness, surrender, and forgiveness.

The transformational stage is where the shift takes place. Only through the body can the gateway to healing spiritually and energetically be conducted.

Our beliefs act like filters through which we perceive reality. Some of our beliefs are formed from suppressed energy caused from painful experiences. This leads to irrational, limited, and destructive behaviors. Suppression is a psychological mechanism which begins with resistance. It works internally as well as externally. Internally, it is felt as detachment and negative emotions. Outwardly, suppression of negative emotions manifests as imbalanced relationships, physical imbalances, and undesirable life experiences. Suppression leads to repression, which manifests as conditions such as neurosis, addiction, and depression, to name just a few. Addiction exaggerates duality.

In order to heal, one must learn to use the negative attributes they find proactively by understanding the dualistic components.

Feeling Through the Body and the Body/Mind Connection

This stage of integration is where one works with the body to see psychological change. Many times, we turn away from feelings to protect ourselves from perceived pain, leading to a lack of body awareness. Body/mind medicine and energy psychology are two modalities that help to integrate the body and mind back into balance.

Our chakras are our psychic/spiritual center, but each chakra also represents a physical aspect of self. Our chakras are directly linked to specific organs and systems within the body. Negative energy stored within the body becomes trapped in muscle tissue and organ tissues, causing physical imbalances that lead to circulation problems and physical illness.

Repeated karmic patterns are considered karmic loops. Karmic contracts are unconscious decisions, beliefs, perceptions, and attitudes which bind us to people. Codependent relationships that are polarizing are an example of karmic contracts. Every time a karmic block gets activated by triggers, the block accumulates more emotional energy. Over time the energy becomes solidified, giving it a magnetic pull, bringing those same frequencies to us. Since beliefs hold emotional reactions, one must learn what their underlying beliefs are and how they cause us to react emotionally.

The first steps in this clearing process are:

1) Ask yourself what you believe about your situation.

2) Describe in a few words how you feel.

3) Let go of judgments so you can identify the limiting patterns.

4) Forgive yourself.

5) Forgive others.

6) Verbalize out loud a forgiveness statement.

7) Transcend the negative effects of karma by surrendering.

8) Exhale with a big belly breath. (This activates the nervous system to detox and relax.)

It is important to note that our emotional body lives in the past and remembers habits and conditions we formed then. Many times, this occurred in our childhood to support our well-being. Unfortunately, what was supportive in childhood is not always supportive in the present. Letting go of these attachments allows us to be in alignment with our true self so we can co-create with God and the universe successfully, which leads to living in one's bliss.

Soul Relationships, Spiritual Tests, Karmic Programs, and Humanity's Evolution

Karmic relationships are a big part of our spiritual evolution. We can experience a karmic relationship with anyone—a child, parent, friend, lover, or even someone you work with.

All karmic relationships are gifts that teach us about ourselves, God, and our union together. Many times, karmic associations are difficult and challenging because of emotional ups and downs. The emotional roller coaster is a manifestation of the psychological and emotional imbalances within each person. The imbalance is normally caused because the relationship is lacking on a spiritual and mental level and yet there is a strong physical and emotional connection.

Most of the time, karmic relationships are established because we see something in the other person which we believe can help us overcome our own karma and/or perceived limitations.

Not all karmic relationships are soulmate or "twin flame" relationships. Before we incarnated, we each made a conscious choice to come together with another soul so that we could share, support, learn, forgive, grow, heal, and resolve past-life issues. In short, to expand conscious and spiritual awareness.

There are several defining characteristics of karmic relationships. I have listed the most obvious ones below.

1. Instant familiarity and recognition of each other on some level, especially when there is no way you have ever met before

2. Strong and often unexplainable attraction

3. An intensity to the relationship, either positive or negative

4. A tendency for the relationship to become the most dominant

5. A deep emotional or physical connection that often has an addictive quality

6. An ability to really press each other's buttons

7. An inability to easily walk away, regardless of how toxic

8. A feeling of the need to stay so that you can work through or resolve something

9. Codependency

Usually, karmic relationships serve to bring people together for a definite purpose. Once the purpose has been fulfilled, the intense karmic connection is usually broken.

It is important to know that we have many soul mates. Soul mates are usually a karmic-based relationship. This means that we have karmic debts or lessons to learn from the other person.

Usually, the other person has as much to learn as we do. If you have karma to resolve in a close relationship, it is easy to get sucked into a whirlpool of repetitive past patterns and behaviors; you are compelled to do this because they are familiar.

Making new patterns takes much more effort—and can bring unsettling change. It could mean having to look at yourself in a new light, which can feel daunting and emotionally taxing.

I have definitely had my share of soul relationships. Some were short lived and wonderful, while others were a chaotic, hot mess from the beginning. Nevertheless, they all helped me spiritually evolve enough to trust myself and know exactly what I need and want in all my relationships. Those gifts can't be bought, and they have brought me the most satisfaction and fulfillment to date.

Relationship problems? Heal yourself of negative karmic relationships, cut psychic cords, remove entities with a psychic spiritual reading and spiritual clearing.

Psychic Cords

(Healing Yourself of Toxic Relationships and Healing Second-Chakra Imbalances)

There are many ways to describe a psychic experience, but the simplest definition is understanding or knowing through sensing. Reading psychic energy is like learning an energetic language. We receive information through our five senses—sight, sound, taste, touch, and smell—as well as through our inner knowing.

Intuition, telepathy, and empathy are each referred to as a sixth sense. Psychic energy is free-flowing energy. It's considered creative energy and is more like daydreaming and imagination than logical thinking.

Throughout history, psychics, mystics, witches, wizards, and sorcerers have known about psychic chords. Psychic chords are energetic ties between people. They are not seen with our eyes; they are sensed and felt. Cords are energetically connected to the spirit body, otherwise known as our chakras.

Psychic cords work like an energetic umbilical cord between two people who can send and receive information to each other. Some examples are mother and daughter, lovers, friends, and siblings. Psychic cords give and take energy telepathically and act as an energetic link between two people.

We are all connected to one another through energetic and emotional energy. Each and every time we interact with another, we create an energetic exchange on a subtle level. Even when we separate, energetic and emotional ties many times remain. Energetic ties are not restricted by time and space, so you can be connected to someone from your past, someone who lives far away, and even to someone who is no longer living.

Between two people, emotional and energetic ties are structures of energy which cause negative patterns from the past to constantly be relived. Cords and attachments are open channels that flow with and without conscious knowledge from either person. Cords connect through subtle energy.

When you establish any kind of relationship, two structures are formed. The first one is of divine energy for the spirit part of self. This is known as a soul's bond. The second structure contains negative patterns and dynamics of the relationship. This is called attachment cords. The astral-level attachments contribute negative patterns which affect both people.

Patterns of negative thoughts and emotions circulate in cords. And some cords aren't just draining; they can cause negative behaviors, as well. Psychic cords are not always negative, however. Some are a result of an emotional exchange.

Negative cords will continually take and drain energy until they are removed and energy is no longer feeding them. Individuals who have removed their cords feel lighter, have more energy, focus, and clarity and have an overall sense of power.

Many times, we are not conscious of energetic ties, so they repeat. A good way to see if you have a cord is to think of a person involved in an emotionally draining situation you've experienced. Then see what negative emotions bubble up and linger. When negative emotions arise, it shows there is still an energetic investment you have with this person.

When we feel drained after spending time around certain people, it's a sign that energy is leaking. Feeling brain-fogged, confused, disoriented, angry, or fatigued are all clear indicators of unhealthy cords.

People prone to draining energy through cords include those who are chronically physically, mentally, or emotionally sick, drug abusers, alcoholics, emotionally needy, fearful, aggressive and argumentative, victims, and complainers.

Negative cords help us grow spiritually. They help us evolve and strive for better life experiences and relationships. We learn that in dealing with the negative aspects of cords we expand in consciousness and grow spiritually.

It is very important to know that in order for a cord to be fully severed, one has to understand the energies which have formed it. Cutting an energy cord does not affect the other person, however. You can only change your own energy and emotions because everyone has free will.

It is not necessary to believe in cord cutting in order for it to work, although understanding the spiritual dynamic makes healing faster and easier.

There are many different methods of cord cutting, and there is no incorrect way. The most important part of cutting a cord is having the intention to do so. The most important factors are finding out what was contained within the cord and what changes will occur within your life after the cord is cut.

Cords represent spiritual lessons which lead to self-healing and our evolution.

Steps to Cutting Cords:

1. Sit quietly in a place where you are unlikely to be disturbed. Try to ensure that no one else is likely to sit where you regularly choose to meditate by moving the sofa or your chair for meditation.

2. Close your eyes and ask for protection on all levels. Start with a prayer: "Please send me protection on all levels from the

source, the manifestation of the source, and the energy behind the source."

3. Offer thanks for the protection you are receiving.

4. Ask for the light to enter your crown chakra and to pass through your body, out through your feet, and into the earth.

5. Offer thanks for the light three times.

6. Feel the light entering your crown and pouring down through your body, cleansing and re-balancing you as it sweeps through your head, neck, shoulders, chest and lungs, spine, your lower torso, your legs, feet, and toes.

7. In case you need to clear a path for the light to enter your crown, take a deep breath and imagine a small whirlwind of white light spinning from your crown, the center of the top of your head.

8. Spend a few minutes becoming aware of the light as it sweeps through your body. If you feel tension or imbalances in any part of your body, concentrate the light on those areas to ensure that they return to balance.

9. When you feel relaxed and calm, take another deep breath.

10. As you release this breath, force a whirlwind of white light out through your third-eye chakra (at the center of your forehead).

11. Now allow this whirlwind of white light to pass around your body from right to left, cutting all of your cords as it does so.

12. When the whirlwind has encircled your body three times, mentally direct it out the window and off into space.

13. Return your awareness to your physical body by thinking of your body. Allow the white light to flow more freely down through your body for a few minutes now.

(After you have cut psychic cords to your body, it becomes easier to concentrate and to enjoy a deep meditation. Often it is our psychic cords to others which prevent us from being centered in the present.)

14. Prepare to end your meditation by offering thanks and requesting that the light cease to flow through your body. If it continues to flow through your body at the rate it does in this meditation, you'll become a beacon for lost souls, and needy friends and strangers are likely to cord you for your energy.

15. Offer thanks for this three times.

16. Prepare to close your chakras to contain the energies you have just received. This is done from the feet up, by concentrating on your feet chakras and visualizing them shrinking to around 2 centimeters (1/2 an inch) in diameter.

17. Finally, close your crown chakra to the same size as the others.

18. Take three deep breaths and open your eyes.

Take a moment to notice how you feel after this process. If you have effectively completed each step, you are likely to feel calm, centered, and at peace with yourself.

The purpose of asking for protection from advanced spiritual beings such as Jesus, Buddha, Mohammed, or any of the ascended masters is to protect you from spiritual entities which may seek to distract you from your spiritual purpose. It is simply the process of requesting support from a more experienced spiritual being.

Healing Depersonalization Disorder (Healing First-, Second-, and Third-Chakra Imbalances)

Have you ever felt disconnected from your body, almost as if you were watching yourself on a movie screen? Depersonalization disorder occurs from trauma and in most cases, it occurs from psychological, physical, and/or emotional abuse.

I have spent a large part of my healing journey learning about depersonalization disorder in order to heal myself as well as many of my clients.

Having depersonalization disorder myself, I know that we wind up watching our lives instead of living them. It is as if our lives unfold into situations that we had no control over. This causes us to not trust ourselves and over time to manifest physical and emotional imbalances. Some manifestations of imbalances are anxiety and depression as well as other negative emotions which eventually turn into physical ailments, addictions, and disorders.

Until a person recognizes and heals from depersonalization disorder, they will continue to form negative habits, conditions, and reflexes. These patterns mirror previous events and situations. Having depersonalization disorder causes people to "check out." For many people, it is a way of dealing with their trauma.

Thankfully, learning about depersonalization disorder allowed me to understand that becoming detached is a normal psychological and physical response to being traumatized.

Understanding what depersonalization disorder is, is crucial for the overall healing process—for the millions of people who suffered from psychological, physical, or emotional trauma and for those who have done healing work but haven't seen results they desire.

Depersonalization disorder causes individuals to become robbed of life, making life impossible to enjoy. It causes individuals to have intense fear, making them feel unstable and not in control of their life.

The first step to healing is awareness. Symptoms in the physical body are also good indicators of what needs to be healed in the spirit body. Some manifestations of having depersonalization disorder are lack of concentration and focus, learning issues, digestive and immune-system disorders, anxiety, depression, brain fog, fatigue, forgetfulness, feeling spacey, low self-esteem, and feeling out of touch with the world and yourself.

Healing depersonalization disorder is slow and needs constant reinforcement, but it is possible and can be done.

I have found through my own healing of depersonalization disorder that releasing emotions in a ritualistic manner such as journaling, automatic writing, dream therapy, and clearing meditations were all helpful. Also, separating from who and what caused depersonalization disorder is imperative.

For healing depersonalization disorder, it is also important to mention that yoga and stretching along with breath work help assist in removing any negative emotional energy which is left in the energy body. This will also help the nervous system to become balanced.

After experiencing emotional abuse, healing the physical body through nutrition and lifestyle changes and spiritual rituals are all essential ways of clearing the physical body of left-over karmic residue caused by the events manifested by depersonalization disorder.

Doing grounding exercises upon waking in the morning is also extremely helpful in staying present and proactive in life. There are plenty of free grounding exercises on the internet.

Reciting positive affirmations, doing good deeds, surrounding yourself with positive people, joining clubs, and/or doing activities are all helpful for individuals with depersonalization disorder.

Workshops offered in holistic and spiritual healing for depersonalization disorder are offered through my meet-up http://www.meetup.com/holistic-and-spiritual-transitions/.

If you or someone you know is interested in healing depersonalization disorder, please contact me at http://www.pureenergyhealer.com. Soul readings, crystal healing, and karmic clearing are available for healing soul wounds and depersonalization disorder.

Healing and Full Body Consciousness
(Healing Root-Chakra Imbalances)

The definition of full body consciousness is knowing and being in tune with your body on a body, mind, and spirit level. Our bodies speak to us through sensations mostly known as our emotions and feelings.

Feelings such as tension, stress, butterflies, headaches, and nausea are just a few ways our body communicates to us that a situation, experience, person, or thing is not good for us. Just the same as feelings of happiness, joy, love, and excitement translate to something positive.

Having full body consciousness is to be aware of the messages you unconsciously broadcast out into the world. Most people are so busy in their everyday responsibilities of family, relationships, work, bills, etc., that they become disconnected from their bodies.

Negative emotions like fear, anger, jealousy, resentment, etc., are all emotions which create energy imbalances.

When experiencing a negative emotion, most people's energy goes up in their heads, causing them to think a lot. When our mind is stuck in a spin cycle of thought, we are no longer in the present moment. When we are not in the present moment, we are not in full body consciousness.

Individuals who need spiritual healing have a hard time staying in full body consciousness. Emotional, psychological, spiritual, and physical abuse and/or physical trauma cause depersonalization disorder, a form of detachment. This is where the person who has experienced the trauma becomes disconnected from the details, feelings, emotions, and sensations around the trauma.

The negative energy which was caused by the experience is then held within all layers of our aura until we have learned and integrated its spiritual lesson. If we do not process the energy, it becomes stagnant within our energy body, causing energy blockages.

Energy blockages affect the spirit body through our chakras, our energy body through our meridians, our emotional body through our nervous system, our mental body through our thoughts, and our physical body through our cells. Spiritual healing is when we become the witness to how we feel and are able to take the appropriate actions to create balance—physically, mentally, psychologically, emotionally, and/or spiritually.

Being in full body consciousness allows us to direct our energy toward our dreams and desires instead of getting lost in the stories and chatter of the mind. Being aware of the body allows us to be present and proactive in the now. It is only in the now that the universe brings us the right experiences to help us achieve our physical goals and evolve spiritually.

The term *grounded* refers to mentally and emotionally being stable. Grounding is the awareness that we are in physical form called a body, which helps us evolve as spiritual beings. Some common symptoms of not being grounded are dizziness, daydreaming, weight gain, being accident prone, having anxiety, having depression, and being forgetful. These are just some manifestations of being out of balance. Grounding, on the other hand, makes it possible to detach from emotional pain and thus allows us to logically think in stressful and emotionally trying times.

Grounding can be done anytime and anywhere. The key to grounding is to focus on something in the now, such as your breath. are perceived. Some easy grounding techniques are to walk barefoot, sit on the ground, lean on a tree, do gardening and put your hands in dirt, dance, or simply breathe and pay attention to what you feel physically in the moment.

Some tips for staying grounded are:

1. Be around loving and supportive people and get rid of toxic relationships.
2. Work on building a strong sense of self and individual character.
3. Do something physical.
4. Look at emotionally charged situations through a different perspective by taking a step back.
5. Ask friends or family for their opinions on how your reactions are perceived.

When we are in full body consciousness, we are aware of our posture, the way we breathe, and how we interact with our environment and the people in it. We can create full body consciousness by setting goals, creating spiritual rituals which align habits to desires, and tapping into our own intuitive guidance.

Also, journaling and working with a partner or video to help create awareness are very helpful.

Being aware of the dialogue you have with your body is the best way to become conscious of what you are broadcasting out.

Being aware of how you speak about your body, what verbal tones you use, involuntary movements, body postures, and breathing are all a reflection of how a person feels about themselves. Many people unconsciously broadcast their wounds, perceptions, and beliefs, manifesting undesirable life experiences.

Your body is always sending out messages and signals as a way of communicating. The way we feel creates a state of mind and body on an unconscious level. A person's personality is comprised of attitudes, beliefs, behavioral patterns, emotional responses, social roles, and ancestral roles. Being in full body consciousness allows us to express ourselves proactively through our body's personality.

Finding Your Soul's Purpose

Two common questions I am asked as a spiritual advisor and psychic healer are: "What is my purpose?" and "Why am I here?"

So I have decided to write in response these because I am hearing them more frequently, especially with the world going through a paradigm shift, i.e., an awakening. Many people today feel very disconnected, not only from the earth but from themselves as well.

The reason is because they do not understand they are not here by chance but as part of God's and the universe's grand design. Unfortunately, society has taught us instead that the answer for our livelihood, success, and even our stability comes from resources that are outside of ourselves.

Spirituality as well as universal and metaphysical laws teach us that this left-brain way of thinking is limited and a poverty-conscious way of thinking. This makes people feel defective because it causes individuals to suffer with feelings that they aren't capable. This way of thinking causes anxiety and unnecessary feelings of being victimized instead of looking to what special traits, hobbies, gifts, or knowledge can be utilized to co-create with the universe.

It is through our own unique individuality and creativity we have free will to choose how we will contribute to humanity. It is through the spiritual law of *dharma* we know there is such a thing as a soul's path. Dharma basically means living "rightly" or in accordance with cosmic law. It is associated with terms like virtue, duty, conduct, purpose, and order.

Each of us was made in God's image, here to manifest in physical form, to fulfill a unique purpose, our dharma, our souls' purpose. Only then can we truly experience complete fulfillment.

When you live in the synchronicity flow of dharma, the entire field of new opportunities in alignment with your spiritual purpose opens. You're able to create abundance in wealth and emotional fulfillment because you're aligned with the Holy Spirit, an unlimited source of all manifestation.

The spiritual law of dharma lays out the three steps needed to align with Spirit and fulfill your life's purpose effortlessly. The first step is making the decision to seek your higher self. You come into the awareness that you are a spiritual being having a human experience. The spirit part of self is what is able to express itself creatively through our divinity.

The second step of the law of dharma is finding your unique talent or gift. The dharma says that there's at least one thing you can do better than anyone else on the entire planet. When you're completely absorbed in expression, time seems to stand still. You love what you're doing and you enter the universal state of timeless awareness of love.

To take the third step of the law of dharma, ask yourself these questions: "How can I use my unique talent to serve humanity? How can I help others?" When you are living it, you are living in the flow of the universe. When you put the law of dharma into action, you no longer struggle or worry and instead begin to experience your life as an ecstatic expression of divinity.

Unfortunately, without knowing or understanding the spiritual law of dharma, many people are ignorant to mastering their lives. Ironically, they would rather have someone tell them what to do to create fulfillment and security for themselves. This eventually leads to many spiritual imbalances which manifest into physical imbalances as well as undesirable life experiences.

The root causes of imbalances which manifest in the body, mind, and spirit come from depression. If we do not like many of our life experiences, we have to look at the way we think so we can begin to analyze our choices. Many of us have been taught what to think instead of how to think. This is the main reason so many people are unhappy.

If you have been struggling to find your purpose, you need ask yourself the following three questions. They will help you discover the qualities you possess that can be successfully translated into a career, profession, or your soul's purpose.

1) Where is your focus? Focus on the big picture rather than the specifics. The details will fill themselves in over time. Focus on the general direction you feel most drawn towards. Have a niche. Where do you lose your time, energy, focus, and money?

2) Connect the dots of your life experiences. Are you being led? What has created meaning in your life? Or what has affected you? Know your life's path or soul's purpose could evolve from a traumatic experience, such as recovering from an illness, losing a loved one, overcoming a learning disability, losing a home or child. The answer to how we use these traumatic events to find our soul's path often comes from learning how we overcame these hardships.

3) What hobbies and interests have you always had?

As for me, I was always into witches, the color purple, being sensitive and intuitive, creative, imaginative, and childlike.

All these characteristics are of an empathic psychic healer.

And by the way, purple is the color of healing, spirituality, and witchcraft.

There are many more stumbling blocks to manifesting than I have listed in my blog, but typically the ones listed below are the ones most people experience and struggle with. Removing these blocks initially unlocks your true potential.

1) Believing that one only need think of something for it to magically appear in their lives

2) Doubting one's ability to manifest

3) Not having the discipline to maintain the mindset and rituals of a true manifestor

4) Not knowing what is truly desired

5) Desiring to manifest from a place of lacking, rather than a place of abundance

6) Having a poverty-consciousness mentality

The Healing and Therapeutic Benefits of Drumming
(Healing the Body/Mind Connection)

Music is a universal language that transcends all barriers of race, culture, nation, and age. The word *rhythm* in the Greek dictionary means *flow*. Drums have been used for thousands of years for many purposes in many different cultures around the world. Healers known as shamans or witch doctors have used drums to help get into trance and reach different altered states of consciousness where they can connect to different cosmic and spiritual dimensions.

Drumming has many therapeutic effects on the body, mind, and spirit. It can be used as a powerful tool in reconditioning the body/mind connection and helps individuals who have post-traumatic stress disorder. Drumming also synchronizes non-verbal, lower parts of the brain with the language and reasoning parts of the brain, known as the frontal cortex.

Drumming is a workout for the mind that increases mindfulness and creativity because the coordination across both sides of the brain allows us to have insight. The transmission of rhythmic movement to the brain synchronizes the left logical hemisphere with the right intuitive hemisphere.

Drumming also creates deeper self-awareness by inducing synchronous brain activity. The sound waves produced by the drum impart their energy to the resonating systems of the body, mind, and spirit, making them vibrate in sympathy. When we drum, our energetic body, brainwaves, and spiritual energy centers begin to vibrate and hold the same resonance.

Trauma held in the body over time holds a dense, heavy, and lower energetic vibration. It is felt as stress. Drumming can shift, transmute, and transcend energy. The benefits of sympathetic resonance healing's effects last up to seventy-two hours after a drum session. These powerful effects influence the subtle energy centers known as chakras.

The physiological system that seems to correspond most directly with the chakras is the endocrine system. The endocrine system is a system of internal glands releasing messenger molecules into the bloodstream. Those molecules communicate with other organs and the nervous system and are known as hormones. There are many glands, as there are many chakras, but in biology, just like in spirituality, the focus is on seven that run from the base of the spine to the crown of your head.

Endocrine System/Chakras/Psychological and Physical Chakra

Healthy Integrated Function

Pineal/7th/Crown

The lymphatic system, body clock, fear of death/faith, inspiration, selfless service

Pituitary/6th/Brow

Soul realization, wisdom, peace of mind, 'boss' of the endocrine system, conscious living

Thyroid, Parathyroid, Hypothalamus/5th/Throat

Power of spoken word, creative expression, devotion to self, suffocation of life, involuntary systems (breathing, heart rate)

Thymus/8th/Christ Consciousness

Slow to mature, fear of rejection, self-acceptance, constant evolution, the bridge between dualities, creator of own world

Heart/4th/Heart

Understanding, group consciousness, ONE with ALL

Pancreas, Spleen/3rd/Solar plexus

Change, moodiness, personal power, authority, self-control, transformation, awakening

Ovaries, Testes/2nd/Sacral

Give/receive, movement, family, in/tolerance, harmony within a group

Adrenals/1st/Root

The material world, mastery of the physical world, overindulgence, fight/flight

Research has found that drummers have higher levels of a brain substance in the spinal cord that helps them solve their problems faster and more efficiently and helps their body produce white blood cells that protect them from cancer cells. Drumming is a moving meditation which not only helps to balance the left and right hemispheres of the brain but also helps reduce stress and enhance immune function.

Blood samples from participants of an hour-long drumming session revealed a reversal of the hormonal stress response and an increase in natural killer-cell activities.

Individuals who drummed in a weekly music therapy group were less anxious, less distressed, had higher self-esteem, and have shown an increase in natural killer-cell activity and an enhanced immune system.

The predictability of rhythm may provide the framework for repetitive responses that make few cognitive demands on people with dementia and reduce Alzheimer's disease. Rhythmic cues can help retrain the brain after a stroke or other neurological impairment, as well. Researchers have discovered that hearing slow, steady rhythms, such as drumbeats, allows Parkinson patients to move more steadily.

Drumming not only provides a medium for healing physical issues but also allows individual self-realization. Drumming helps us to reconnect to our core, enhancing healing while empowering and stimulating creative expression. Drumming is a channel for self-expression. It is non-verbal, emotion based, and sound mediated.

Each person in a drum circle can express themselves through their drum while listening to the other drums at the same time. Each person can drum out their feelings without having to reveal their issues. Group drumming complements traditional talk therapy methods. It provides a means of exploring and developing the inner self. It serves as a vehicle for personal transformation, consciousness expansion, and community building.

Healing Colon Cancer
(Healing Root-Chakra Imbalance)

Any cancer denotes longstanding resentment for some past experience that one is stuck in or can't move past. When dealing with a debilitating disease like colon cancer, it is advised to forgive yourself as well as others for all the sufferings that you have endured. While analyzing the metaphysical causes of disease, know that the right side of the body is associated with physical energies whereas the left side is related to emotional energies.

Poor digestion and constipation are manifestations of spiritual blocks of fear of the future and holding on to old ideas and feelings that no longer support one's highest good. These are also the spiritual and energetic causes of colon cancer.

The large intestine symbolizes the unconscious mind and shadow side of ourselves. Colon cancer is caused by suppressing negative emotions of fear and anger from the past. Problems of the colon stem from an unwillingness to or not knowing how to let go of the past. Clearing and reconditioning feelings of unworthiness, lacking, and limitation in the root chakra is the first place to start.

The first chakra/root chakra symbolizes support, money, family, DNA, structural, cultural, mother, father, the earth, and one's connection to the earth. This root chakra is formed in childhood, so on an energetic level, that would be your feelings, thoughts, and emotions. To spiritually heal the root chakra, we have to get a better connection to God and our own physical body. One cannot go back in time to treat most root-chakra imbalances which were caused in childhood. Thankfully, we do not need to. Just establishing an intimate and personal relationship with God allows us to heal this center.

God the Father works through everyone and everything because the Holy Spirit lives within all of us. To heal colon cancer on the spiritual level, one must create a daily practice of self-love. To see if you love yourself enough, look at your lifestyle habits, how you eat, how you care for your body, how you care for your spiritual and emotional well-being.

Having a strong spiritual and energetic body is essential for supporting our physical, mental, and emotional selves. Consider the relationship of a strong foundation to a house. If the wood is rotted, the house will collapse. Having a strong connection to your body as well as the physical world is essential to a successful and emotionally fulfilling life.

Understand that the body's energy body/circulatory system is felt in the nervous system. Chi, oxygen, and bio-plasma are other words for the Holy Spirit. As mentioned above, the Holy Spirit works within as without. Energy blocks are spiritual blocks and psychological blocks. God created man in his image, in the image of God created he him; male and female created he them. We are incarnated on the physical plane to learn different spiritual lessons to help us cultivate the traits of Jesus Christ and to learn through personal experience that we aren't separate from God. We learn how to build the internal character traits of Jesus Christ through the trials and tribulations we go through.

To learn is to heal, which manifests as seeing a different perspective. (God is all knowing, but we are limited from our life and life experiences.) If we change our habits, it changes our life. A daily practice to help recondition the body-mind connection allows us to feel the constant connection to God. In the moment, God gives us direct and divine guidance and wisdom. Reading scripture, writing in a journal, doing transcendental meditation (mantra) twice a day and when feeling stressed are all secure practices to help heal. Most people forget our choice of focus is our greatest tool in relieving stress!

Having a passion, direction, and vision is hugely important in the recovery of any cancer. Make more time for friends, family, and interests. Healing anything with the colon or related to the colon means you need to create balance and support and deal with stress more productively—all need to be looked at.

Our biggest weapons against sickness and all things created from lower energies are love and passion. God is love. To give and receive love is to provide yourself with greater immunity and better digestive health and to allow yourself to be open to receiving.

We can learn to be accessible through our passions, hobbies, and interests. Doing basic yoga, for example, creates balance in your life. Individuals who have colon and other digestive-tract problems need to get better lifestyle habits:

- Daily practice of holistic and spiritually healthy things like dry brushing and tongue scraping are beneficial.
- Before eating in the morning, drink kombucha (fermented tea) to put the good bacteria back into your digestive system.

Nutrition, Dietary Recommendations, and Herbal Medicine for the Colon

It is a good idea to keep a food journal because *when* you eat and *what* you eat have an effect on your colon. A food journal may help to identify food allergies and inflammation patterns and thus help you recognize a food that needs to be removed from your diet. Make sure you are not eating anything you're allergic to.

Also, remember when the body is healing it is best to give your digestion a break by incorporating and replacing some meals with juices and smoothies in your diet.

Because the colon plays such a significant role in digestion, your body will not get the necessary fats and proteins it needs while fighting cancer.

For colon health, your eating habits should include a high-fiber and low-residue diet. Fiber is found in plants and has a number of benefits for immune and digestive health.

There are three basic types of fiber: insoluble, soluble, and resistant starch:

Insoluble Fiber: The body does not digest insoluble fiber, which passes through the intestine more easily. Sources include whole-grain bread, brown rice, and whole-wheat pasta. These foods leave residue fiber in the bowels that helps prevent constipation and gastrointestinal blockage.

Soluble Fiber: Soluble fiber gets partially digested and fermented in the colon and may reduce the amount of cholesterol in the blood as well as preventing blood-sugar spikes. Oats are good examples. They leave a gel-like residue fiber in bowels.

Resistant Starch: Resistant starch is a fermentable soluble fiber which helps increase levels of good bacteria in the colon. Rice, cooled cooked pasta, cooled cooked potatoes, oats, lentils, and green peas are good sources of this.

More Dietary Recommendations

Eat more of these: Celery, ginger, garlic, kale, avocados, asparagus tips, cucumber, any dark-green leafy vegetable, dandelion, root vegetables, artichoke, lima beans, fennel, garlic, pureed spinach, eggplant (peeled), green beans, bananas, applesauce, ripe melon, peaches, nectarines, papaya, and plums. Green bananas reduce problems with loose stool.

Avoid: Figs, pineapple, dried fruit and prunes, alcohol, processed foods, sugar, processed meats, trans fats, artificial chemicals and preservatives like BHA, BHT, MSG, and food coloring, processed milk, smoked and canned meats

Drink green drinks: These clarify and detoxify to heal and rebuild healthy cells—wheatgrass, chlorophyll, kelp, alfalfa, barley, parsley, and chaga mushrooms.

Selected supplements: Ashwagandha, betaine HCl, cayenne, calcium D-gluconate, CoQ10, cinnamon, essential fatty acids (omega 6, 8, and 9), black currant and primrose, flax seed and oil, ginseng, milk thistle, passion flower, turmeric

Lean proteins: Chicken, duck, eggs, goose, quail, fish, lamb, grass-fed beef, tilapia, trout, wild Pacific salmon

Condiments: Apple cider vinegar, balsamic vinegar, Bragg's liquid amino acids, natural mustard, olives, homemade salsa (no sugar), tahini, non-iodized sea salt, Celtic and kelp salt, black pepper, seaweed

Sweeteners: Organic honey, organic grade A maple syrup, brown rice syrup, blackstrap molasses, applesauce, agave nectar, stevia

Oils: Coconut oil, ghee, grape seed oil, and always buy cold-pressed olive oil, almond, avocado, sunflower, cod liver, and wheat-germ oil

Spices: Basil, dill, rosemary, chives, cilantro

Teas to invigorate: Cinnamon, ginger, green, fennel, lemongrass, Gotu Kola, peppermint, slippery elm, sage, yerba mate

Teas to detoxify: Alfalfa, anise, dandelion, fenugreek, gingko, licorice, nettle, parsley, and red clover

Teas to boost immunity: Birch bark, echinacea, elder, feverfew, garlic, goldenseal, horehound, hyssop, marshmallow, and pau d'arco

Teas to calm: Borage, chamomile, dong quai, hops, kava kava, St. John's wort, valerian

Complex grains: Wild and brown rice, mixed grains, whole wheat, buckwheat, oats, rye, spelts, quinoa, millet, barley, groats

Nuts and nut butter: As long as you are not allergic to these

Sweet treats: Dark chocolate, unsweetened whipped cream

In closing, colon cancer surgery can damage the lining of the colon, thus interfering with the body's ability to process nutrients in foods and supplements. Incorporating spiritual and holistic practices into your daily life can ensure the balance needed to repair and heal not only colon cancer but to also assist the body in recovering from colon cancer surgery.

Healing Inflammation Holistically
(First Chakra)

Inflammation is the sign of an overactive immune system.

Inflammation is the body's attempt at self-protection. Therefore, when eliminating it, the aim is to remove harmful stimuli—including damaged cells, irritants, or pathogens—and begin the healing process.

All chronic illness begins with inflammation. Everything from obesity, ADD/ADHD, and diabetes to heart disease, thyroid issues, and dental issues. It is so common that most of us know someone who is suffering from a disorder caused by inflammation. And most doctors prescribe pharmaceuticals to just control inflammation, which doesn't heal the root cause but rather only suppresses the systems.

Inflammatory diseases usually start in the gut with an autoimmune reaction which progresses into systemic inflammation. To truly heal a disease is to address it holistically and spiritually. Incorporating good lifestyle habits, following good nutrition habits, and employing ways to eliminate stress have all proven to play a part in minimizing inflammation.

First, let's take a look at how stress and the survival hormone cortisol, as well as thyroid and other fluctuating hormones, contribute to inflammation. When the body initiates an attack on foreign invaders, it responds with inflammation, allergic reactions, and other symptoms we relate to a variety of diseases. Since your immune system can become overburdened, inflammatory triggers are continuously circulated through our blood where they affect nerves, organs, connective tissues, joints, and muscles.

Inflammation Triggers the Symptoms of Disease

The presence of inflammation is what makes most disease perceptible to an individual.

The Best Natural Weapons against Inflammation

Fruits:

Acerola cherries, apples, avocados, black currants, blueberries, fresh pineapple, lemons, limes, mulberries, oranges, strawberries, rhubarb, tomatoes, papaya, kumquats, raspberries

Vegetables:

Bell peppers, bok choy, broccoli, Brussels sprouts, cabbage, chard, cauliflower, collards, fennel bulb, garlic, green beans, kale, leeks, olives, spinach, sweet potatoes, turnips

Seafood:

Cod, halibut, herring, oysters, rainbow trout, salmon, sardines, snapper, striped bass, tuna, whitefish

Herbs, Spices, and Others:

Basil, chili peppers, cinnamon, cloves, cocoa, licorice, mint, oregano, parsley, rosemary, thyme, turmeric, almonds, avocado oil, cat's claw, flaxseed, ginger, green tea, hazelnuts, krill oil, olive oil, sunflower seeds, walnuts

Yoga Positions:

Seated spinal twist, sage pose, boat pose, shoulder stand, head stand

Inversion and twist poses are great for the circulatory system, stimulate abdomen muscles, calm the brain, and improve digestion.

Aromatherapy Oils:

Chamomile, lavender, sweet marjoram, eucalyptus, clary sage, frankincense, and yarrow

Put five drops of aromatherapy oil in a bath and soak for 20 to 30 minutes. You can also mix three drops into massage oil or apply it to a cold or hot compress held on the desired area for 20 to 30 minutes.

Emotional Intelligence

(Sacred Chakra)

Emotional intelligence is about being aware of feelings in yourself and others and understanding their impact.

Developing emotional intelligence is a valuable skill that not only allows you to know yourself better and helps you control your emotions but also helps you use social skills in a more effective but simple way.

All energy is consciousness. Belief is the key to expanding your brain's functioning and helps you to achieve what you really want out of your life.

The core issue in many unhappy conditions and sabotaging behaviorisms comes from the misuse of spiritual laws. We live in an intelligent universe which responds to our mental state. Learning to control our thoughts allows us to automatically have a lot more control in our environment.

In the bible, Jesus said, "It is done unto you as you believe." This means that we do not create on our own. We use the power of the one mind/God mind/unity consciousness, also known as the universal mind, which creates for us.

All our beliefs, fears, hurts, and deep-seated convictions reflect themselves in our experiences, our environment, and our physical and mental health conditions.

The activity of consciousness flows through us. Spirit cannot do for us only what it can do through us. Without providing consciousness, Spirit cannot provide us with what we are asking for. God is personal to us by being personified through us.

Thought form creates vibration, and the physical universe is Spirit in form. We all are immersed in the energies of our own thinking, which is a direct result of whatever we have said and done through our life since coming into consciousness.

Thought attracts what it is like and repels what it is unlike. Since man was made in God's image, which is love, any lower vibrational emotion creates spiritual blocks which over time cause sickness.

Health and sickness are largely externalizations of our most dominant and mental states. Modern psychology also backs up this fact by saying all thoughts and emotions we have ever experienced are still present and active in the mind. They manifest as subjective tendencies which mold the body in health or sickness as well as determining our most dominant reactions to our life experiences.

Our emotions and behaviorisms are formed by many factors: the beliefs and principles we hold about ourselves, other people, and the way we perceive life; the way we want to be seen by others; the lessons we learned both in childhood and later in life; our need for affection; and of course, our goals and sense of purpose all contribute to how much emotional intelligence we have to work with.

There are many benefits to obtaining emotional intelligence:

1. It helps us to express ourselves warmly and clearly.

2. It helps build better relationships.

3. It helps us to become resilient in difficult times.

4. It increases well-being.

Acknowledgments

I thank God for getting me to and guiding me along my path.

I would also like to thank Om Wellness and the spiritual communities I have learned from over the years.

And thank you to my readers. I hope this book will help you in your journey to healing.

Please contact me at www.pureenergyhealer.com for more information on the many services I can provide as a Master Psychic Healer.

www.ingramcontent.com/pod-product-compliance
Lightning Source LLC
Chambersburg PA
CBHW071335150426
43191CB00007B/740